The Bible Speaks Today

Series Editors: J. A. Motyer (OT)
John R. W. Stott (NT)

The Message of Thessalonians

The Gospel & the End of Time

Kevin Ray

Titles in this series

The Message of Thessalonians

The Gospel & the End of Time

John R. W. Stott

With Study Guide

Inter-Varsity Press
Leicester, England
Downers Grove, Illinois, U.S.A.

InterVarsity Press
38 De Montfort Street, Leicester LE1 7GP, England
P.O. Box 1400, Downers Grove, Illinois 60515, U.S.A.

InterVarsity Press®, USA, is the book-publishing division of InterVarsity Christian Fellowship®, a student movement active on campus at hundreds of universities, colleges and schools of nursing in the United States of America, and a member movement of the International Fellowship of Evangelical Students. For information about local and regional activities, write Public Relations Dept., InterVarsity Christian Fellowship, 6400 Schroeder Rd., P.O. Box 7895, Madison, WI 53707-7895.

Inter-Varsity Press, England, is the publishing division of the Universities and Colleges Christian Fellowship (formerly the Inter-Varsity Fellowship), a student movement linking Christian Unions in universities and colleges throughout the United Kingdom and the Republic of Ireland, and a member movement of the International Fellowship of Evangelical Students. For information about local and national activities in Great Britain write to UCCF, 38 De Montfort Street, Leicester LE1 7GP.

USA ISBN 0-8308-1237-7
USA ISBN 0-87784-925-0 (set of The Bible Speaks Today)
UK ISBN 0-85110-696-X

Printed in the United States of America ∞

Library of Congress Cataloging-in-Publication Data

Stott, John R. W.
    [Gospel & the end of time]
    The message of Thessalonians: the gospel and the end of time/
John Stott.
        p.   cm—(The Bible speaks today)
    Originally published as The gospel & the end of time, 1991.
    Includes bibliographical references.
    ISBN 0-8308-1237-7
    1. Bible. N.T. Thessalonians—Commentaries. I. Title.
II. Series.
    [BS2725.3.S767 1994]
    227'.81077—dc20   *94-427*
                                                              CIP

British Library Cataloguing in Publication Data

A catalogue record for this book is available from the British Library.

16	15	14	13	12	11	10	9	8	7	6	5	4
07	06	05	04	03	02	01						

General preface

The Bible Speaks Today describes a series of both Old Testament and New Testament expositions, which are characterized by a threefold ideal: to expound the biblical text with accuracy, to relate it to contemporary life and to be readable.

These books are, therefore, not 'commentaries', for the commentary seeks rather to elucidate the text than to apply it, and tends to be a work rather of reference than of literature. Nor, on the other hand, do they contain the kind of 'sermons' which attempt to be contemporary and readable without taking Scripture seriously enough.

The contributors to this series are all united in their convictions that God still speaks through what he has spoken, and that nothing is more necessary for the life, health and growth of Christians than that they should hear what the Spirit is saying to them through his ancient – yet ever modern – Word.

J. A. MOTYER
J. R. W. STOTT
Series Editors

AUTHOR'S PREFACE

'There is a kind of unmingled sweetness in this epistle', wrote Bengel about 1 Thessalonians in the eighteenth century.[1] I agree. Indeed, I have found much sweetness in both letters as, for many years now, I have reflected on their meaning and message. Their value, I suggest, lies in three related areas.

First, these letters reveal the authentic Paul. Not that he is ever inauthentic. But sometimes the human Paul is obscured by his apostolic office and authority. To be sure, in the Thessalonian letters he issues commands and demands obedience. More often, however, he writes like the pastor he is, indeed like the Thessalonians' mother and father, which is what he claims to be (1 Thes. 2:7, 11). He loves them, gives himself for them, is anxiously concerned for their welfare, teaches and admonishes them, begs them to stand firm, and prays for them constantly, urgently and personally. We can hear his heart-beat and see his tears. It would be hard to find a finer model for ministry than Paul.

Secondly, these letters address a local church, and the life of the local church is of increasing concern to many people today. When we affirm (as we should) that the church is central to the historical purpose of God, we are not referring only to its universal aspect, but also to its concrete, local, colourful manifestations. But what is to be our vision for the local church, and how is its life to be developed? Paul's letters to the Thessalonian church throw valuable light on such

[1] Bengel, p. 190.

aspects as its continuous evangelism, pastoral care, ethical standards, reciprocal fellowship, public worship, obedience to apostolic teaching, and future hope. I cannot imagine how any church member or leader could fail to find both direction and inspiration in these letters for the life of their local church.

Thirdly, these letters set the church in a theological, indeed an eschatological, context. Paul is emphatically not a pragmatist. He is first and foremost a believer, who is concerned to allow his beliefs to determine his actions. Again and again he returns to the central verities of the Christian faith, that Christ died for our sins, that he was raised from the dead, and that he is coming back. One can almost hear the threefold acclamation, in which many Anglicans join at the Lord's Supper:

> Christ has died!
> Christ is risen!
> Christ will come again!

It is these truths which stimulate evangelism, promote holiness, deepen fellowship, inform worship and inspire hope. In other words, it is the gospel which shapes the church, just as it is the church which spreads the gospel. This seems to me to be the underlying theme of the Thessalonian letters.

I am particularly grateful to the church family of All Souls Church, Langham Place, London, of which I have now been a privileged member for forty-five years (five as curate, twenty-five as Rector, and fifteen as Rector Emeritus) for the vision they have helped to give me of God's purpose for the local church; to Frances Whitehead for typing yet another manuscript with undiminished efficiency, energy and eagerness; to Jo Bramwell for putting together the study guide; and to Todd Shy for his characteristically painstaking work in reading and commenting, compiling the bibliography and the list of abbreviations, checking the typescript and correcting the proofs.

JOHN STOTT
August 1990

CHIEF ABBREVIATIONS

AV The Authorized (King James') Version of the Bible (1611).

BAGD Walter Bauer, *A Greek-English Lexicon of the New Testament and Other Early Christian Literature*, translated and adapted by William F. Arndt and F. Wilbur Gingrich, 2nd edition, revised and augmented by Gingrich and Frederick W. Danker from Bauer's fifth edition, 1958 (University of Chicago Press, 1979).

GNB The Good News Bible (NT 1966, 4th edition 1976; OT 1976).

GT *A Greek-English Lexicon of the New Testament* by C. L. W. Grimm and J. H. Thayer (T. & T. Clark, 1901).

JB The Jerusalem Bible (1966).

JBP *The New Testament in Modern English* by J. B. Phillips (Collins, 1958).

LXX The Old Testament in Greek according to the Septuagint, 3rd century BC.

MM *The Vocabulary of the Greek New Testament* by J. H. Moulton and G. Milligan (Hodder & Stoughton, one volume edition, 1930).

NEB The New English Bible (NT 1961, 2nd edition 1970; OT 1970).

NIV The New International Version of the Bible (1973, 1978, 1984).

REB The Revised English Bible (1989).

11

RSV   The Revised Standard Version of the Bible (NT 1946, 2nd edition 1971; OT 1952).

TDNT   *Theological Dictionary of the New Testament*, ed. G. Kittel and G. Friedrich, translated into English by G. W. Bromiley, 10 vols. (Eerdmans, 1964–76).

SELECT BIBLIOGRAPHY

Alford, Henry, *The Greek Testament*, vol. 3 (Rivingtons, 1865).

Bengel, Johann Albrecht, *Gnomon of the New Testament*, vol. 4, 1759; translated into English by Rev. James Bryce, revised and edited by Rev. Andrew Fausset (T. & T. Clark, 1866).

Berkouwer, G. C., *The Return of Christ* (1961 and 1963; Eerdmans, 1972).

Best, Ernest, *A Commentary on the First and Second Epistles to the Thessalonians* (Black's New Testament Commentary; A. & C. Black, 1972).

Bicknell, E. J., *The First and Second Epistles to the Thessalonians* (Westminster Commentary; Methuen, 1932).

Bruce, F. F., *1 & 2 Thessalonians* (Word Biblical Commentary; Word, 1982).

Calvin, John, *The Epistles of Paul the Apostle to the Romans and to the Thessalonians*, translated by Ross Mackenzie (Oliver and Boyd, 1961). The commentary on 1 and 2 Thessalonians was first published in Geneva, 1550.

Chrysostom, John, *Homilies on the Epistles of St. Paul the Apostle to the Thessalonians*, preached in Constantinople, c. AD 400. From *A Select Library of the Nicene and Post-Nicene Fathers of the Christian Church*, ed. Philip Schaff, vol. 13 (Eerdmans, 1976).

Deissmann, Adolf, *Light from the Ancient East* (1908; translated into English by L. R. M. Strachan; Hodder & Stoughton, 1927).

13

Denney, James, *The Epistles to the Thessalonians* (Expositor's Bible; Hodder & Stoughton, 1902).

Findlay, George G., *The Epistles of Paul the Apostle to the Thessalonians* (Cambridge Greek Testament; Cambridge University Press, 1904).

The Epistles to the Thessalonians (Cambridge Bible; Cambridge University Press, 1891).

Frame, J. E., *A Critical and Exegetical Commentary on the Epistles of St. Paul to the Thessalonians* (International Critical Commentary; T. & T. Clark, 1912).

Hendriksen, William, *Exposition of I and II Thessalonians* (New Testament Commentary; Baker, 1955).

Jeremias, Joachim, *The Unknown Sayings of Jesus* (SPCK, 1957).

Josephus, Flavius, *The Antiquities of the Jews, c.* AD 93–94, translated by William Whiston, 1737; from *Josephus: Complete Works* (Pickering & Inglis, 1981).

The Wars of the Jews, c. 78–79, translated by William Whiston, 1737; from *Josephus: Complete Works* (Pickering & Inglis, 1981).

Lightfoot, J. B., *Biblical Essays* (Macmillan, 1893).

Notes on Epistles of St. Paul (Macmillan, 1895).

Marshall, I. Howard, *1 and 2 Thessalonians* (New Century Bible Commentary; Eerdmans/Marshall, Morgan & Scott, 1983).

Martin, Ralph P., *Worship in the Early Church* (1964; Marshall, Morgan & Scott, 1974).

Metzger, Bruce M., *A Textual Commentary on the Greek New Testament* (United Bible Societies, corrected edition, 1975).

Milligan, George, *St. Paul's Epistles to the Thessalonians* (1908; Revell reprint).

Moffatt, James, *The First and Second Epistles to the Thessalonians* (Expositor's Greek Testament; Hodder & Stoughton, 1910).

Morris, Leon, *1 and 2 Thessalonians* (Tyndale New Testament Commentary; 2nd ed. IVP, 1985).

The First and Second Epistles to the Thessalonians (New International Commentary on the New Testament; Eerdmans, 1959).

Plummer, Alfred, *A Commentary on St. Paul's First Epistle to the Thessalonians* (Robert Scott, 1918).

A Commentary on St. Paul's Second Epistle to the Thessalonians (Robert Scott, 1918).

Travis, Stephen H., *I Believe in the Second Coming of Jesus* (1982; Hodder & Stoughton, 1988).

Vos, Geerhardus, *The Pauline Eschatology* (1930; Baker, 1979).

INTRODUCTION

When Paul and his companions visited Thessalonica in AD 49 or 50, it was already a well-established city with a long history. It had been founded in the fourth century BC by Cassander, one of Alexander the Great's army officers. He named it after his wife, Thessalonica, who was Alexander's half-sister. It occupied a strategic position, for it boasted a good natural harbour at the head of the Thermaic Gulf, and it was situated on the *Via Egnatia* which was the main route between Rome and the East. Thessalonica became the capital of the Roman province of Macedonia. Lightfoot described it as 'the key to the whole of Macedonia', and added that 'it narrowly escaped being made the capital of the world'.[1] Today as Thessaloniki it is the second most important city of Greece.

Luke tells us in Acts 17 how Thessalonica came to be evangelized. It happened during Paul's second missionary journey, which followed soon after the Council of Jerusalem. Silas was his chief missionary partner from the beginning.[2] In Lystra he invited the young man Timothy to join them,[3] and in Troas Luke was added to the team.[4] So Paul, Silas, Timothy and Luke were the four missionaries who sailed across the Northern Aegean Sea into Europe. After a remarkably successful mission in Philippi, Paul, Silas and Timothy moved on in a south-westerly direction to Thessalonica,[5]

[1] Lightfoot, *Essays*, pp. 254–255.   [2] Acts 15:40.   [3] Acts 16:1–3.
[4] Acts 16:11, where Luke begins to use the pronoun 'we'.
[5] Acts 17:1.

while Luke stayed behind.

The Jewish population of Thessalonica was large enough to justify a synagogue, and here Paul preached on three successive sabbaths. Luke describes his approach.[6] First, he argued from the Old Testament Scriptures that the expected Christ (*i.e.* the Messiah) had to suffer and rise from the dead. Next, he proclaimed Jesus of Nazareth to them, doubtless telling the story of his life, death and resurrection. And thirdly, he put his first and second points together, and declared that this Jesus was that Christ. In other words, Old Testament prophecy had been fulfilled in Jesus, so that the Jesus of history and the Christ of Scripture were the same person. Some of his Jewish listeners were convinced, and joined the missionaries. So did 'a large number of God-fearing Greeks', Gentiles on the fringe of the synagogue, 'and not a few prominent women'.[7] This may mean (as is implied by the reference to idolatry in 1 Thes. 1:9) that the Jewish mission was followed by a Gentile mission and that Paul stayed in Thessalonica several months, rather than just three weeks.

It was not long before opposition arose. Jealous of Paul's influence in the city, the Jews recruited a gang of thugs and started a riot. Not finding Paul or Silas in Jason's house, where they were staying, the ringleaders dragged Jason and some other believers before the city magistrates (whom Luke correctly calls 'politarchs') and lodged a serious accusation against them: 'These men who have caused trouble all over the world have now come here, and Jason has welcomed them into his house. They are all defying Caesar's decrees, saying that there is another king, one called Jesus.'[8] This allegation threw the city into an uproar. Jason and his friends were put on bail, and that night under cover of darkness Paul and Silas had to be smuggled out of town.[9]

They went south to Berea for a short mission. But the Jews followed them there, so that Paul had to continue his southward journey to Athens, where his escort left him. Soon after, at his request, Silas and Timothy rejoined him. But so anxious was he about the situation in Macedonia that he sent them north again in order to find out what was happening, even though it meant that he was again left in Athens alone.

[6] Acts 17:2–3.   [7] Acts 17:4.   [8] Acts 17:6–7.   [9] Acts 17:5–10.

Timothy went to Thessalonica, and Silas probably to Philippi. By the time they were ready to return south with news, Paul had moved on once more. So it was in Corinth that their reunion took place,[10] and that Paul wrote his first letter to the Thessalonian church (1 Thes. 3:6). It was one of his earliest letters – his second, in fact, on the assumption that Galatians was written just before the Jerusalem Council.

The apostle responded in this letter to the information he had received from Timothy. On the one hand, Timothy had brought good news of the Thessalonians' 'faith and love', their loyalty and steadfastness under persecution (1 Thes. 3:6–8). On the other, he had reported that Paul was being criticized for insincerity and ulterior motives (2:2–6), and for his failure to return to Thessalonica (2:17 – 3:5). In addition, the Thessalonians needed correction and instruction in the areas of sexual morality, earning their own living, preparing for the second coming (*parousia*) of Jesus, and tensions in the fellowship.

In the light of this background, it would be possible to divide 1 Thessalonians into two, naming the first half 'Narrative' (looking back to the missionaries' visit) and the second 'Exhortation' (addressing the Thessalonians' problems):

I. Narrative (1 Thes. 1:1 – 3:13)

Paul reminds the Thessalonians:

1. of their conversion and subsequent evangelism (1:1–10)

2. of his and his fellow-missionaries' conduct during their visit and subsequently (2:1 – 3:13)

II. Exhortation (1 Thes. 4:1 – 5:28)

Paul urges the Thessalonians:

1. to sexual self-control (4:1–8)

2. to brotherly love and daily work (4:9–12)

3. to steadfastness in bereavement (4:13–18)

[10] Acts 18:5; *cf.* 2 Cor. 1:19.

4. to righteousness in view of the unexpectedness of the Parousia (5:1–11)

5. to fellowship and worship in the church (5:12–28)

This kind of analysis is entirely appropriate if our interest in the letter is historical, even antiquarian. But the *Bible Speaks Today* series is above all concerned with the contemporary application of the biblical documents. So in our study of 1 Thessalonians we shall be asking ourselves what lessons it is legitimate to draw from this letter for local Christian churches today.

For 1 Thessalonians opens a window on to a newly planted church in the middle of the first century AD. It tells us how it came into being, what the apostle taught it, what were its strengths and weaknesses, its theological and moral problems, and how it was spreading the gospel.

What is of particular interest, because it applies to Christian communities in every age and place, is the interaction which the apostle portrays between the church and the gospel. He shows how the gospel creates the church and the church spreads the gospel, and how the gospel shapes the church, as the church seeks to live a life that is worthy of the gospel. This theme suggests a different analysis:

The gospel and the church

1. Christian Evangelism, or how the church spreads the gospel (1:1–10)

2. Christian Ministry, or how pastors serve both the gospel and the church (2:1 – 3:13)

3. Christian Behaviour, or how the church must live according to the gospel (4:1–12)

4. Christian Hope, or how the gospel should inspire the church (4:13 – 5:11)

5. Christian Community, or how to be a gospel church (5:12–28)

It seems certain that Paul, Silas and Timothy were still in Corinth when the Thessalonians' response to Paul's first letter arrived. For he stayed in the city about two years.[11] The news they received was mixed, as is clear from Paul's second letter which it prompted. On the one hand, he and his co-workers were deeply thankful to learn of the Thessalonians' growing faith and love, and of their perseverance under persecution (2 Thes. 1:3–4). On the other hand, there was cause for anxiety because the church was being disturbed in three particular ways. First, the persecution was so severe that Paul felt the need to explain why God allows his people to suffer for the kingdom and how he will put wrongs right when Jesus comes (2 Thes. 1:5–10).

Secondly, the Thessalonians were in danger of being deceived by false teaching, which had reached them through a communication which purported to come from Paul but was a forgery (2 Thes. 2:1–3a). In particular, they were being told that the day of the Lord had already come. So Paul needed to remind them of God's eschatological calendar, and especially that the revelation of Christ would be preceded by the rebellion of Antichrist (2 Thes. 2:3b–12).

Thirdly, the group of 'idlers', who (for whatever reason) had given up their work, had not all followed Paul's instruction to return to it. So he had some stern words in his second letter to and about this disobedient minority (2 Thes. 3:4–12). Paul also entreated the Thessalonians in this as in all matters to be loyal to his teaching (2:13–15). And he took the opportunity to express both his continuing prayers for them (1:11–12; 2:16–17; 3:16–18) and his need for their prayers (3:1–3).

All three chapters of the second letter allude to the Parousia. Indeed Paul sets the current problems of the Thessalonian church firmly in the context of the historical process and of its climax when Christ comes. As in his first letter, his preoccupation is still the church and the gospel, but now he relates them more clearly to the unfolding of history. He writes in turn about the revelation of Christ (chapter 1), the rebellion of Antichrist (chapter 2), and, in the light of these, the responsibility of Christians meanwhile (chapter 3).

[11] Acts 18:11, 18.

A. THE MESSAGE OF 1 THESSALONIANS

THE GOSPEL AND THE CHURCH

1 THESSALONIANS 1:1-10

1. CHRISTIAN EVANGELISM
or HOW THE CHURCH SPREADS THE GOSPEL

Introduction (1:1a)

Paul, Silas and Timothy . . .

It was customary in the ancient world for all letters to begin in the same way. Correspondents would announce first themselves, then the person(s) to whom they were writing, next a greeting, and lastly (though not always) either a thanksgiving or a wish for the reader's welfare. Paul follows the same pattern, but Christianizes it.

As we have already seen, *Paul, Silas* (as he is called in the Acts, although the Greek here has the Latin form 'Silvanus') *and Timothy* were the missionary team who evangelized Thessalonica. It is natural, therefore, for Paul to associate Silas and Timothy with him in both his letters to the Thessalonians. This does not necessarily mean that they shared in composing them; it is more likely to have been a courteous gesture, since Silas and Timothy were so well known in the Thessalonian church, together with a general indication that they were in agreement with what Paul wrote. See the Additional Note on Paul's use of 'we' (pages 71–74).

We also notice that in associating Silas and Timothy with him, Paul does not distinguish himself from them by calling himself an apostle, which they were not. Probably he omitted a reference to his apostleship here because what was being challenged in Thessalonica was his behaviour, not his authority. In other letters, however, if his special commission was being questioned, he both asserted and defended his apostleship, and in so doing distinguished himself from those he

25

mentioned in the address. Already in Galatians, while including 'all the brothers with him' in his greeting, he called himself an apostle who owed his appointment not to any human source but to Jesus Christ and to God the Father.[1] Similarly, in his two Corinthian letters he deliberately contrasted the designations 'apostle' and 'brother'. In both cases he styled himself 'Paul, (called to be) an apostle of Christ Jesus by the will of God' and then added 'and our brother Sosthenes'[2] or 'and Timothy our brother'.[3] There is no reason to suppose that the situation was different in Thessalonica; it is simply that he saw no need to spell out the distinction.

In this first chapter Paul refers to both the church and the gospel. He begins by describing the church of God, which the gospel has brought into being (1–4), and goes on to describe the gospel of God which the church has received and is spreading (5–10). Thus the gospel creates the church, which spreads the gospel, which creates more churches, which in their turn spread the gospel further *ad infinitum*. This is God's plan for ongoing evangelism through local churches.

1. The church of God (1:1b–4)

To the church of the Thessalonians in God the Father and the Lord Jesus Christ:

Grace and peace to you.

[2]We always thank God for all of you, mentioning you in our prayers. [3]We continually remember before our God and Father your work produced by faith, your labour prompted by love, and your endurance inspired by hope in our Lord Jesus Christ.

[4]For we know, brothers loved by God, that he has chosen you . . .

It is truly remarkable to read Paul's comprehensive portrayal of the Thessalonian church. It is only a few months old. Its members are newborn Christians, freshly converted from either Judaism or paganism. Their Christian convictions have been newly acquired. Their Christian moral standards have

---

[1] Gal. 1:1.   [2] 1 Cor. 1:1.   [3] 2 Cor. 1:1.

been recently adopted. And they are being sorely tested by persecution. You would expect it to be a very wobbly church in a very precarious condition. But no. Paul is confident about it, because he knows it is God's church, and because he has confidence in God. He delineates it in three ways.

a. The church is a community which lives in God the Father and the Lord Jesus Christ (1:1b)

We notice in passing the unselfconscious way in which Paul brackets 'God the Father' and 'the Lord Jesus Christ', as being together the source of the church's life. Later (in verse 10) he will call Jesus the 'Son' of God. Already within twenty years of the death and resurrection of Jesus the coupling of the Father and the Son as equal is the universal faith of the church. This simple fact is enough to undermine the teaching of those who claim that the New Testament nowhere attributes deity to Jesus.

The Greek word for 'church' is *ekklēsia*, which means 'an assembly'. In those days it was used in a variety of contexts, religious and secular. As Chrysostom wrote, 'there were many assemblies, both Jewish and Grecian'.[4] What, then, was distinctive about the *ekklēsia* to which Paul is writing? It is this. It is 'in' the Father and the Son. What kind of relationship has he in mind by the preposition 'in'? It is certainly not spatial, as if the church were somehow 'inside' God. Nor does it seem to mean that the church is 'founded on' God (JBP) or that its members 'belong to' God (REB) or simply that they 'have God as Father and Jesus Christ as Lord',[5] true as all these statements are. Nor does it seem natural to take 'in' as instrumental and translate the phrase 'brought into being by' God.[6]

If the phrase had been only 'in the Lord Jesus Christ', without reference to the Father, commentators would probably agree about its meaning because to be 'in Christ' is a familiar and favourite expression of Paul's, and because in 2:14 the churches of Judea are described as being 'in Christ Jesus'. Two New Testament metaphors explain this usage, the first developed by Jesus and the second by Paul. Jesus

---

[4] Chrysostom, p. 324.   [5] Plummer, p. 3.   [6] Best, p. 62.

spoke of his disciples being 'in' him as branches are 'in' the vine,[7] while Paul sees us as being 'in Christ' as limbs are 'in' the body.[8] In both cases the relationship in mind is a vital, organic union which makes possible the sharing of a common life. The fact that Paul here adds 'in God the Father' seems no reason why the 'in' relationship should mean something different. Elsewhere Paul describes our new life as 'hidden with Christ in God';[9] is this not almost the same as saying that the church is *in God the Father and the Lord Jesus Christ*? Perhaps, then, we should paraphrase the preposition 'in' as meaning 'living in', 'rooted in' or 'drawing its life from'.

In later letters Paul's description of the church would be the other way round, namely 'the church of God in Corinth'.[10] He might therefore have written to 'the church of God in Thessalonica', since he referred to 'God's churches' in Judea (1 Thes. 2:14) and in other places (2 Thes. 1:4). Instead, he wrote to *the church of the Thessalonians in God* (see 2 Thes. 1:1 too). Both accounts of the church are true. For God's church was living in Thessalonica, and the Thessalonians' church was living in God. To be sure, the preposition 'in' has a different nuance in these statements, since the church is 'in' God as the source from which its life comes, whereas it is 'in' the world only as the sphere in which it lives. Nevertheless, it is still correct to say that every church has two homes, two environments, two habitats. It lives in God and it lives in the world.[11]

Why, then, did Paul choose to describe the Thessalonian church in the way he did? Since he does not tell us, we can only guess. But it is at least plausible to suggest that, because he knew the insecurity felt by a young and persecuted church, he wanted to remind them that in the midst of their trials their security was in God. It is from him, from the Father and the Son ('through the Spirit', we might wish to add), that every church derives its life, strength and stability.

To this church Paul now sends his greeting *Grace and peace*. It seems to be a combination of the Jewish greeting *shalom* ('Peace!') and the Greek greeting *chairein* ('Rejoice!'

[7] John 15.   [8] 1 Cor. 12.   [9] Col. 3:3.
[10] 1 Cor. 1:2; 2 Cor. 1:1.
[11] *Cf.* 'in Christ at Philippi', Phil. 1:1, and 'in Christ at Colosse', Col. 1:2.

or 'Hail!'),[12] now Christianized as *charis*, 'grace'. It is as if Paul is saying 'We send you the new greeting with the old'.[13] Still today we can desire for the church no greater blessings than grace and peace. God's 'peace' is not just the absence of conflict, but the fullness of health and harmony through reconciliation with him and with each other. 'The entire gospel is involved in this word', writes Ernest Best.[14] And God's 'grace' is his free, undeserved favour through Christ which confers this peace and sustains it.

b. The church is a community which is distinguished by faith, hope and love (1:3)

After identifying the letter-writer and the recipients, and sending a greeting, ancient correspondents, as we saw, normally continued with an expression of thanksgiving, a wish or a prayer. Paul Christianizes this custom too. He tells the Thessalonians that he, Silas and Timothy – whether together, separately or both – (1) always thanked God for them all, (2) mentioned them in their prayers, and (3) continually remembered them before God (*i.e.* in his presence). Thus memory, thanksgiving and prayer belong together. Perhaps we need to pray and work for better memories. For it is when we remember people (their faces, names and needs) that we are prompted both to thank God and to pray for them.

What Paul and his companions especially remembered about the Thessalonians was the three most eminent Christian graces (faith, love and hope) which characterized their lives. Apart from Galatians 5:5–6 where they are mentioned, though not in a recognizable triad, this verse (with 5:8) is their first occurrence in Paul's letters. He will refer to them again in varying degrees of clarity,[15] and elaborate them in 1 Corinthians 13. They also occur in Peter's first letter and in the Letter to the Hebrews.[16] Two aspects of these Christian qualities need to be noted.

First, each is outgoing. Faith is directed towards God, love

[12] *Chairein* is used as the greeting at the beginning of two letters in the Acts (15:23; 23:26) and of the Letter of James (1:1).
[13] Milligan, p. 3. [14] Best, p. 64.
[15] Eph. 4:2–5; Col. 1:4–5; Rom. 5:1–5.
[16] 1 Pet. 1:3–8; Heb. 6:10–12 and 10:22–24.

towards others (both within the Christian fellowship and beyond it), and hope towards the future, in particular the glorious coming of *our Lord Jesus Christ*. Similarly, 'faith rests on the past; love works in the present; hope looks to the future'.[17] Every Christian without exception is a believer, a lover and a hoper (not necessarily an optimist, since 'optimism' is a matter of temperament, 'hope' of theology). Faith, hope and love are thus sure evidences of regeneration by the Holy Spirit. Together they completely reorientate our lives, as we find ourselves being drawn up towards God in faith, out towards others in love and on towards the Parousia in hope. The new birth means little or nothing if it does not pull us out of our fallen introversion and redirect us towards God, Christ and our fellow human beings.

Secondly, each is productive. It is this that Paul emphasizes. Faith, hope and love sound rather abstract qualities, but they have concrete, practical results. Faith works, love labours and hope endures. A true *faith* in God leads to good works, and without works faith is dead. Here Paul and James are seen to agree, even if Paul usually stresses the faith which issues in works and James the works which issue from faith.[18] A true *love* for people leads to labour for them; otherwise it degenerates into mere sentimentality. Moreover, this 'labour' is *kopos*, which denotes 'either the fatiguing nature of what is done or the magnitude of the exertion required'.[19] And a true *hope*, which looks expectantly for the Lord's return, leads to endurance (*hypomonē*), which is patient fortitude in the face of opposition.

So comprehensive is the vision conjured up by *your work produced by faith, your labour prompted by love, and your endurance inspired by hope in our Lord Jesus Christ* that Calvin did not exaggerate when he called it 'a brief definition of true Christianity'.[20] Bengel similarly affirmed that 'in these (*sc.* faith, hope and love) the whole of Christianity . . . consists'.[21]

---

[17] J. B. Lightfoot, *St Paul's Epistles to the Colossians and to Philemon* (1875; Macmillan, 7th ed., 1884), p. 134.
[18] *E.g.* Jas. 2:18.   [19] Best, p. 68.   [20] Calvin, p. 335.
[21] Bengel, p. 45 (commenting on Gal. 5:6).

c. The church is a community which is loved and chosen by God (1:4)

To whatever denomination or tradition we may belong, the doctrine of election causes us difficulties and questions. To be sure, it is a truth which runs through Scripture, beginning with God's call of Abraham[22] and later his choice of Israel 'out of all nations' to be his 'treasured possession . . . a kingdom of priests and a holy nation'.[23] This vocabulary is deliberately transferred in the New Testament to the Christian community.[24] Moreover, the topic of election is nearly always introduced for a practical purpose, in order to foster assurance (not presumption), holiness (not moral apathy), humility (not pride) and witness (not lazy selfishness). But still no explanation of God's election is given except God's love. This is clear in Deuteronomy: 'The LORD did not set his affection on you and choose you because you were more numerous than other peoples, for you were the fewest of all peoples. But it was because the LORD loved you . . .'.[25] Similarly in 1 Thessalonians 1:4 Paul unites the love of God and the election of God.[26] That is, he chose us because he loves us, and he loves us because he loves us. He does not love us because we are lovable, but only because he is love. And with that mystery we must rest content.

But before we leave this subject, we need to note the assertion made by Paul, Silas and Timothy that they *know* their brothers and sisters in Thessalonica to have been loved and chosen by God. God's election, however, is essentially a secret known to him alone.[27] So how could the missionaries possibly dare to claim that they knew it? They tell us. They give two bases for their knowledge, the first in the following verse (5), relating to their evangelism, and the second in the previous verse (3), relating to the Thessalonians' holiness. Both were evidences of the activities of the Holy Spirit, first in the missionaries (giving power to their preaching) and secondly in the converts (producing in them faith, love and hope), and therefore of the election of the Thessalonians. This shows that the doctrine of election, far from making evangelism unnecessary, makes it indispensable. For it is only

[22] Gn. 12:1ff.   [23] Ex. 19:5–6.   [24] *E.g.* 1 Pet. 2:5, 9–10.
[25] Dt. 7:7–8; *cf.* 4:37.   [26] As in 2 Thes. 2:13 and Eph. 1:4.
[27] 2 Tim. 2:19.

through the preaching and receiving of the gospel that God's secret purpose comes to be revealed and known.

Here, then, is Paul's threefold delineation of the church. It is a community beloved and chosen by God in a past eternity, rooted in God and drawing its life from him, and exhibiting this life of God in a faith which works, a love which labours and a hope which endures. What stands out of Paul's vision of the church is its God-centredness. He does not think of it as a human institution, but as the divine society. No wonder he could be confident in its stability!

The fourth part of Paul's representation of the church is that it is a community which receives and transmits the gospel. But this belongs to the next section, as we turn from the church of God to the gospel of God.

2. The gospel of God (1:5–10)

It is true that the message which Paul often called 'the gospel' (*e.g.* 2:4) he sometimes named 'our gospel' because he and his companions proclaimed it (5)[28] and even 'my gospel'[29] because its distinctive truth that in Christ Jews and Gentiles are equal had been disclosed and entrusted to him.[30] Nevertheless, he knew that above all it was 'the gospel of God' because he had revealed it (2:2, 8, 9)[31] and 'the gospel of Christ' because the good news focused on him (3:2).[32] Thus God was the author, Christ the substance and the apostles the primary agents (as we are secondary agents) of the gospel.

It was natural for Paul to move on in his mind from God's church to God's gospel because he could not think of either without the other. It is by the gospel that the church exists and by the church that the gospel spreads. Each depends on the other. Each serves the other.

In verses 5–10 the apostle outlines in three clear stages the progress of the gospel in Thessalonica. First, 'our gospel came to you' (5). Secondly, 'you welcomed the message' (6). Thirdly, 'the Lord's message rang out from you' (8). Thus it came to you, you received it, and you passed it on. This sequence is God's continuing purpose throughout the world.

---

[28] *Cf.* 2 Thes. 2:14; 2 Cor. 4:3.   [29] Rom. 2:16; 16:25; 2 Tim. 2:8.
[30] Eph. 3:2–7.   [31] *Cf.* Rom. 1:1.   [32] *Cf.* 2 Thes. 1:8; Gal. 1:7.

. . . because our gospel came to you not simply with words, but also with power, with the Holy Spirit and with deep conviction. You know how we lived among you for your sake. ⁶You became imitators of us and of the Lord; in spite of severe suffering, you welcomed the message with the joy given by the Holy Spirit. ⁷And so you became a model to all the believers in Macedonia and Achaia. ⁸The Lord's message rang out from you not only in Macedonia and Achaia – your faith in God has become known everywhere. Therefore we do not need to say anything about it, ⁹for they themselves report what kind of reception you gave us. They tell how you turned to God from idols to serve the living and true God, ¹⁰and to wait for his Son from heaven, whom he raised from the dead – Jesus, who rescues us from the coming wrath.

a. Our gospel came to you (1:5)

Of course, it did not come by itself. It did not drop by parachute from heaven. No, Paul, Silas and Timothy brought it. Before they arrived in Thessalonica there was no church; when they left, the church had been planted and had taken root. How did this happen? The planting of the church was the direct result of the preaching of the gospel, which Paul now depicts by four expressions.

(i) . . . with words

True, the gospel did *not* come *with words only*, but it did come to them with words. For the gospel is itself a word or message, indeed 'the word' (6, RSV), 'the word of the Lord' (8, RSV) or 'the word of God' (2:13, RSV). So we must not acquiesce in the contemporary disenchantment with words. Words matter. They are the building blocks of sentences by which we communicate with one another. And the gospel has a specific content. That is why it must be articulated, verbalized. Of course it can and must be dramatized too. For images are sometimes more powerful than words. Yet images also have to be interpreted by words. So in all our evangelism, whether in public preaching or in private witnessing, we need to take trouble with our choice of words.

(ii) . . . also with power

Words by themselves are seldom enough, even in secular

discourse. Because they may be misunderstood or disregarded, they need somehow to be enforced. This is even more the case in Christian communication, since blind eyes and hard hearts do not appreciate the gospel. So words spoken in human weakness need to be confirmed with divine power. The reference is probably not to external miracles which are normally designated by the plural word 'powers' (*dynameis*), but to the internal operation of the Holy Spirit. It is only by his power that the Word can penetrate people's mind, heart, conscience and will. Paul wrote the same thing to the Corinthian church,[33] and it is from Corinth that he is writing to the Thessalonians. We must never divorce what God has married, namely his Word and his Spirit. The Word of God is the Spirit's sword.[34] The Spirit without the Word is weaponless; the Word without the Spirit is powerless.

(iii) . . . and with deep conviction

I omit for the moment Paul's reference to the Holy Spirit, which comes next in verse 5, in order to bring together the words 'power' and 'conviction'. 'Power' describes the objective result of the preaching, 'conviction' the subjective state of the preacher. Paul's preaching was not only powerful in its effect but confident in its presentation. He was sure of his message, of its truth and its relevance, and in consequence was bold in proclaiming it. Yet this confidence and this courage are precisely what many modern preachers seem to lack.

(iv) . . . with the Holy Spirit

I deliberately take this expression last because it seems to me to belong to all the other three. That is to say, the truth of the Word, the conviction with which we speak it, and the power of its impact on others all come from the Holy Spirit. It is he who illumines our minds, so that we formulate our message with integrity and clarity. It is he whose inward witness assures us of its truth, so that we preach it with conviction. And it is he who carries it home with power, so that the hearers respond to it in penitence, faith and obedience. As the 1974 Lausanne Covenant put it, 'without his witness ours is futile'.[35]

Here then are three characteristics of all authentic preach-

[33] 1 Cor. 2:1–5.   [34] Eph. 6:17.   [35] Lausanne Covenant, para. 14.

ing (truth, conviction and power), all three springing from the ministry of the Holy Spirit. Paul then adds *You know how we lived among you for your sake*. He was not making claims which could not be substantiated. His and his companions' ministry was exercised in public and was witnessed. The Thessalonians remembered it well. God grant that our evangelism may also be so evidently characterized by truth, assurance and power, that like Paul we may be able to appeal to others to testify to it.

b. You welcomed the message (1:6)

As Paul has given a description of his preaching of the gospel, so now he gives an equally full description of the Thessalonians' receiving of it. His first thought is to link it with their afflictions.

(i) . . . in spite of severe suffering

There had been considerable opposition in Thessalonica to the gospel, and so also to those who preached it and those who embraced it. The authentic gospel always arouses hostility (not least because it challenges human pride and self-indulgence), although the opposition it provokes takes different forms. But persecution had not deterred the Thessalonians. They had *welcomed the message* in spite of the suffering involved.

(ii) . . . with the joy given by the Holy Spirit

We must not miss this second reference to the Holy Spirit within two verses. The same Spirit who gave power to those who preached the gospel gave joy to those who received it. He was working at both ends, so to speak, in the speakers and in the hearers. And it is not surprising to read of the converts' joy, for joy is a fruit of the Spirit.[36] Wherever the gospel goes and people respond, there is joy – joy in heaven among the angels over sinners repenting, as Jesus said,[37] and joy on earth among the people of God.[38] This pattern of outward opposition and inward joy has often been repeated in the long history of the church.[39]

[36] Gal. 5:22.   [37] Lk. 15:7, 10.   [38] Acts 8:8, 39; 13:52; 16:34.
[39] Jn. 16:33.

(iii) You became imitators of us and of the Lord
This is an earlier expression, which comes at the beginning
of verse 6. It indicates the profound change which came over
the lives of the converts. They began to follow the example
as well as the teaching of the apostles (*us*), and so of Jesus (*the
Lord*), whose apostles they were. To 'welcome the message'
includes this. It is no mere intellectual acquiescence in the
truth of the gospel; it is a complete transformation of
behaviour through a close following of Christ and his
apostles. We often think about the imitation of Christ,[40] but
probably do not pay sufficient attention to Paul's repeated
exhortation to the churches to imitate him,[41] as he imitated
Christ.[42]

*(iv) And so you became a model to all the believers in
Macedonia and Achaia*
As Dr Leon Morris has put it, 'the imitators in their turn
were imitated'.[43] For those who take Christ and his apostles
as their model inevitably themselves become a model to
others. And the singular 'model' probably signifies 'a model
community'.[44]

It is marvellous to see the effect of the gospel on those
who receive it. It may mean persecution and consequent
suffering. But it also involves inward joy through the Holy
Spirit, the imitation of Christ and the apostles in changed
lives, and the setting of an example to others. Four new
relationships seem to be implied – the opposition of the
world, the joy of the Holy Spirit, the imitation of the Lord
and his apostles, and being a model to the rest of the church.
If the preachers were marked by truth, conviction and power,
the converts were marked by joy, courage and obedience. Let
nobody say that the gospel is devoid of wholesome effects!

3. The Lord's message rang out from you (1:8)

The Greek word is *exēcheō*, which occurs nowhere else in
the New Testament. It is derived from *ēchos*, an echo or
noise. According to *TDNT*, it can mean to 'sound, ring, peal

[40] *E.g.* Eph. 5:1–2; 1 Jn. 2:6; 3:3.
[41] 'I urge you to imitate me', 1 Cor. 4:16; *cf.* 2 Thes. 3:7; Gal. 4:12;
Phil. 3:17; 4:9.
[42] 1 Cor. 11:1.   [43] Morris, NICNT, p. 59.   [44] Frame, pp. 73, 85.

or boom'. It was used in LXX of bells, zithers, trumpets and other loud noises. In the New Testament the weaker verb *ēcheō* relates to the noise of a resounding gong[45] and of the roaring sea.[46] Chrysostom thought that Paul was likening the preaching of the gospel to 'the sound of a loud trumpet'.[47] The verb is also used of 'a great thunder',[48] and Jerome described Paul's writings as *non verba sed tonitrua*, 'not words but thunderclaps'.[49] At all events, whether Paul is thinking of thunder or trumpets, the gospel proclaimed by the Thessalonians made a loud noise, which seemed to reverberate through the hills and valleys of Greece.

But there was something more than that: *your faith in God has become known everywhere* (8). We must notice carefully the threefold contrast in verse 8 between the two means by which the gospel spread from Thessalonica. The first is between 'the word of the Lord' (direct preaching) and 'your faith in God' (an indirect report). The second is between the loud 'ringing out' of the gospel and the much quieter 'becoming known' of their faith. And the third is between the local provinces of Macedonia and Achaia which the preaching reached, and 'everywhere' to which the news of their faith had penetrated.[50] Even if Paul's 'everywhere' is hyperbole, he is certainly saying that the Thessalonians' faith was becoming known far beyond Greece, maybe west by land to Rome and east by sea to Ephesus.

There is an important lesson to learn here. We are a very media-conscious generation. We know the power of the mass media on the public mind. Consequently, we want to use the media in evangelism. By print and tape, by audio and video cassettes, by radio and television we would like to saturate the world with the good news. And rightly so. In principle nobody should quarrel with this ambition. We should harness to the service of the gospel every modern medium of communication which is available to us.

Nevertheless there is another way, which (if we must compare them) is still more effective. It requires no complicated electronic gadgetry; it is very simple. It is neither organized nor computerized; it is spontaneous. And it is not expensive;

---

[45] 1 Cor. 13:1.   [46] Lk. 21:25; *cf.* Ps. 65:7.
[47] Chrysostom, p. 327; *cf.* Ex. 19:16; Heb. 12:19; Rev. 1:10.
[48] Ecclus. 40:13; *cf.* 46:17.   [49] Quoted by Lightfoot, *Notes*, p. 15.
[50] *Cf.* Rom. 1:8.

it costs precisely nothing. We might call it 'holy gossip'. It is the excited transmission from mouth to mouth of the impact which the good news is making on people. 'Have you heard what has happened to so and so? Did you know that such and such a person has come to believe in God and has been completely transformed? Something extraordinary is going on in Thessalonica: a new society is coming into being, with new values and standards, characterized by faith, love and hope.'

The result of such gratuitous publicity was tremendous. *Therefore we do not need to say anything about it, for they themselves report what kind of reception you gave us* (8b–9a). Better, 'we do not need to tell other people about it: other people tell us . . .' (JB). Not only were the media redundant; the missionaries felt redundant also! For the message was spreading without them, and everybody seemed to know it already.

Mind you, I think the apostle Paul may be forgiven for a little harmless exaggeration. He did not mean literally that he was no longer necessary. At least he did not resign, or apply for indefinite furlough. No. He carried on preaching the gospel, but especially where Christ was not known.[51] For we take his point: the good news was advancing spontaneously.

Exactly what was the news which was spreading far and wide from Thessalonica? According to verse 8 it was their *faith in God*. But according to verse 9 what people were hearing and reporting was *what kind of reception you gave us* and how the Thessalonians were converted. Paul then goes on in verses 9b and 10 to give a three-part analysis of Christian conversion, which is arguably the fullest account of it in the New Testament. It indicates that conversion involves (1) a decisive break with idols, (2) an active service of God, and (3) a patient waiting for Christ. These three steps are summed up in the verbs 'you turned . . . to serve . . . and to wait . . .'. Indeed, this succinct threefold statement has suggested to several commentators that Paul was making use of an already existing formula.

[51] Rom. 15:20.

a. You turned to God from idols (1:9a)

The verb translated 'turn' (*epistrephō*) became an almost technical term for conversion, which is a turn from sin to Christ, from darkness to light,[52] and from idols to God. Luke in particular uses it repeatedly in Acts.[53] It would be difficult to exaggerate how radical is the change of allegiance which is implied by the turn from idols to *the living and true God*.[54] For idols are dead; God is living. Idols are false; God is true. Idols are many; God is one. Idols are visible and tangible; God is invisible and intangible, beyond the reach of sight and touch. Idols are creatures, the work of human hands; God is the Creator of the universe and of all humankind. Besides, Paul knew what he was talking about. Not only had he inveighed against idolatry when addressing the pagans of Lystra[55] and the philosophers of Athens,[56] but the Thessalonians could themselves see Mount Olympus, about fifty miles south of their city, where the Greek gods were supposed to live.

Modern missionaries, especially in areas of 'animism', which is now usually termed 'traditional religion', know all about the power of idols, and of the spirits which are believed to lurk behind them. A tribe's traditional idols have a tremendous hold over the people's minds, hearts and lives. For centuries they have lived in superstitious dread of them and in obsequious submission to them. The very thought of breaking away from them fills them with alarm, as they fear the spirits' revenge.

And the more sophisticated idols (that is, God-substitutes) of modern secular cities are equally powerful. Some people are eaten up with a selfish ambition for money, power or fame. Others are obsessed with their work, or with sport or television, or are infatuated with a person, or addicted to food, alcohol, hard drugs or sex. Both immorality and greed are later pronounced by Paul to be forms of idolatry,[57] because they demand an allegiance which is due to God alone. So every idolater is a prisoner, held in humiliating bondage.

Then, through the gospel and the grace of God, in many cases suddenly and completely, the prisoner turns to God

[52] Acts 26:18; Col. 1:13; 1 Pet. 2:9.
[53] Acts 3:19; 9:35; 11:21; 14:15; 15:19; 26:18, 20; 28:27.
[54] *Cf.* Je. 10:10.   [55] Acts 14.   [56] Acts 17.   [57] Eph. 5:5.

from the idols (whether superstitious or sophisticated) which have so far controlled his or her life. The experts call it a 'power encounter', for it is a personal encounter with Jesus Christ in which the spell of the idol is broken and the superior power of the living and true God is demonstrated. People are amazed and filled with awe, and they spread the good news.

The history of Christian missions contains many examples of such power encounters. In each case a deliberate Christian challenge is thrown down to the false gods which previously held sway in the community. Sometimes the challenge is conversion itself, as people are rescued by Christ from an evil power which can no longer hold them. At other times the challenge is made by new converts who dare to defy their former gods. Then, when no harm follows, the supremacy of Christ is acknowledged and more conversions take place.

As an example of the first I would like to quote from the letter of a young Burmese national, who a few years ago went with some friends to evangelize a village inhabited by animists:

> We explained to them the pure simple gospel and Christ's lordship over the devil and all evil foes, after which they were counselled to confess and forsake their evil deeds and to receive Christ Jesus as their Saviour and Lord. With brokenness and tears and guilt they responded. Then we burned up the charms and amulets, took a wood-cutting knife, and broke down a spirit's house made of bamboo and wood, claiming the lordship of Jesus Christ, and singing Christ's victory songs, and putting all of ourselves under the blood of the Lamb of God and the rule of the Holy Spirit, and claiming God's protection.

Examples of the second kind of power encounter, which took place in Oceania at the beginning of the last century, have been documented by the distinguished Australian missionary and anthropologist, Dr Alan R. Tippett. He tells how Pomare II, the Christian chief of Tahiti, baked and ate a sacred turtle without first observing the customary rituals; how Taufa'ahau, chief of Tonga, struck the priestess of his old god with a soft banana club, saying, 'I will strike the devil-god with this'; and how Malietoa, paramount chief of

Samoa, taking no precautions, ate a sacred mullet, which was forbidden food. These were deliberately daring and provocative acts. They were performed in public, with relatives and friends watching in silent apprehension of the god's revenge. They were also symbolic, each being 'a public rejection of a power which had bound them all for ages'. And when no fatal consequences followed, the people were convinced, conversions took place and the church grew. The Southern Polynesians knew, writes Dr Tippett, that 'the only real and effective way of proving the power of their new faith was to demonstrate that the old religion had lost its power and fear'. As a missionary leader commented at the time, 'idolatry bows and expires at Jesus' name'.[58]

Truly, now that the strong man (the devil) has been overpowered by one stronger than he (Jesus Christ), his palace can be raided and his prisoners set free.[59]

b. . . . to serve the living and true God (1:9b)

The claim to have turned to God from idols is manifestly bogus if it does not result in serving the God to whom we have turned. We must not think of conversion only in negative terms as a turning away from the old life, but also positively as the beginning of a new life of service. We could say that it is the exchange of one slavery for another, so long as we add that the new slavery is the real freedom.[60] In this way authentic conversion involves a double liberation, both *from* the thraldom of the idols whose slaves we were and *into* the service of God whose children we become.

c. . . . and to wait for his Son from heaven (1:10)

It is immediately noteworthy that 'serving' and 'waiting' go together in the experience of converted people. Indeed, this

---

[58] Alan R. Tippett, *People Movements in Southern Polynesia*, 'a study in church growth' (Moody, 1971), pp. 16, 81–83, 91, 160–164, 205–206. See also his *Deep Sea Canoe*, the story of Third World missionaries in the South Pacific (William Carey Library, 1977). For the example of Boniface, the 8th-century pioneer missionary bishop in Germany, who deliberately felled the sacred oak of Thor in Hesse, see S. C. Neill, *A History of Christian Missions* (Penguin, 1964), pp. 74–75.

[59] Lk. 11:21–22.   [60] Rom. 6:15–23.

is at first sight surprising, since 'serving' is active, while 'waiting' is passive. In Christian terms 'serving' is getting busy for Christ on earth, while 'waiting' is looking for Christ to come from heaven. Yet these two are not incompatible. On the contrary, each balances the other. On the one hand, however hard we work and serve, there are limits to what we can accomplish. We can only improve society; we cannot perfect it. We shall never build a utopia on earth. For that we have to wait for Christ to come. Only then will he secure the final triumph of God's reign of justice and peace.[61] On the other hand, although we must look expectantly for the coming of Christ, we have no liberty to wait in idleness, with arms folded and eyes closed, indifferent to the needs of the world around us. Instead, we must work even while we wait, for we are called to serve the living and true God.

Thus working and waiting belong together. In combination they will deliver us both from the presumption which thinks we can do everything and from the pessimism which thinks we can do nothing.

In this first reference of the letter to the Parousia (which is hereafter mentioned in every chapter of both letters), Paul tells us two truths about him for whom we are waiting.

First, Jesus is the one, *whom he* [God] *raised from the dead*. The Resurrection not only publicly declared Jesus to be the Son of God[62] but was also the beginning of God's new creation, the pledge that he will complete what he has begun. The resurrection from the dead assures us of the return from heaven.

Secondly, *Jesus* is the one *who rescues us from the coming wrath*. This statement is surely a play on the name 'Jesus', which means 'saviour'.[63] Already he has delivered us from the condemnation of our sins and the power of our idols. But when he comes, he will accomplish the final stage of our salvation: he will rescue us from the outpouring of the wrath of God. God's wrath is neither an impersonal process of cause and effect (as some scholars have tried to argue), nor a passionate, arbitrary or vindictive outburst of temper, but his holy and uncompromising antagonism to evil, with which he refuses to negotiate. One day his judgment will fall.[64] It is from this terrible event that Jesus is our deliverer.

---

[61] 2 Pet. 3:13.   [62] Rom. 1:4.   [63] Mt. 1:21.   [64] *Cf.* Rom. 2:5, 16.

It is evident that Paul has a lofty view of the Person for whose coming we wait. In verse 10 he calls him both 'Jesus' (his human name) and 'God's Son' (his divine dignity), adding that he is the Saviour who rescues us, and the Christ (1, 3) whom the Scriptures foretold. Putting these four epithets together, we have 'Jesus Christ, Son of God and Saviour' or (in the Greek acrostic) ICHTHUS, the word for fish which the early Christians chose as their secret symbol.

We are now in a position to summarize the report about the Thessalonians which was being widely disseminated, and so the essentials of Christian conversion, namely the turning from idols, the serving of God and the waiting for Christ. Some students have detected a correspondence between these and the triad of faith, hope and love. For the turning to God is certainly faith, and the serving of God could be seen as the fruit of love, while the waiting for Christ is the essence of hope. Be that as it may, Paul has shown us in the Thessalonians a model of conversion which is invariable. There will, of course, be different idols from which people need to turn, and different forms in which they will express their service of God, but always the break with the past will be decisive ('you turned from idols'), the experience of the present will be liberating ('to serve the living and true God') and the look to the future will be expectant ('to wait for his Son from heaven'). And without this turning, serving and waiting one can scarcely claim to have been converted.

Conclusion

Looking back over the chapter we note again the vital relationship between the church and the gospel. Two points stand out.

a. The church which receives the gospel must pass it on

Nothing is more impressive in 1 Thessalonians 1 than the sequence 'our gospel came to you – you welcomed it – it rang out from you'. God intends every church to be like a sounding board, bouncing off the vibrations of the gospel, or like a telecommunications satellite which first receives and then transmits messages. In fact, this is God's simplest plan for world evangelization. If every church had been faithful, the world would long ago have been evangelized.

b. The church which passes on the gospel must embody it

We have noted that what went forth from Thessalonica was not only 'the word of the Lord' (verbal evangelism) but also the news of their conversion (rumour evangelism). Everybody heard about this new community which had come into being in Thessalonica, its bold rejection of idolatry, its joy in the midst of opposition, its transformed values, its faith and love. People were so impressed by what they heard that many must have come to see for themselves. Then they were convinced not by what they had heard (either from or about the Thessalonian church) but by what they had seen with their own eyes. As Douglas Webster has written:

> the communication of the gospel is by seeing as well as hearing. This double strand runs all through the Bible: image and word, vision and voice, opening the eyes of the blind and unstopping the ears of the deaf. Jesus is the Word of God and the Image of God. The Word became visible, the Image audible ... We are familiar enough with the verbal element in evangelism. Where is the visual?[65]

No church can spread the gospel with any degree of integrity, let alone credibility, unless it has been visibly changed by the gospel it preaches. We need to look like what we are talking about. It is not enough to receive the gospel and pass it on; we must embody it in our common life of faith, love, joy, peace, righteousness and hope.[66]

[65] Douglas Webster, from *I Will Heal their Land*, report of the South African Congress on Evangelism, ed. Michael Cassidy (Africa Enterprise, 1974), p. 96.
[66] See also *Manila Manifesto*, para. 7, 'The Integrity of the Witnesses' (published by the Lausanne Committee for World Evangelization).

2. CHRISTIAN MINISTRY
or HOW PASTORS SERVE BOTH THE GOSPEL AND THE CHURCH

Introduction

Part of the abiding value of 1 Thessalonians 2 and 3 is the insight it gives us into Paul's pastoral heart. In these chapters, more perhaps than anywhere else in his letters, he discloses his mind, expresses his emotions and bares his soul. No-one who is engaged in any form of pastoral ministry (ordained or lay) can fail to be touched and challenged by what Paul writes here.

True, he was an apostle and we are not. That is, we have neither seen the risen Lord, nor been commissioned to be his eye-witnesses, nor received a special inspiration of the Holy Spirit to teach with authority or contribute to the New Testament – which were some of the distinctive privileges of the apostles of Christ, especially the Twelve and Paul. Nevertheless, other aspects of the apostles' ministry were not unique to them, for example their pastoral concern and care, of which they provide an excellent model for us to copy, not least in these two chapters of 1 Thessalonians.

Before we consider their contemporary application, we need to recall their historical background. The brief mission in Thessalonica had been brought to an ignominious end. The public riot and the legal charges against the missionaries were so serious that they were persuaded to make a humiliating night flight from the city. Paul's critics took full advantage of his sudden disappearance. In order to undermine his authority and his gospel, they determined to discredit him. So they launched a malicious smear campaign. By studying

Paul's self-defence it is possible for us to reconstruct their slanders. 'He ran away', they sneered, 'and hasn't been seen or heard of since. Obviously he's insincere, impelled by the basest motives. He's just one more of those many phoney teachers who tramp up and down the Egnatian Way. In a word, he's a charlatan. He's in his job only for what he can get out of it in terms of sex, money, prestige or power. So when opposition arose, and he found himself in personal danger, he took to his heels and ran! He doesn't care about you Thessalonian disciples of his; he has abandoned you! He's much more concerned about his own skin than your welfare.'

It seems likely that some of the Thessalonians were being carried away by this torrent of abuse. The facts of Paul's abrupt departure and failure to return seemed to fit the accusations being made against him. His critics' case sounded pretty plausible. So Paul must have found this personal attack extremely painful. Perhaps he drew comfort from his knowledge that Jesus had himself been misrepresented as being a glutton and a wine-bibber, a law-breaker, seditious, in league with the devil, and even mad. Paul also determined to reply to the charges which were being levelled at him, not out of pique or vanity, but because the truth of the gospel and the future of the church were at stake. Chapters two and three of 1 Thessalonians are, in fact, his *apologia pro vita sua*. First, he defends his conduct when he was in Thessalonica (2:1–16). Secondly, he explains his involuntary departure from the city, his subsequent inability to go back and his determination to visit them again as soon as he can (2:17 – 3:13).

Before we are ready to consider his case, however, we need to note two general and preliminary points which he makes, namely the openness of his ministry and his willingness to suffer.

You know, brothers, that our visit to you was not a failure. [2]We had previously suffered and been insulted in Philippi, as you know, but with the help of our God we dared to tell you his gospel in spite of strong opposition.

According to the Greek sentence, Paul is making a clear-cut contrast between verses 1 and 2, for verse 1 contains a 'not' and verse 2 begins with the strong adversative *alla*, 'but', which NIV omits. He is saying that his visit to Thessalonica was not one thing but another. It was not *kenos*, 'empty'. That much is clear. But empty of what? Most commentators translate it 'empty of results' (as in 3:5), 'a failure' (NIV), 'fruitless' (REB), 'ineffectual' (JB). The problem with this interpretation, however, is that verse 2 does not contrast with it. To say that Paul's visit was not a failure, but that he dared to preach does not really make sense, since the result of the preaching is not mentioned in verse 2. The alternative is to render *kenos* 'empty of purpose' not 'empty of result', 'aimless' not 'fruitless'. Lightfoot explained *kenos* in this way, namely 'hollow, empty, wanting in purpose and earnestness'.[1] Then verses 1 and 2 hold together. Far from being empty-handed on arrival in Thessalonica, with nothing to say or bring, Paul had had the courage to preach the gospel and risk the persecution.

a. Paul's openness

With the help of our God we dared to tell you his gospel (2). The verb translated 'dared' is *parrēsiazomai*, which means to 'speak freely, openly, fearlessly' (BAGD), indeed to speak with *parrēsia*, which is 'outspokenness, frankness, plainness of speech' (BAGD), and so with courage. This characteristic of his preaching Paul goes on to emphasize. He has already written: '*You know* how we lived among you for your sake' (1:5). Now he repeats five times that they are his witnesses, and twice that God is as well: '*You know*, brothers, that our visit to you was not a failure' (1). 'We had previously suffered ... *as you know*' (2). '*You know* we never used flattery ... *God is our witness*' (5). 'Surely *you remember* ...' (9). '*You are witnesses*, and *so is God* ...' (10). Paul's ministry in Thessalonica had been public. It was exercised in the open before God and human beings, for he had nothing whatever to hide. Happy are those Christian leaders today, who hate hypocrisy and love integrity, who have nothing to conceal or be ashamed of, who are well known for who and what they are, and who are able to appeal without fear to God and the public as their witnesses! We need more transparency and openness of this kind today.

[1] Lightfoot, *Notes*, p. 18.

b. Paul's sufferings

Before reaching Thessalonica Paul had suffered both injury and insult in Philippi (2). He and Silas had been stripped, beaten, thrown into prison, and their feet fastened in the stocks. It had not only been an extremely painful experience, but humiliating as well, since they were flogged naked in public, without trial, and in spite of their Roman citizenship. In Thessalonica too Paul had met *strong opposition* (2). Yet these afflictions did not deter him. On the contrary, God gave him courage to go on preaching the gospel, whatever the consequences might be. This, then, was the second evidence of Paul's genuineness. People are prepared to suffer only for what they believe in. Thus Paul appeals both to his openness and to his sufferings as tokens of his sincerity.

Having considered these two preliminary points, we are ready to follow Paul's *apologia* in its two main stages, in which he alludes first to his visit, and secondly to his absence, together with his intended return. He describes his integrity when he was with them, his anxiety while he was separated from them, and his determination to see them again.

1. Paul defends his visit (2:3–16)

For the appeal we make does not spring from error or impure motives, nor are we trying to trick you. ⁴*On the contrary, we speak as men approved by God to be entrusted with the gospel. We are not trying to please men but God, who tests our hearts.* ⁵*You know we never used flattery, nor did we put on a mask to cover up greed – God is our witness.* ⁶*We were not looking for praise from men, not from you or anyone else.*

As apostles of Christ we could have been a burden to you, ⁷*but we were gentle among you, like a mother caring for her little children.* ⁸*We loved you so much that we were delighted to share with you not only the gospel of God but our lives as well, because you had become so dear to us.* ⁹*Surely you remember, brothers, our toil and hardship; we worked night and day in order not to be a burden to anyone while we preached the gospel of God to you.*

¹⁰*You are witnesses, and so is God, of how holy, righteous and blameless we were among you who believed.* ¹¹*For you know that we dealt with each of you as a father deals with*

his own children, *¹²encouraging, comforting and urging you to live lives worthy of God, who calls you into his kingdom and glory.*

¹³And we also thank God continually because, when you received the word of God, which you heard from us, you accepted it not as the word of men, but as it actually is, the word of God, which is at work in you who believe. ¹⁴For you, brothers, became imitators of God's churches in Judea, which are in Christ Jesus: You suffered from your own countrymen the same things those churches suffered from the Jews . . .

As the apostle recalls his visit to Thessalonica, he seems to depict it by four metaphors, two of which are quite explicit, while the other two are clearly implied. He likens himself successively to a steward (3–4), a mother (5–8), a father (9–12) and a herald (13–16).

a. A steward (2:3–4)

It is true that the word 'steward' does not occur in the text. But the concept of stewardship is implicit in the phrase *entrusted with the gospel* (4). God had entrusted the gospel to Paul, as a householder entrusts his property to his steward. The apostle reverts a number of times to this concept when he wishes to express either his sense of privilege in having had the gospel committed to him,[2] or his sense of responsibility to be faithful to his stewardship.[3]

Before he develops his positive ministry of trusteeship, however, his sense of accountability to God for the gospel, he has some negative disclaimers to make in verse 3. His *appeal*, he maintains, did not and *does not spring from error*, since his message – the gospel of God – was true. Nor was it due to *impure motives*. The Greek is the single word *akatharsia*, which means 'impurity, uncleanness'. It can refer to sexual immorality (as it does in 4:7), and it is possible that Paul's detractors were hinting at this, since it was not uncommon among travelling teachers. Were they even insinuating that there was something suspicious about the 'not a few prominent women' who had been converted?[4] But

---

[2] Gal. 2:7; 1 Tim. 1:11; Tit. 1:3.
[3] *E.g.* 1 Cor. 4:1–2; 9:17; 2 Tim. 2:2.   [4] Acts 17:4.

probably NIV is right to render the word *impure motives*, alluding to such evils as 'ambition, pride, greed, popularity'.[5] Thirdly, the missionaries' appeal was not 'made with guile' (RSV): *nor are we trying to trick you.* That is, there was nothing devious about their methods. They made no attempt to induce conversions, for example, either by concealing the cost of discipleship or by offering fraudulent blessings.

Here, then, is a tremendous threefold claim. Paul insists that his message was true, his motives were pure and his methods were open and above-board. In these three areas his conscience was entirely clear. In what he said, and in why and how he said it, he was free from anything underhand.

It is over against error, impurity and guile, which he disclaims, that Paul now develops the stewardship metaphor: *On the contrary, we speak as men approved by God to be entrusted with the gospel* (4). His emphasis is on God as the person to whom he was responsible. First, God had *approved* him. *Dokimazō* can mean both to 'put to the test, examine' and especially, as a result of the examination, to 'accept as proved' or 'approve' (BAGD). More simply still, it means to test and find genuine, and was used of both coins and people. Milligan refers to its technical use to describe 'the passing (of somebody) as fit for election to a public office'.[6] Just so, God had tested Paul and found him fit.

Secondly, as a result of the successful test, God had *entrusted* him *with the gospel*, making him a steward of it. Thirdly, God was the person he was *trying to please*, not men.[7] Fourthly, it is God who *tests our hearts*. This present continuous tense at the end of the verse is added to the perfect tense of the same verb at its beginning, because the divine examination is never final. *We speak*, therefore, writes Paul, as men who are tested by God, approved by God, trusted by God and are seeking to please God. No secret of Christian ministry is more important than its fundamental God-centredness. The stewards of the gospel are primarily responsible neither to the church, nor to its synods or leaders, but to God himself. On the one hand, this is a disconcerting fact, because God scrutinizes our hearts and their secrets, and his standards are very high. On the other hand, it is marvellously liberating, since God is a more knowledgeable,

---

[5] Best, p. 94.   [6] Milligan, p. 18.   [7] *Cf.* Gal. 1:10.

impartial and merciful judge than any human being or ecclesiastical court or committee. To be accountable to him is to be delivered from the tyranny of human criticism.

b. A mother (2:5–8)

The apostle again begins negatively. He is about to declare his mother-like love for the Thessalonians as his motivation in serving them, but before this he repeats his claim to be free of unworthy motives. Verse 5: *you know we never used flattery*, a word (*kolakia*) which occurs nowhere else in the New Testament and which expresses 'the tortuous methods by which one man seeks to gain influence over another, generally for selfish ends'.[8] *Nor did we put on a mask to cover up greed – God is our witness*, pretending to serve while in reality wishing to be served. *We were not looking for praise from men, not from you or anyone else* (6). All three evils (the flattery, the mask and the hunger for compliments) are illicit ways of using others to build up ourselves.

Paul now mentions one other trap which he and his companions avoided, which they could have fallen into as *apostles of Christ*. Since Silas and Timothy are both mentioned many times in the New Testament, but never as apostles like Paul and the Twelve, Paul is either using the plural of authority like the royal 'we' (saying 'we' but meaning 'I') or he is using the word 'apostles' in its more general sense of 'messengers', 'missionaries' or 'envoys'.[9] Personally, I prefer the former explanation, which seems to have a parallel in 3:1 ('we thought it best to be left by ourselves', when it is almost certain that Paul was left alone). What he might have done as an apostle was to be *a burden* to the Thessalonians, either by standing on his dignity and issuing orders, or by insisting on being paid (*cf.* v. 9 and 2 Thes. 3:8). Lightfoot thinks it 'safer' to include 'both these royal prerogatives, so to speak, of the apostleship, the assertion of authority and the levying of contributions'.[10]

Instead, *we were gentle among you, like a mother caring for her little children* (7). The general contrast between an apostle's authority and a mother's tenderness is clear enough.

---

[8] Milligan, p. 19.
[9] *Cf.* Acts 14:4, 14. See the Additional Note on pages 71–74.
[10] Lightfoot, *Notes*, p. 24.

But the precise application of the mother metaphor is uncertain, since some manuscripts read 'gentle' (*ēpioi*), while others startle us by reading 'babies' (*nēpioi*). Textually speaking, either could be correct. The previous word in the Greek sentence ends in 'n'. If *ēpioi* was original, then *nēpioi* is explained by a copyist mistakenly repeating the 'n'. If *nēpioi* was original, then *ēpioi* is explained by a copyist mistakenly omitting the second 'n'. Which is the more likely of the two readings? Because the manuscript support for *nēpioi* ('babies') is older and stronger, and because such a bold image of being 'babies like a mother' is unlikely to be due to a scribal error, some scholars favour its adoption. Mixed metaphors are frequent in Paul, they argue, and the imagery is appropriate, even 'beautifully correct. A mother fondling her children comes down to their level, uses their language, and plays their games'.[11] She becomes 'childlike with her children'.[12] On the other hand, *ēpios* occurs elsewhere of the necessary gentleness of Christian leaders (even if only once),[13] and *nēpios* ('baby'), though it occurs several times in Paul's letters, is always used in a derogatory way of the immaturity of his converts; he never applies it to himself. 'Gentle' certainly seems a more appropriate contrast with an apostle's authority and a more natural development of the mother metaphor.

Paul adds that he was not only as gentle as a mother with them, but as affectionate and sacrificial too: *We loved you so much that we were delighted to share with you not only the gospel of God but our lives as well, because you had become so dear to us* (8). Far from using them to minister to himself, he gave himself to minister to them. It is a lovely thing that. a man as tough and masculine as the apostle Paul should have used this feminine metaphor. Some Christian leaders become both self-centred and autocratic. The more their authority is challenged, the more they assert it. We all need to cultivate more, in our pastoral ministry, of the gentleness, love and self-sacrifice of a mother.

c. A father (2:9–12)

It is striking that Paul likens himself to their father as well as their mother. And in doing so, for the third time he begins

---

[11] Plummer, p. 23.　　[12] Findlay, *Greek*, p. 42.　　[13] 2 Tim. 2:24.

negatively. He reverts to the fact, already mentioned in verse 6, that he had *not* been *a burden to anyone* in Thessalonica, even while he *preached the gospel of God* to them. Indeed, it was in order deliberately to avoid being dependent on them financially that he and his companions had *worked night and day*. Probably they preached by day and laboured by night. For Paul anyway (we do not know about the others) his work was tent-making,[14] by which he earned his living and presumably paid Jason for his board and lodging (2 Thes. 3:8). They would *surely . . . remember . . .* his *toil and hardship* (9). Although we know that some gifts were sent to him from the Philippian church, even while he was in Thessalonica,[15] these were evidently inadequate for his needs, perhaps because the Macedonian churches suffered from 'extreme poverty'.[16] So in these circumstances Paul could have made himself a burden to the Thessalonian Christians by asking them for money, but he determined not to do so.

Instead of being a burden to them, he had been like a father to them, by both his example and his instruction. As for his example, they and God were together *witnesses . . . how holy, righteous and blameless* he had been among the believers (10). Although we should not attempt to distinguish too neatly between these three words, yet 'holy' (*hosios*) seems to refer to our being 'devout, pious, pleasing to God' (BAGD), 'righteous' to our dealings with our neighbour, and 'blameless' to our public reputation. Paul evidently saw his example as part of his paternal duty, so that he continued: *For you know that we dealt with each of you as a father deals with his own children* (11), *encouraging, comforting and urging you to live lives worthy of God, who calls you into his kingdom and glory* (12).

Paul seems to be thinking specially of the educational role of fathers, who, in addition to setting their children a consistent example (10), should also encourage, comfort and exhort them. In the apostle's case, he found himself urging the Thessalonians to live worthily of God and his kingdom, and even 'insisting'[17] on it. Since it was part of his teaching that the kingdom of God has both a present manifestation[18] and a future glory,[19] we may assume that he appealed to the

---

[14] Acts 18:3; 20:34–35. [15] Phil. 4:16. [16] 2 Cor. 8:1–2.
[17] Best, p. 107. [18] *E.g.* Col. 1:13. [19] *E.g.* 2 Thes. 1:5; 1 Cor. 6:9.

Thessalonians to live a life worthy both of their dignity now and of their destiny at the end.

There is no need to deduce from the two metaphors which Paul had developed in verses 7 and 11 that he was laying down a stereotype of sexual roles in the home, the mother feeding and the father educating their children. For mothers certainly have an indispensable part in the mental and moral upbringing of their children, while there is no reason (except cultural tradition) why fathers should not take their turn at feeding and bathing the babies. Indeed, Scripture encourages rather than discourages this sharing of responsibilities. What is impressive is that, in his pastoral care of the Thessalonians, Paul could claim to have combined both the father's and the mother's roles.

d. A herald (2:13–16)

It is well known that the commonest New Testament word for preaching is *kēryssō*, to act like a herald (*kēryx*) and make a public proclamation. The verb occurs in verse 9, 'we preached [*ekēruxamen*] the gospel of God to you', and the concept lies behind verse 13: *And we also thank God continually because, when you received the word of God, which you heard from us, you accepted it not as the word of men, but as it actually is, the word of God, which is at work in you who believe.* There is a deliberate interplay in this important statement between 'God', 'us' and 'you'. What you received (the technical term for receiving a tradition which is being handed on), namely what you heard *from us* (the apostle), you accepted as the word *of God*, which is effectively at work *in you*. The message came from God through the apostle to the Thessalonians and was changing them.

This is an umambiguous assertion by Paul that the gospel he preached was the word of God. We are familiar with the claims of the Old Testament prophets that they were bearers of the word of God, for they introduced their oracles with formulas like 'the word of the Lord came to me', 'listen to the word of the Lord', and 'thus says the Lord'. But here in verse 13 is a comparable claim by a New Testament apostle. Paul does not rebuke the Thessalonians for regarding his message too highly. On the contrary, he commends them for having recognized it as what it truly is (God's word) and for having accepted it as such. More than that, he actually thanks God constantly that they have done so, and adds that the gospel authenticates its divine origin by its transforming power in their lives. This is a clear indication of Paul's self-conscious apostolic authority. He knew who he was (an apostle of Christ) and he knew what his message was (the word of God). And the Thessalonians knew these things as well.

The efficacy of the gospel in the believers was seen in the fact that they *became imitators of God's churches in Judea, which are in Christ Jesus* (14a). The Judean churches are probably singled out for mention because they were the first to be planted. And the 'imitation' of them by the Thessalonians was an unwitting rather than a deliberate one. All true churches, which belong to God and live in Christ, are bound on that account, in spite of cultural differences, to display a certain similarity to one another. This similarity was seen not only in their receiving the word, but also in their suffering for it: *You* (Thessalonians, mostly of Gentile stock) *have suffered from your own countrymen the same things those* (Judean) *churches suffered from the Jews* (14b).

But what sufferings at the hand of the Jews does Paul have in mind? He tells us:

. . . *15who killed the Lord Jesus and the prophets and also drove us out. They displease God and are hostile to all men 16in their effort to keep us from speaking to the Gentiles so that they may be saved. In this way they always heap up their sins to the limit. The wrath of God has come upon them at last.*

These two verses, sometimes called 'the Pauline polemic against the Jews', have been described as 'violent', 'vehement', 'vindictive', 'passionate', 'intemperate', 'bitter' and 'harsh'. So incongruous do some commentators feel them to be in one of Paul's letters, that they attribute them to an anti-Jewish interpolator. But there is no manuscript evidence that they were added by a later hand.

We must begin our evaluation of these verses by studying what Paul actually wrote and by setting it against the background of the most recent Jewish persecution which he had experienced. Luke makes it clear in Acts 17 and 18 that it was Jewish opponents of the gospel who pursued Paul from Thessalonica to Berea and from Berea to Athens. Then after his arrival in Corinth (from which he wrote 1 Thessalonians) it was Jewish opposition which led him to take the drastic step of turning to the Gentiles. In his indictment of the Jews in verse 15, he accuses them of five things, which remind us of Stephen's speech before the Sandhedrin.[20] First, they had *killed the Lord Jesus*. To say such a thing today would be regarded as a very reprehensible, anti-semitic statement. And it is true that the Romans were also implicated in Jesus' death. So are all of us for whose sins he died. Indeed, Paul included himself personally in this,[21] and never forgot that he had once been 'a blasphemer and a persecutor'.[22] Nevertheless, the Jewish people as a whole shared in the blame and said so.[23] While implicating ourselves, we cannot exonerate them. Secondly, they *killed . . . the prophets*, which Jesus himself had accused them of doing.[24] Thirdly, they *also drove us out*, which seems to put the apostles on a level with the prophets.[25] Fourthly, *they displease God*, especially by rejecting his Messiah, and lastly they *are hostile to all men*. This phrase has reminded many commentators of Tacitus' famous description of the Jews: 'Towards all other people (*i.e.* except their fellow-Jews) they feel only hatred and hostility.'[26] Further, Paul explains their hostility to the human race in terms of their attempt to stop the apostles from preaching the gospel and so to stop the Gentiles from being saved.[27] Paul saw this policy as the appalling thing it was. The Jews had not only killed the Messiah and persecuted the prophets and the apostles. They were also obstructing the spread of the gospel and so the work of salvation.

As a result of their antagonism, *they always heap up their sins to the limit*. Just as God's judgment fell on the Amorites when their sin 'had reached its full measure',[28] so it would fall on the Jewish people when they had filled up the measure of their sins and those of their forefathers.[29] Then it can be said that *The wrath of God has come upon them at last* (16). According to 1:10 God's wrath is future, but here it appears to be past. Ernest Best explains that although *phthanō* means

---

[20] Acts 7.   [21] Gal. 2:20.   [22] 1 Tim. 1:13.   [23] Mt. 27:25.
[24] Mt. 23:29–31; Lk. 13:34.   [25] *Cf.* 1 Cor. 4:9.   [26] Tacitus, *History*, v.5.   [27] *Cf.* Mt. 23:13.   [28] Gn. 15:16.
[29] Mt. 23:32.

to arrive, it can express an arrival with or without 'participation in whatever experience lies at the destination'. Thus, Jesus' statement in Matthew 12:28 that 'the kingdom of God has come upon you' (*ephthasen*, the same verb in the same tense), affirms its arrival, while leaving open whether people have yet received it or not. Similarly, Paul's statement about God's wrath could mean either that it 'has fallen on them and they now experience it', or that it 'hangs over them and is just about to fall upon them'.[30] If the former is right, then (commentators suggest) Paul may be seeing the arrival of God's judgment in such events as the unprecedented famine in Judea of AD 45–47,[31] the brutal massacre of Jews in the temple precincts at Passover in AD 49 (described by Josephus), and in the same year the expulsion of the Jews from Rome by the emperor Claudius.[32] Since 1 Thessalonians was probably written in AD 50, these were all at the time vivid, recent events.

The other translation seems to me more likely, however, namely that 'the wrath of God is over their heads' (JBP), though it has not yet engulfed them. The destruction of Jerusalem in AD 70 was still twenty years away. But the reference in 2 Thessalonians 2:4 to Antichrist setting himself up in God's temple strongly suggests that Paul was familiar with at least some of the apocalyptic warnings of Jesus.[33] So Jesus' epigrammatic sayings about God's coming judgment on the nation had surely become current, like 'the kingdom of God will be taken away from you',[34] 'your house is left to you desolate',[35] and 'Daughters of Jerusalem, do not weep for me; weep for yourselves and for your children'.[36] If the tradition of such predictions of judgment was part of the background of Paul's thinking, then the Jews' continuing rejection of the gospel would surely make him think this judgment to be imminent, which indeed it was. In this case the final words *eis telos* are likely to mean neither 'decisively, completely, to the uttermost', nor 'for ever', but 'finally', *i.e.* 'the wrath of God hangs over their heads at last'.

However we interpret the last two sentences of verse 16, they are extremely solemn words. Yet anti-Semitism cannot find any possible justification in them. No Christian can read

---

[30] Best, p. 119.   [31] Acts 11:27–28.   [32] Acts 18:2.
[33] *E.g.* Mk. 13:14.   [34] Mt. 21:43.   [35] Mt. 23:38.   [36] Lk. 23:28.

the long history of anti-Judaism in the church without feeling profoundly ashamed. The worst example among the Fathers was Chrysostom, who in AD 386–88 in Antioch preached eight virulent sermons against the Jews. He likened them to animals, and made wild accusations against them, ranging from gluttony, drunkenness and immorality to infanticide and even cannibalism. In the Middle Ages four repressive regulations of the Fourth Lateran Council (1215) obliged Jews to live in ghettos and wear distinctive dress, while during the Crusades the church failed to restrain the popular fanaticism which led to pogrom and pillage in Jewish communities. More embarrassing still is Luther's intemperate treatise *On the Jews and their Lies* (1543). It is true that his health was declining, not long before his death, and that he was disillusioned over his earlier hopes for the conversion of the Jews. Yet these things do not exonerate him for his diatribe against them, or for his call to set fire to their synagogues, destroy their homes, confiscate their Talmudic books and silence their Rabbis.

Only one clarification helps to lighten our Christian sense of guilt. It is that what some Fathers, medieval churchmen and Reformers were expressing was anti-Judaism not anti-Semitism, a theological conviction not a racial prejudice. Thus Chrysostom reserved his bitterest invective for 'Judaizing' Christians who tried to combine church and synagogue. And Luther's overriding concern was the honour of God's Son, whom the Jews denied. Even Rosemary R. Ruether, in her violent critique of the Christian anti-Jewish record, *Faith and Fratricide* (1975), concedes this: 'There is no way to rid Christianity of its anti-Judaism, which constantly takes social expression in anti-Semitism, without grappling finally with its christological hermeneutic itself.'[37]

By Christianity's 'christological hermeneutic' Professor Ruether is referring to our belief that Jesus is the Messiah, that those who deny Christ are Antichrist, and that only those who acknowledge the Son have the Father also.[38] Such convictions may help to explain some Christian attitudes of antipathy towards the Jews; they certainly do not excuse them.

[37] Rosemary R. Ruether, *Faith and Fratricide: The Theological Roots of Anti-Semitism* (Search Press, 1975), p. 116.
[38] *E.g.* 1 Jn. 2:22–23.

Returning now to Paul's statements in 1 Thessalonians 2:15–16, we need to remember that he himself was a patriotic Jew, as we learn particularly from Romans 3:1–4 and 9:1 – 11:36. He gloried in his Jewish ancestry. He longed with anguish for the salvation of his people. He declared that he was willing even to forfeit his own salvation if only thereby they might be saved.[39] He also taught that God had not cast off his people, because his gifts and call are irrevocable, and that he intended to include them again, if they did not persist in unbelief. Metaphorically speaking, his plan was to graft back into the olive tree the natural branches which had been temporarily cut off.[40] So we have to balance 1 Thessalonians 2:15–16 with everything Paul wrote a few years later in Romans 9 – 11. There is no evidence that he changed his mind during the interval, and so contradicted himself, or that in 1 Thessalonians his statements are vengeful, or incompatible with the mind of Christ. No. Paul is simply stating bald facts. Many of his Jewish contemporaries were rejecting Christ, opposing the gospel and hindering Gentiles from being saved. In consequence, God's wrath had come upon them, as Jesus himself had warned.

How is it possible, however, to reconcile the horizons of 1 Thessalonians (which predicts, even declares, God's judgment) and of Romans 11 (which affirms the continuing validity of God's covenant and the assurance of Israel's salvation)? Are not the warning of judgment and the promise of salvation equally irrevocable and therefore contradictory? Perhaps the solution to this problem is to be found in the difference of Paul's terminology between God's wrath upon 'the Jews' individually (1 Thes. 2:14) and his salvation of 'Israel' collectively.[41] Paul had not come to believe, when writing to the Thessalonians, that henceforth all Jews could expect nothing but judgment, and that no Jew could be saved. This is plain from the fact that, when he moved on from Corinth to Ephesus, he continued his policy of evangelizing the synagogue first.[42] And even when he reached Rome, he called the leaders of the Jews together (it was his first act) and 'explained and declared to them the kingdom of God and tried to convince them about Jesus from the Law of

---

[39] Rom. 9:1–5; 10:1.   [40] Rom. 11.   [41] Rom. 11:25–26.
[42] Acts 19:8; cf. Rom. 1:16 'to the Jew first'.

Moses and from the Prophets'. Moreover, 'some were convinced'. It was those who rejected Christ who were themselves rejected, and on whom God's judgment fell.[43]

2. Paul explains his absence (2:17 – 3:13)

Paul returns from his digression about the Jews to his *apologia* for himself. His detractors were criticizing him not only for his motives and conduct during his visit to Thessalonica, but also for his precipitate departure and his irresponsible failure to return. Either he had now abandoned and even forgotten the Thessalonians, they seem to have been saying, or he was too craven to go back. So the apostle defends himself against this further calumny. If 2:1–16 is his *apologia pro vita sua*, 2:17 – 3:13 is his *apologia pro absentia sua*.[44]

But, brothers, when we were torn away from you for a short time (in person, not in thought), out of our intense longing we made every effort to see you. [18]For we wanted to come to you – certainly I, Paul, did, again and again – but Satan stopped us. [19]For what is our hope, our joy, or the crown in which we will glory in the presence of our Lord Jesus Christ when he comes? Is it not you? [20]Indeed, you are our glory and joy.

[3:1]So when we could stand it no longer, we thought it best to be left by ourselves in Athens. [2]We sent Timothy, who is our brother and God's fellow-worker in spreading the gospel of Christ, to strengthen and encourage you in your faith, [3]so that no-one would be unsettled by these trials. You know quite well that we were destined for them. [4]In fact, when we were with you, we kept telling you that we would be persecuted. And it turned out that way, as you well know. [5]For this reason, when I could stand it no longer, I sent to find out about your faith. I was afraid that in some way the tempter might have tempted you and our efforts might have been useless.

[6]But Timothy has just now come to us from you and has brought good news about your faith and love. He has told us that you always have pleasant memories of us and that you

---

[43] Acts 28:16–31.   [44] Hendriksen, p. 74.

long to see us, just as we also long to see you. ⁷Therefore,
brothers, in all our distress and persecution we were encour-
aged about you because of your faith. ⁸For now we really live,
since you are standing firm in the Lord. ⁹How can we thank
God enough for you in return for all the joy we have in the
presence of our God because of you? ¹⁰Night and day we pray
most earnestly that we may see you again and supply what is
lacking in your faith.

¹¹Now may our God and Father himself and our Lord Jesus
clear the way for us to come to you. ¹²May the Lord make
your love increase and overflow for each other and for every-
one else, just as ours does for you. ¹³May he strengthen your
hearts so that you will be blameless and holy in the presence
of our God and Father when our Lord Jesus comes with all
his holy ones.

Addressing his Thessalonian readers affectionately as
'brothers' (17), as he has done previously in verse 1, Paul
develops a telling fivefold rebuttal of his critics' arguments,
while at the same time advancing evidence of his genuine love
for the Thessalonians.

a. He had left them with great reluctance (2:17a)

It had given Paul no pleasure to leave the city. He had not
gone voluntarily. On the contrary, *we were torn away from*
you, he writes. The Greek verb is *aporphanizomai*, whose
only New Testament occurrence is in this verse. Since
orphanos normally means an orphan, namely a parentless
child, some commentators take this as a further example of
Paul's love of mixing metaphors. Having called himself their
father, mother, even baby (7, 11), and brother (1, 17), he
now also pictures himself as their orphaned child. But the
word has a wider sense than children deprived of their parents; it 'applies also to parents deprived of children',[45] which
would link more easily with the earlier father and mother
metaphors. But Lightfoot broadens the word further still to
include bereavement in general, 'the loss of any friend or
relation'.[46] Hence the modern translations 'we were bereft of
you' (RSV) and 'you were lost to us' (REB). The emphasis is

---

[45] Best, p. 124.   [46] Lightfoot, *Notes*, p. 36.

on an unnatural separation, both forcible and painful. At the same time, Paul felt sure that it was only temporary (*for a short time*), and he assured them that it was *in person not in thought*, which Bicknell neatly renders 'out of sight but never out of mind'.[47]

b. He had made repeated efforts to return to them (2:17b–20)

Paul writes of his *intense longing* to see them, which lay behind his efforts to return (17b). *For*, he goes on, *we wanted to come to you – certainly I, Paul, did, again and again – but Satan stopped us* (18). It is not clear whether the change from 'we' to 'I, Paul' is meant to distinguish the pronouns ('we all wanted to visit you, but I specially') or to identify them ('we wanted to come, by which I really mean that I did'). I will come back to this question later. Meanwhile, we observe that the apostle blames the devil for the failure of his attempts to return. Satan 'thwarted us' (REB) or 'prevented' us (JBP, JB), he says, using a verb (*enkoptō*, to cut into) which could be applied either to 'breaking up a road to render it impassable'[48] or to an athlete 'cutting in' during a race.[49]

A number of conjectures have been made as to precisely how Satan hindered the apostle's return to Thessalonica. (1) Some think it was continuing Jewish opposition, even 'a plot . . . being formed against him by the Jews'.[50] (2) Others (*e.g.* Lightfoot)[51] guess that it was his 'thorn in the flesh', and that this was a debilitating illness which he later called 'a messenger of Satan'.[52] (3) William Ramsay suggested that the satanic hindrance was the legal ban which the plutarchs of Thessalonica had put on Jason. They 'took security from Jason and the others before letting them go',[53] with severe penalties if Paul were to return. 'This ingenious device put an impassable chasm between Paul and the Thessalonians'.[54] (4) Another possibility is that Paul was referring to 'some sin

---

[47] Bicknell, p. 28.   [48] Milligan, p. 34.   [49] Gal. 5:7.
[50] Chrysostom, p. 334.   [51] Lightfoot, *Notes*, p. 38.
[52] 2 Cor. 12:7; Gal. 4:13–14.
[53] Acts 17:9, REB; or NEB, 'They bound over Jason and the others'.
[54] Sir William M. Ramsay, *St Paul the Traveller and the Roman Citizen* (Hodder and Stoughton, 1895; 11th ed. undated), p. 231.

or scandal that detained him in Corinth'.[55] Presumably both Paul and the Thessalonians knew well what the interference was. Since we lack this information, it is better for us to confess our ignorance than express an unwarranted confidence.

A more important question is why Paul attributed this blockage to Satan, while attributing others to God.[56] One answer could be that God gave Paul spiritual discernment to distinguish between providential and demonic happenings. Another is that the attribution could be made only with the benefit of hindsight. 'It was probably evident – in retrospect, if not immediately – that the one check worked out for the advance of the gospel and the other for its hindrance'.[57] A third and more theological perspective is to say that 'both statements are true. Although Satan does his part, God still retains supreme authority . . .'.[58] At all events, Paul's purpose is to affirm that his inability to return to them was not due to any indifference on his part, but rather to the malign influence of the devil.

In verses 19 and 20, unconsciously supplying evidence that he really has longed and tried to revisit them, Paul asks rhetorical, unanswerable questions which express his great love for them: *For what is our hope, our joy, or the crown in which we will glory* [our 'triumphal crown' (REB)] *in the presence of our Lord Jesus Christ when he comes? Is it not you? Indeed, you are our glory and joy.*[59] The double reference to joy perhaps refers to the present, while the double reference to glory certainly refers to the future when Christ comes again. We must not interpret Paul's glory in the Thessalonians in a way which conflicts with his affirmations that he will glory only in Christ and his cross.[60] For the Thessalonians are trophies of Christ crucified. What Paul seems to mean, in this transport of love, is that his joy in this world and his glory in the next are tied up with the Thessalonians, whom Christ through the apostle's ministry has so signally transformed.

---

[55] Denney, p. 104.   [56] *E.g.* Acts 16:6–7, 10, and probably Rom 1:13.
[57] Bruce, p. 58.   [58] Calvin, p. 351.   [59] *Cf.* Phil. 4:1.
[60] *E.g.* 1 Cor. 1:31; Gal. 6:14.

c. He had sent Timothy to them (3:1–5)

Paul's repeated efforts to revisit Thessalonica were made more frustrating by the lack of news about the church there. So the suspense grew until *we could stand it no longer* (1a). Something simply had to be done to relieve the tension. So, since Paul could not go himself, the decision was taken to send Timothy in his place. It seemed 'the best plan' (JBP), although it was a costly sacrifice on Paul's part because it meant that he would have 'to stay on alone at Athens' (1b, REB). He had been alone there once before, since on arrival his escort had left him,[61] and a very painful experience it had proved. His whole being had felt oppressed and provoked by the city's prevailing idolatry.[62] Soon, however, in keeping with his instructions for Silas and Timothy to join him as soon as possible,[63] at least Timothy did so (without bringing any news, however). But must Paul now send Timothy away and be left a second time isolated from Christian fellowship in the idolatrous city? His sensitive spirit shrank from this further ordeal. But he could bear another bout of loneliness better than a further period of suspense over the Thessalonians.

So *we sent Timothy*, whose fellowship would have meant much to Paul, for he is *our brother and God's fellow-worker in spreading the gospel of Christ* (2a). Perhaps Paul gave Timothy this exalted description because he wanted to show that in sending him he had sent a gifted and qualified representative. Otherwise, we might have expected Paul to describe him as 'our brother and *our* fellow-worker'; it was a daring assertion to say that he was *God's*. Indeed, some later scribes did not like it. So 'in order to remove the objectionable character which the bold designation *synergos tou theou* ("God's fellow-worker") appeared to have', some copyists deleted the words 'of God', while others replaced 'fellow-worker' with 'servant'.[64]

Paul had three reasons for sending Timothy on this mission to Thessalonica. The first was *to strengthen and encourage you in your faith* (2b). The verb to strengthen (*stērixai*) was an almost technical term for the consolidation and building

---

[61] Acts 17:15.   [62] Acts 17:16.   [63] Acts 17:15.   [64] Metzger, p. 631.

up of new converts.[65] Timothy was to do more than establish the Thessalonians in their faith; he was also to encourage, comfort or cheer them (*parakaleō*). Paul's second concern was *that no-one would be unsettled by these trials* (3a). To 'unsettle' is *sainō*, which was used at first of dogs wagging their tail, and so came to mean to 'flatter', 'fawn upon' and therefore 'deceive' (BAGD). Paul was worried that the Thessalonians' sufferings might lead them astray from Christ. Perhaps the best way to protect people from being upset by tribulation is to remind them that it is a necessary part of our Christian vocation. This Paul proceeded to do: *You know quite well that we were destined for them* (3b), for 'these are the terms on which we are Christians'.[66] *In fact, when we were with you*, Paul continues, *we kept telling you that we would be persecuted. And it turned out that way, as you well know* (4). It is very interesting to learn that a regular topic of Paul's instruction to converts was the inevitability of suffering. But Jesus had plainly taught it.[67] So Paul taught it too. 'We must go through many hardships to enter the kingdom of God', he said.[68]

Then Paul had a third objective in sending Timothy: *For this reason, when I could stand it no longer* (he repeats the reference to the intolerable suspense, but now makes it personal, 'I' not 'we'), *I sent to find out about your faith*, how it was 'standing the strain' (JBP). *I was afraid that in some way the tempter might have tempted you and our efforts might have been useless* (5) or 'wasted' (JB). The apostle refers again to the devil. He is not ignorant of his devices, whether in hindering the apostle's ministry or in tempting his converts to renounce their faith. So Timothy had been sent on both a nurturing and a fact-finding mission. His brief had been to stabilize the Thessalonians in their faith, to remind them that suffering for Christ was unavoidable, and to come back with news of how they were doing.

d. He had been overjoyed by Timothy's good news (3:6–10)

But Timothy has just now come to us from you, only a short time before Paul sat down to write this letter, *and has brought*

[65] *E.g.* Acts 14:22; 15:32; Rom. 1:11; 16:25; 2 Thes. 2:17.
[66] Calvin, p. 353.   [67] *E.g.* Mt. 5:11; Jn. 15:20; 16:33.
[68] Acts 14:22; *cf.* Rom. 8:17; Phil. 1:29; 2 Tim. 3:12.

good news (literally, 'evangelized', the only time the word is used in the New Testament when it does not refer to the gospel) *about your faith and love* (6a), 'the sum total of godliness'.[69] In addition, *He has told us that you always have pleasant memories of us and*, as a further item of good news, *that you long to see us, just as we also long to see you* (6b). These three pieces of information almost overwhelmed the apostle. He could not contain himself. He breaks out: *Therefore, brothers, in all our distress and persecution we were encouraged about you because of your faith* (7). Why should *your* faith encourage *us*, do you ask? Because our life is bound up in yours. *For now we really live*, 'now we can breathe again' (JB), now we have been given 'a new lease of life',[70] *since you are standing firm in the Lord* (8). The good news also leads Paul to thanksgiving: *How can we thank God enough for you in return for all the joy we have in the presence of our God because of you?* (9). And next the apostle is prompted to pray: *Night and day we pray most earnestly that we may see you again and supply what is lacking in your faith* (10). Since earlier in the letter Paul has described himself as having 'worked night and day' (2:9), partly in preaching, partly in tent-making, it is difficult to see how he could pray night and day as well. Perhaps his activities overlapped one another, so that he found he could pray even while he was engaged in his tent-making. What he says he prayed for was that now, in defiance of Satan's hindrances, he might be able to visit them in order to make up their spiritual deficiencies. 'Supply' is *katartizō*, meaning to restore, equip, or complete. It was used in various contexts, for example of a fisherman repairing his nets,[71] a surgeon setting bones, and a politician reconciling factions. The deficiencies Paul detected in their faith will have been 'gaps' (JB, footnote)[72] both in their doctrinal and in their ethical understanding. He longed to see them complete, whole, mature Christians. Hence his intended visit. Prayer for the increase of their faith was vital. Letters too can encourage and establish people in their faith. But there is no substitute for the stimulus of face-to-face fellowship, when we are 'mutually encouraged by each other's faith'.[73]

---

[69] Calvin, p. 354.   [70] Milligan, p. 40.   [71] Mk. 1:19.
[72] JB, 1 Thes. 3:10, note c.   [73] Rom. 1:12.

e. He had been praying for them all the time (3:11–13)

Having mentioned in verse 10 his earnest and continuous prayers, he immediately breaks into prayer in his letter. He expresses three precise and particular petitions, namely that God will bring him to see the Thessalonians again, and that he will increase both their love and their holiness. First, *Now may our God and Father himself and our Lord Jesus clear the way for us to come to you* (11). It is an amazing bracketing on a level of equality, as in 1:1, of God the Father and Jesus the Lord, and this time it is the more remarkable because the double subject (Father and Son) is followed by a singular verb (*kateuthynai*). There follows a wish in the form of a prayer, that God will 'make straight' or level the way which Satan has cut up, or remove the obstacles with which he has strewn it (2:18). Paul's prayer was answered, although only (so far as we know) about five years later when he visited Macedonia twice towards the end of his third missionary journey.[74]

Secondly, Paul prays: *May the Lord* (meaning Jesus, as almost always in the New Testament when 'the Lord' occurs without further designation) *make your love increase and overflow for each other*, in the Christian community, *and for everyone else*, 'the whole human race' (JB), *just as ours does for you* (12). It is impressive to note this prayer's double progress, on the one hand from each other to everybody and on the other from increasing to overflowing, the latter 'implying an *overplus* of love'.[75]

Thirdly, Paul prays: *May he strengthen* (*stērizai* again, as in 3:2) *your hearts so that you will be blameless and holy in the presence of our God and Father when our Lord Jesus comes with all his holy ones* (13), which could mean 'angels' or 'saints', but is best understood as including both, namely 'all who belong to him' (JBP). There is no greater stimulus to holiness than the vision of the Parousia, when Jesus comes in glory with his holy ones. In order that we may be 'blameless and holy' then, Paul prays that we may be inwardly strengthened now. For sanctification is a present, continuing process; perfection awaits the Parousia. The 'Amen' of JB (footnote)[76] is omitted from nearly all English versions. But

---

[74] Acts 20:1–3.   [75] Milligan, p. 43.   [76] JB, 1 Thes. 3:13, note e.

it is quite well attested, and it seems a fitting climax to Paul's prayer.

Conclusion: a double commitment

We have seen how Paul responds to his critics. He both defends his visit (2:1–16) and explains his non-return (2:17 – 3:13). In the course of his double *apologia* he has illustrated his pastoral ministry by four metaphors – the steward, the mother, the father and the herald. Like a steward he was faithful in guarding the gospel; like a mother he was gentle in caring for his converts; like a father he was diligent in educating them; and like a herald he was bold in proclaiming God's word. From these four metaphors we may discern the two major responsibilities of pastoral ministry for today. The first is to the Word of God (as both a steward to guard it and a herald to proclaim it), and the second to the people of God (as their mother and father, to love, nurture and teach them).

First comes *our commitment to the Word of God*. In 1 Thessalonians 2, Paul refers to his message three times as 'the gospel of God' (2, 8, 9) and twice as 'the word of God' (13). It was Paul's firm assurance that his message came from God, and that 'his' gospel was in reality 'God's' gospel. He had not invented it. He was only a steward entrusted with it and a herald commissioned to proclaim it. He must above all else be faithful.

Every authentic Christian ministry begins here, with the conviction that we have been called to handle God's Word as its guardians and heralds. We must not be satisfied with 'rumours of God' as a substitute for 'good news from God'. For, as Calvin put it, 'the gospel . . . is as far removed from conjecture as heaven is from the earth'.[77] Of course we are not apostles of Christ like Paul. But we believe that in the New Testament the teaching of the apostles has been preserved and is now bequeathed to us in its definitive form. We are therefore trustees of this apostolic faith, which is the Word of God and which works powerfully in those who believe. Our task is to keep it, study it, expound it, apply it and obey it.

[77] Calvin, p. 347

Secondly, there is *our commitment to the people of God*. We have seen that Paul expressed his deep love and care for the Thessalonians by likening himself to their mother and father. He felt and acted towards them as if they were his own children, which indeed they were, since he had introduced them to Christ. So he fed and taught them; he earned his own living so as not to be a burden to them; he was concerned to see them grow into maturity; and he was gentle and sacrificial in all his dealings with them.

Then in 2:17 – 3:13, it seems quite unselfconsciously, Paul gives a moving illustration of what he has been writing about. He lays bare his heart of love for them. He had left them only with the greatest reluctance, and had in fact been torn away from them against his will. He had then tried hard to visit them, but all his attempts had been thwarted. Waiting for news of them, he had found the suspense unbearable and so, though at great personal cost, he had sent Timothy to encourage them and find out how they were. When Timothy came back with good news, he was over the moon with joy and thanksgiving. And all the time he had been pouring out his heart for them in prayer. The fact is that his life was inextricably bound up with theirs. 'For now we really live', he wrote, 'since you are standing firm in the Lord' (3:8).

What is this extravagant language? I have sometimes asked myself. What is this loving and longing; this intolerable suspense when there was no news and this overwhelming joy when the news was good; this affectionate care and fervent prayer; this sense of intimate solidarity with them, so that his life was wrapped up in their life and theirs in his? My answer is that it is the language of parents, who are separated from their children, who miss them dreadfully, and are profoundly anxious when they have had no recent news of them. Pastoral love is parental love; that is its quality.

Chrysostom (about AD 400) understood this, when commenting on Paul's statement that the Thessalonians were his hope, joy and crown: 'Of what fiery warmth is this! Never could either mother, or father, yea if they even met together, and commingled their love, have shown their own affection to be equivalent to that of Paul.'[78] And in another homily he spoke of his own pastoral devotion to his congregation:

[78] Chrysostom, p. 334.

69

There is nothing I love more than you, no, not even light itself. I would gladly have my eyes put out ten thousand times over, if it were possible by this means to convert your souls; so much is your salvation dearer to me than light itself. . . . This one thing is the burden of my prayers, that I long for your advancement. But that in which I strive with all is this, that I love you, that I am wrapped up in you, that you are my all, father, mother, brethren, children.[79]

Another and more recent example I would like to mention is that of Charles Simeon, Vicar of Holy Trinity Church, Cambridge, for fifty-four years in the first half of the nineteenth century. An American bishop twice visited him in his old age and wrote: 'the sweet, affectionate expression of his face, and the welcoming tone of his voice, united with the great softness and childlike simplicity of his manners, instantly made me feel as if I was in the presence of a father . . .'.[80] And Simeon himself, preferring rather to commend truth and goodness than to castigate error and evil, used to beg younger clergy to 'be gentle among your people' as a mother with her family.[81]

Here, then, is the double commitment of Christian pastoral leaders, first to the Word of God (as stewards and heralds) and secondly to the people of God (as mothers and fathers). We are ministers of the Word and ministers of the church. Another way of expressing the same thing is that the two chief characteristics of pastoral ministry are truth and love. It is these which build up the church, especially in association with each other. It is by 'speaking [or maintaining] the truth in love' that we 'grow up into him who is the Head, that is, Christ'.[82] Yet this combination is rare in the contemporary church. Some leaders are great champions of the truth and anxious to fight for it, but display little love. Others are great advocates of love, but have no equal commitment to truth, as Jesus and his apostles had. Truth is hard if it is not softened by love, and love is soft if it is not strengthened by the truth.

If, finally, we ask how we may develop this double com-

---

[79] Towards the end of Homily III on Acts 1:12–26.

[80] Hugh Evans Hopkins, *Charles Simeon of Cambridge* (Hodder and Stoughton, 1977), p. 209.

[81] *Ibid.*, p. 205.   [82] Eph. 4:15

mitment to Word and church, this balanced combination of truth and love, there is only one possible answer, namely by the power of the Holy Spirit, since he is the source of both. He is 'the Spirit of truth'[83] and 'the fruit of the Spirit is love'.[84] Pastoral leaders, therefore, have no greater need than the fullness of the Spirit, who alone can lead us in the single path of truth and love.

Additional Note on Paul's use of 'we'

Is it legitimate, however, to apply 1 Thessalonians 2:13 in particular to Paul, since in it he writes in the plural that 'we thank God' and that 'you received the word of God from us'? Are we to understand the plural form, which is used almost invariably throughout both letters, to indicate that Paul, Silas and Timothy were joint authors? Or is Paul in reality the author, who uses an epistolary 'we' by which to refer to himself? Neither extreme position seems right. But these questions, briefly alluded to already in the exposition of 1:1 and 2:18, must now be more thoroughly explored.

Certainly Silas and Timothy arrived in Thessalonica with Paul and shared with him in evangelizing the city. Timothy too had subsequently revisited the Thessalonians and brought back the news which prompted the writing of the first letter.[85] It is not in the least surprising, therefore, that all three names head both letters. Paul wanted in this way to acknowledge the labours of Silas and Timothy and to indicate their endorsement of what had been written.

This does not mean, however, that we have to adopt a new title 'The Letters of Paul, Silas and Timothy to the Thessalonians'. Nor need we deny Paul's leading role in the writing of both of them. The use of the plural 'we' does not require these drastic conclusions. The position of leadership and the voice of authority still belong to Paul. The evidence for this is both internal and external.

Internally, within the letters themselves, the personality of Paul not infrequently shines through:

1. It is he who was the main preacher when 'our gospel came to you' (1:5) and who regularly claimed that the

---

[83] *E.g.* Jn. 14:17.   [84] Gal. 5:22.
[85] *Cf.* 1 Thes. 3:2–6; Acts 18:5; 2 Cor. 1:19.

gospel had been uniquely entrusted to him (2:4). It is also he who felt towards the Thessalonians as their mother and father (2:7, 11).

2. Although he wrote that 'we wanted to come to you', he then added 'certainly I, Paul, did again and again' (2:18). By this he was not correcting himself, to the effect that he wanted to revisit them, while Silas and Timothy did not. He was rather clarifying that by 'we' he really meant 'I'.

3. Although he first wrote 'when we could stand it no longer' (3:1), he repeated this by saying 'when I could stand it no longer' (3:5). Again he was clarifying his meaning: the unbearable suspense was his.

4. Although he wrote 'we thought it best to be left by ourselves in Athens' and 'We sent Timothy' (3:1–2), he meant that he was left by himself alone because he had sent Timothy to them. Timothy did not send himself! And Silas had been sent away too, probably to Philippi. Chrysostom took this explanation for granted. Without justifying his paraphrase, he reworded Paul's statement: 'When I could no longer forbear, I sent Timothy that I might know your faith.'[86]

5. In 1 Thessalonians 5:27 he wrote 'I charge you before the Lord to have this letter read to all the brothers.' The names of Silas and Timothy may have been included in the opening greeting, but it is Paul who takes responsibility for the letter and who solemnly requires the Thessalonians to read it in the public assembly.

6. When in his second letter he waxes eloquent about the anti-God rebellion of the man of lawlessness, he cannot restrain himself from breaking out into a highly personal expostulation: 'Don't you remember that when I was with you I used to tell you these things?' (2 Thes. 2:5).

7. When he reaches the end of 2 Thessalonians, he not only seizes the scribe's pen and writes his signature in his own hand ('I, Paul'), but sufficiently forgets himself and his 'we'-style as to call it 'the distinguishing mark in all *my* letters' (2 Thes. 3:17). So it is *his* letter after all! It is not just that he gives it his imprimatur, but that the authorship and therefore the authority are ultimately his.

Turning from internal to external evidence to substantiate the essential Pauline authorship of the Thessalonian letters,

---

[86] Chrysostom, p. 339.

three points may be made. First, Luke in Acts is quite clear that Paul was the leader of his mission team. Silas had been chosen to replace Mark, and Mark had been only a 'helper'.[87] Timothy, though much loved, was clearly a junior.[88] Luke does indeed couple 'Paul and Silas' as fellow prisoners,[89] Roman citizens,[90] and co-labourers.[91] Yet he makes it clear that Paul did the preaching, in both the Thessalonian and the Berean synagogues.[92] If, then, he was the leading preacher, it is all but certain that he was the leading writer too.

Secondly, Paul was an apostle, whereas Silas and Timothy were not. True, Silas was a leader in the Jerusalem church, an official delegate of the Jerusalem Council and a prophet,[93] but he is never named an apostle. Nor is Timothy. In fact, in later letters Paul deliberately distinguishes himself from Timothy in this respect by writing 'Paul, an apostle of Christ Jesus and Timothy our brother'.[94] It is in the light of this that we must understand the surprising expression 'as apostles of Christ we could have been a burden to you' (1 Thes. 2:6b). Either Paul was using the word 'apostles' here in its broader sense of 'missionaries',[95] or he was referring to himself as the apostle but was forced by grammar to write 'apostles' in the plural, in order to be in apposition to 'we' (rather like 'we were left alone [*monoi*, plural]' in 3:1).

Thirdly, there are many examples in Paul's other letters where he moves from 'I' to 'we' without appearing to change the identity of the subject. For example, after announcing himself to the Romans as having been 'called to be an apostle', he goes on to say that 'we received grace and apostleship'.[96] In his second letter to the Corinthians, after a highly individualistic passage in the first person singular about his relationships with them,[97] Paul changes to 'we',[98] although he is still evidently describing his own apostolic ministry, labours and sufferings. Similarly, at the beginning of 2 Corinthians 10, 'I, Paul'[99] lapses into 'we' from verse 3 to the end of the chapter, and then reverts to 'I' again throughout chapters 11 to 13.

[87] Acts 13:5; 15:37ff. [88] Acts 16:1ff. [89] Acts 16:19, 22, 25, 29.
[90] Acts 16:38. [91] Acts 16:40; 17:4. [92] Acts 17:2–3, 11.
[93] Acts 15:22, 27, 32.
[94] 2 Cor. 1:1; Col. 1:1; *cf.* 1 Cor. 1:1; Phm. 1.
[95] As in Acts 14:4, 14; 2 Cor. 8:23; Phil. 2:25.
[96] Rom. 1:1, 5. [97] 2 Cor. 1:15 – 2:13. [98] 2 Cor. 2:14 – 4:18.
[99] 2 Cor. 10:1.

We may also note the ease with which Paul could slide from the request 'pray for us that God may open a door for our message, so that we may proclaim the mystery of Christ' to the statement 'for which I am in chains'.[100]

One more example, this time from the pen of John, is 3 John 9–10: 'I wrote [singular] to the church, but Diotrephes, who loves to be first, will have nothing to do with us [plural]. So if I come [singular again], I will call attention to what he is doing, gossiping maliciously about us [plural].' It is understandable that RSV preserves the singular throughout, including 'Diotrephes . . . does not acknowledge my authority'. Moreover, this almost interchangeable use of 'I' and 'we' has many parallels in the secular writings of Paul's day. 'There are plenty of examples to hand from the papyri', wrote Bicknell, 'where the writer passes backwards and forwards from the singular to the plural in a single letter.'[101] These are clear cases of the 'epistolary' plural.

To sum up, we should agree with Milligan that there is no 'hard and fast rule', since Paul's use of the 'we' form includes 'a wide variety of *nuances* and shades of meaning'.[102] We have no liberty to say that Paul's plurals are never epistolary, for this position 'does not seem to be tenable'.[103] Nor can we maintain that by 'we' Paul always means 'I', using a 'plural of majesty', of apostolic dignity, for sometimes he is clearly intending to associate Silas and Timothy with him. What we can say is that his use of 'we' is never incompatible with his leadership role in the mission team and never lessens his authority as an apostle of Jesus Christ.

[100] Col. 4:3.
[101] Bicknell, pp. 30–35 ('Additional Note on Apostles of Christ').
[102] Milligan, p. 131.   [103] Morris, NICNT, p. 99.

1 THESSALONIANS 4:1-12

3. CHRISTIAN BEHAVIOUR
or HOW THE CHURCH MUST LIVE ACCORDING TO THE GOSPEL

We have reached the watershed of Paul's first letter to the Thessalonians. There is an abrupt change of topic between chapter 3 and chapter 4. So far (in chapters 1 to 3) Paul has been looking back to his visit and the events which followed it, and has been defending himself against his critics' accusations. Now (in chapters 4 and 5) he looks to the present and future of the Thessalonian church, and addresses himself to certain practical problems of Christian conduct which were evidently troubling them. In so doing he turns from narrative to exhortation, from his *apologia* to his appeal, from explanations regarding his own behaviour to instructions regarding theirs. This change of subject is indicated by the opening words *loipon oun*. They do not introduce Paul's conclusion (he is still two chapters away from this), but only his transition to a new topic, and should therefore be translated not 'Finally' (NIV) but simply 'And now' (REB).

Paul's sudden shift of theme does not mean, however, that there are no links between chapters 3 and 4. For one thing, his prayer that the Lord would cause them to grow in love and holiness (3:12–13) paves the way for his teaching about both (4:3, 9). For another, Timothy must have been the source of Paul's information both about the slanders which he has countered in chapters 1 to 3 and about the deficiencies in the Thessalonians' discipleship (3:10) which he proceeds to remedy in chapters 4 to 5. It seems likely that Timothy brought with him to Corinth not only his own impressions

75

of the Thessalonian church but also some questions from them, whether oral or written. At least the formula 'Now about' (*peri de*), which introduces three sections (4:9, 13; 5:1), is reminiscent of its use in 1 Corinthians where we know that the apostle is responding to questions.[1]

Introduction: the teaching of ethics

One of the great weaknesses of contemporary evangelical Christianity is our comparative neglect of Christian ethics, in both our teaching and our practice. In consequence, we have become known rather as people who preach the gospel than as those who live and adorn it. We are not always conspicuous in the community, as we should be, for our respect for the sanctity and the quality of human life, our commitment to social justice, our personal honesty and integrity in business, our simplicity of lifestyle and happy contentment in contrast to the greed of the consumer society, or for the stability of our homes in which unfaithfulness and divorce are practically unknown and children grow up in the secure love of their parents. At least in the statistics of marriage and family life, Jewish performance is higher than that of Christians. One of the main reasons for this is that our churches do not (on the whole) teach ethics. We are so busy preaching the gospel that we seldom teach the law. We are also afraid of being branded 'legalists'. 'We are not under the law', we say piously, as if we were free to ignore and even disobey it. Whereas what Paul meant is that our acceptance before God is not due to our observance of the law. But Christians are still under obligation to keep God's moral law and commandments. Indeed, the purpose of Christ's death was that 'the righteous requirements of the law might be fully met in us',[2] and the purpose of the Holy Spirit's dwelling in our heart is that he might write God's law there.[3]

To our current neglect of ethics the apostle Paul presents a striking contrast. It is not just that his letters are usually divided into two halves, the first concentrating on doctrine and the second on ethics, but also that he gives detailed instruction in Christian moral behaviour, even to very young

---

[1] 1 Cor. 7:1, 25; 8:1; 12:1.   [2] Rom. 8:3–4.
[3] *E.g.* Je. 31:33; Ezk. 36:27; 2 Cor. 3:3–8.

converts. The *paradosis* (apostolic 'tradition') which he 'passed on' to them, and which they 'received' (2 Thes. 2:15; 3:6), included both the truth of the gospel (1 Thes. 1:5–6; 2:2, 8, 13) and also moral instruction on 'how to live in order to please God' (4:1–2).

In fact, one of the distinctive features of the two Thessalonian letters is the frequency with which the apostle refers back to what he taught them when he was with them. Tell-tale phrases like 'we instructed you how to live' (4:1), 'you know what instructions we gave you' (4:2), 'as we have already told you and warned you' (4:6), and 'just as we told you' (4:11), enable us to reconstruct the content of the apostle's ethical teaching while he was in Thessalonica. He emphasized that Christians must live a life that is 'worthy of God' (2:12) and pleasing to God (4:1); that such a life will be one of moral righteousness; that God's commandments include such mundane matters as our daily work (4:11–12; *cf.* 2:6–9; 2 Thes. 3:7ff.) and penetrate even into the personal privacies of sex and marriage (4:3–6); that God judges those who are sexually selfish (4:6); that uprightness only exempts us from judgment, but not from persecution, since suffering is part of our 'destiny' (3:3–4: as 'we kept telling you'); and that the great stimulus to both holiness and endurance is our expectation of the Lord's return (1:3, 10; 2:12; 5:2–8). Thus, exhortations to holiness, warnings of suffering and promises of the Parousia belonged together in Paul's teaching. Within a few weeks or months he had taught the young Thessalonian converts not only the essence of the good news but also the essence of the good life, not only about faith in Jesus, but also about the necessity of good works by which saving faith is authenticated and without which it is dead (*e.g.* 1:3).

There is an urgent need for us, as pluralism and relativism spread world-wide, to follow Paul's example and give people plain, practical, ethical teaching. Christian parents must teach God's moral law to their children at home. Sunday school and day school teachers must ensure that their pupils know at least the Ten Commandments. Pastors must not be afraid to expound biblical standards of behaviour from the pulpit, so that the congregation grasps the relationship between the gospel and the law. And right from the beginning converts must be told that the new life in Christ is a holy life, a life bent on pleasing God by obeying his commandments.

After this introduction about the importance of Paul's theme, we are ready to study his text. It is divided into three sections in which he urges the Thessalonians (1) to please God (4:1–2), (2) to control themselves (4:3–8) and (3) to love one another (4:9–10), not least in the matter of earning their own living (4:11–12). His instruction applies equally to us.

1. Paul urges us to please God (4:1–2)

Finally, brothers, we instructed you how to live in order to please God, as in fact you are living. Now we ask you and urge you in the Lord Jesus to do this more and more. ²For you know what instructions we gave you by the authority of the Lord Jesus.

This general exhortation by Paul, which precedes his later specific instructions, is particularly noteworthy in two respects: first, for its authoritative tone, and secondly for its emphasis on pleasing God as the foundation on which Christian ethical behaviour is built.

First, we note the authority with which Paul teaches. We have already had occasion to comment on his selfconscious apostolic authority in relation to the gospel (2:13); now we observe it also in relation to his ethical directions (*cf.* 2 Thes. 3:4–15). True, he begins with two quite gentle words (NIV is misleading because it has reversed the order of the sentences): *we ask you and urge you.* The verb *erōtaō* means to make a request, while *parakaleō* means to beseech or exhort. Yet what he asks and urges relates to how Christians 'must' (REB; *dei*) live, and in verse 2 he reminds them of the *instructions* he had given them. This is a much more forceful word. *Parangelia* was often used either for a military command or for a civil order, for example by a court or by magistrates.[4] Moreover, whether Paul is 'urging' or 'instructing', in both cases he boldly associates himself with the Lord Jesus in what he teaches. Thus, his exhortation is made *in the Lord Jesus* (1; *cf.* 2 Thes. 3:12) and his instruction *by the authority of* (literally, 'through') *the Lord Jesus* (2; *cf.* 'In the name of the Lord Jesus Christ', 2 Thes. 3:6). It is clear, then, that when

---

[4] Acts 5:28; 16:24.

Paul is preaching the gospel and when he is teaching ethics, he claims to be speaking with the same divine authority. His gospel is God's word (2:13); his instructions are Christ's commandments (4:1–2).

Secondly, the foundation of Paul's ethical instruction is the necessity of living *in order to please God* (1). Jesus himself had been able to say 'I always do what pleases him [*sc.* the Father]',[5] and this is to be the goal of his disciples. Paul has already affirmed his own resolve to please God not men (2:4),[6] and in his later letters pleasing God becomes both his ambition for himself and his prayer for his friends.[7] Other New Testament authors say the same thing.[8] The terrible alternative is to 'displease God' (2:15)[9] or to 'grieve the Holy Spirit'.[10]

Several points may be made in favour of 'pleasing God' as a guiding principle of Christian behaviour. First, it is a radical concept, for it strikes at the roots of our discipleship and challenges the reality of our profession. How can we claim to know and to love God if we do not seek to please him? Disobedience is ruled out. Secondly, it is a flexible principle. It will rescue us from the rigidities of a Christian Pharisaism which tries to reduce morality to a list of do's and don'ts. True, we still need to be *instructed . . . how to live in order to please God* (1), and this for us will necessitate the developing of a Christian perspective through biblical meditation. Nevertheless, our incentive will be not so much to obey the law as thereby to please the Law-giver, and this will become increasingly a matter of Christian instinct as the Holy Spirit trains Christ's sheep to discern their Shepherd's voice.[11] Thirdly, this principle is progressive. If our goal is to be perfectly pleasing to God, we shall never be able to claim that we have arrived. Instead, we are summoned to please him *more and more* (2).

Here, then, is a very practical ethical guideline for our everyday Christian living. The disciples of Jesus took it much more seriously in earlier centuries than we do today. For example, near the beginning of the seventeenth century a fascinating compendium of the Christian life appeared, which had been written by Lewis Baily, Bishop of Bangor in North

[5] Jn. 8:29. [6] *Cf.* Gal. 1:10. [7] 2 Cor. 5:9; Col. 1:10.
[8] *E.g.* Heb. 11:6; 13:21; 1 Jn. 3:22. [9] *Cf.* 2 Sa. 11:27; Rom. 8:8.
[10] Eph. 4:30. [11] Jn. 10:4–5.

Wales. It was immensely popular and went through seventy-two editions, the last being published in 1842. Its title was *The Practice of Piety*, but its sub-title explained that it was 'directing a Christian how to walk, that he may please God', especially by a disciplined use of the means of grace which he has given us.

From his general exhortation to please God, Paul moves on to some specific ways in which we should do so, especially in the areas of sexual self-control (3–8), daily work (9–12) and bereavement (13–18). It was J. E. Frame who made the attractive suggestion that these were the topics which Paul had in mind when he issued his threefold exhortation in 5:14 to 'warn those who are idle, encourage the timid, help the weak'.[12] For these seem to have been the three groups in the Thessalonian church who needed special help. So Paul urged 'the idlers', who were neglecting their daily work, that if they loved each other they would earn their own living. He reminded 'the timid' or 'the faint-hearted' (RSV, REB), who were anxious in their bereavement about their friends and relatives who had died, of the Christian hope of Christ's return. And to 'the weak', who lacked the strength to resist sexual temptation, he spoke of God's call to purity and honour.

Sex, work and death continue to be three major human preoccupations, so that Paul's teaching on these subjects has about it a ring of relevance.

2. Paul urges us to control ourselves (4:3–8)

It is God's will that you should be sanctified: that you should avoid sexual immorality; ⁴*that each of you should learn to control his own body* [RSV, 'know how to take a wife for himself'] *in a way that is holy and honourable,* ⁵*not in passionate lust like the heathen, who do not know God;* ⁶*and that in this matter no-one should wrong his brother or take advantage of him. The Lord will punish men for all such sins, as we have already told you and warned you.* ⁷*For God did not call us to be impure, but to live a holy life.* ⁸*Therefore, he who rejects this instruction does not reject man but God, who gives you his Holy Spirit.*

---

[12] Frame, pp. 140, 196.

It is not surprising that the apostle begins with sex, not only because it is the most imperious of all our human urges, but also because of the sexual laxity – even promiscuity – of the Graeco-Roman world. Besides, he was writing from Corinth to Thessalonica, and both cities were famed for their immorality. In Corinth Aphrodite, the Greek goddess of sex and beauty, whom the Romans identified with Venus, sent her servants out as prostitutes to roam the streets by night. Thessalonica, on the other hand, was particularly associated with the worship of deities called the Cabiri, in whose rites 'gross immorality was promoted under the name of religion'.[13] It may be doubted, however, whether Corinth and Thessalonica were any worse than other cities of that period in which it was widely accepted that men either could not or would not limit themselves to their wife as their only sexual partner. Professor F. F. Bruce sums up the situation:

A man might have a mistress (*hetaira*) who could provide him also with intellectual companionship; the institution of slavery made it easy for him to have a concubine (*pallakē*), while casual gratification was readily available from a harlot (*pornē*). The function of his wife was to manage his household and to be the mother of his legitimate children and heirs.[14]

In his *History of European Morals* William Lecky paints a lurid picture of sexual licence during the early period of the Roman Empire. The cities of Greece, Asia Minor and Egypt, he writes, 'had become centres of the wildest corruption', and innumerable slaves from these countries had spread their immorality to Rome.[15] Indeed, 'there has probably never been a period when vice was more extravagant or uncontrolled' than it was under the Caesars.[16]

In many cultures and countries today, even where monogamy is officially favoured, deviations from this norm are increasingly tolerated. Christians, by contrast, have a

[13] Lightfoot, 'The Churches of Macedonia' in *Biblical Essays*, pp. 257–258.

[14] Bruce, p. 82.

[15] William Lecky, *History of European Morals*, from Augustus to Charlemagne; 2 volumes in one (Longmans, 1911), vol. 1, p. 263.

[16] *Ibid.*, vol. 2, p. 303.

reputation for being 'puritanical' and 'prudish', and for having a generally negative attitude towards sex. These criticisms are sometimes just. But in self-defence we also claim to be realists. Although we recognize that sex is the good gift of a good Creator, we also know that it has become twisted and distorted by the fall, so that our sexual energies need to be rightly channelled and carefully controlled.

Paul develops his instruction in verses 3 and 4 in three stages. First, he makes a general and positive statement that *God's will* is *that you should be sanctified* or 'holy' (REB). The word is *hagiasmos*, which can refer either to 'a process or, more often, its result (the state of being made holy)' (BAGD). Paul says nothing here about who is to initiate the process, although later he ascribes the work of sanctification to 'God himself, the God of peace' (5:23). Next, he specifies within God's general and positive will a particular prohibition: *that you should avoid sexual immorality* [*porneia*], which includes 'every kind of unlawful sexual intercourse' (BAGD). 'Avoid', however, is too weak a word. The apostle is declaring that God's will entails 'a clean cut' (JBP) with impurity, a total abstinence. As Professor Howard Marshall rightly comments, 'where things are evil the Christian attitude is necessarily one of abstention and not of moderation'.[17] Thirdly, Paul lays down two fundamental, practical principles to guide his readers in their sexual behaviour:

(a) Sex has a God-given context: heterosexual marriage (4a)
(b) Sex has a God-given style: holiness and honour (4b)

a. Sex has a God-given context: marriage (4:4a)

In writing this, it will be seen that I am departing from the NIV rendering *that each of you should learn to control his own body* in favour of the RSV 'that each one of you know how to take a wife for himself'.

The first half of verse 4 contains the most difficult phrase in the whole letter. Literally translated, it reads that 'each of you should learn to acquire his own vessel in holiness and honour'. Throughout church history commentators have

---

[17] Marshall, p. 107.

been divided as to whether the 'vessel' in mind (*skeuos*) is a metaphor for 'wife' or for 'body'. If the former is correct, Paul is urging each Thessalonian believer 'to take a wife for himself' (RSV); if the latter is right, he is 'to gain mastery over his body' (REB), or *control his own body*. There are difficulties with both renderings.

The difficulty with the translation 'take a wife' lies in the noun. For *skeuos* means a vessel, utensil, instrument or container, which appears to express a very derogatory concept of woman in general and of marriage in particular. Reference to woman as a 'container' seems in later Judaism to have been an established (and demeaning) euphemism for sexual intercourse.[18] It is mainly for this reason that some scholars have preferred to see an allusion to the body, even though no parallel use of *skeuos* for 'body' has been found, and to regard the body as the 'container' of the soul is Greek not biblical.

The difficulty with the translation 'control his body' lies in the verb. For *ktaomai* normally means to 'procure for oneself, acquire, get' (BAGD); so it cannot appropriately be applied to our body since we already possess one, whereas it was used in LXX of acquiring a wife.[19] George Milligan suggests from the papyri that *ktaomai* was beginning to be used in popular language for to 'possess' or 'take possession', in the sense of to 'use properly' or 'control', but the evidence is slender.[20]

In this exposition, along with 'the great majority of modern commentators',[21] I am accepting that the reference is to acquiring a wife and that Paul is affirming heterosexual marriage as the only God-given context for sexual intercourse. There are three main arguments. The first concerns *language*. This interpretation preserves the usual meaning of *ktaomai* ('acquire'), and recognizes that *skeuos* ('vessel') is used metaphorically in the New Testament of human beings[22] and once of a wife.[23] It occurs more often in pre-Christian Jewish texts

[18] See Christian Maurer in *TDNT*, pp. 360–362.
[19] *E.g.* Ruth 4:10; Ecclus. 36:24.
[20] Milligan, pp. 48–49. MM also suggests the meaning 'gradually obtain the complete mastery of the body', but gives no parallels.
[21] *Ibid.*, p. 49.
[22] *E.g.* Acts 9:15 'my chosen instrument' and 2 Cor. 4:7 'treasure in earthen vessels'. Also 2 Tim. 2:21.
[23] 1 Pet. 3:7 'the weaker vessel'.

in reference to a wife, as also does its Hebrew equivalent.

The second argument relates to *context*. Since Paul's instruction is the positive counterpart to avoiding *porneia*, which usually means 'fornication' or 'adultery', the natural allusion is to marriage. Again, the contrast in Paul's phrase 'in holiness and honour, not in passionate lust' can readily be understood as presenting alternative views of marriage; they can hardly be seen as alternative styles of self-control. Further, by his emphasis on what is 'holy and honourable' Paul seems deliberately to be purging *skeuos* of any dishonourable associations.[24] Some commentators therefore suggest that *eidenai* in verse 4 should be translated not 'should learn ...' but 'should respect his wife' as in 5:12.[25]

The third argument relates to the analogy of *Scripture*. What Paul writes here is an early, embryonic statement of the more developed position which he expressed a few years later in 1 Corinthians 7: 'Since there is so much immorality, each man should have his own wife, and each woman her own husband ... for it is better to marry than to burn with passion' (verses 2–9). Marriage is thus portrayed in Scripture both as a creation ordinance, intended for companionship and procreation, and also since the fall as a divine remedy against sin.

Paul's first principle, then, is that heterosexual and monogamous marriage is the only context in which God intends sexual intercourse to be experienced, and indeed enjoyed. The corollary is that it is forbidden in every other context, whether with a heterosexual partner before marriage ('fornication') or outside marriage ('adultery'), or in a homosexual relationship.

An additional paragraph is needed for those of us who are single and therefore lack the God-given context for sexual love. What about us? We too must accept this apostolic teaching, however hard it may seem, as God's good purpose both for us and for society. We shall not become a bundle of frustrations and inhibitions if we embrace God's standard, but only if we rebel against it. Christ's yoke is easy, provided that we submit to it. It is possible for human sexual energy to be redirected ('sublimated' would be the Freudian word) both into affectionate relationships with friends of both sexes

[24] See Lightfoot, *Notes*, p. 55. [25] See Frame, pp. 147–148.

and into the loving service of others. Multitudes of Christian singles, both men and women, can testify to this. Alongside a natural loneliness, accompanied sometimes by acute pain, we can find joyful self-fulfilment in the self-giving service of God and other people.

b. Sex has a God-given style: honour (4:4b–8)

The fact that marriage is the only God-given context for sexual intercourse does not mean that within marriage there is no need for restraint. We have all heard or read about, and some have experienced, the selfish sexual demands which are sometimes made by one married partner on the other, in terms of aggression, violence, cruelty and even rape. But marriage is not a form of legalized lust. So Paul proceeds at once from his first principle (each man acquiring his own wife) to his second ('in holiness and honour', RSV). Honourable conduct in marriage he contrasts with *passionate lust like the heathen, who do not know God* (5). He then adds that *in this matter no-one should wrong his brother* (or indeed sister) *or take advantage of him* (or her) (6a). Some expositors have translated the words *in this matter* either 'in his business' or 'in lawsuits' (NEB mg.), which the Greek expression could mean. But both before and after it the subject being handled is sexual behaviour, so that the context really demands that *in this matter* is an allusion to the same topic. Paul is saying, then, that it is possible for sexual partners in marriage to *wrong* or *take advantage of* each other. The first verb (*hyperbainō*) has 'the force . . . of crossing a boundary – here of crossing a forbidden boundary, and hence trespassing (sexually) on territory which is not one's own', while the second verb (*pleonekteō*, to covet) is 'the desire to possess more than one should in any area of life'.[26] Whatever precise meaning should be given to these two verbs, they are evidently incompatible with holy and honourable sexual behaviour.

The fact is that there is a world of difference between lust and love, between dishonourable sexual practices which use the partner and true love-making which honours the partner, between the selfish desire to possess and the unselfish desire to love, cherish and respect. Indeed, *the Lord will punish*

---

[26] Bruce, p. 84.

men for all such sins, as we have already told you and warned you (6b). For the Lord himself sees even the intimacies of the bedroom. He hates every kind of human exploitation, including what is sometimes called 'sexploitation'. There may be no redress for such behaviour in a human lawcourt (in most countries rape in marriage is not a criminal offence), but there will be at the bar of God.[27] And he himself will avenge it because he *did not call us to be impure, but to live a holy life* (7). *Therefore, he who rejects this instruction does not reject man but God, who gives you his Holy Spirit* (8).

Here, then, is a sex ethic for 'the weak', namely that according to God's purpose the context for sex is marriage and the style of sex is honour. It is elementary, no doubt. But it is also plain, frank, practical, authoritative, uninhibited – in fact, just what new converts need, especially if they are exposed to pagan standards and pressures.

What is also impressive about this paragraph is that it is from first to last an example of 'theological ethics', ethics arising out of the Christian doctrine of God. If the heathen behave as they do because they *do not know God* (5),[28] Christians must behave in a completely different way because we do know God, because he is a holy God, because he is our God, and because we want to please him. We have already seen the God-centredness of Paul's view of evangelism (chapter 1 of this book) and Christian ministry (chapter 2); now we note also the God-centredness of his view of morality. He brings together God's will (3), judgment (6), call (7) and Spirit-gift (8), and makes these the ground of his appeal to us to please God. If we rearrange his four points in a theological order, the apostle is making four affirmations. First, God's call is to holiness (7).[29] 'Be holy', he says, 'because I am holy.' Secondly, God's will is our holiness (3). Thirdly, God's Spirit is a holy Spirit (8), who is given to all his people in order to make them holy (2 Thes. 2:13).[30] Fourthly, God's judgment will fall upon all unholiness (6). Therefore, without holiness it is impossible to please God.

---

[27] Cf. Heb. 13:4.   [28] Cf. Gal. 4:8; Rom. 1:28; Eph. 4:17–19.
[29] Cf. 2 Tim. 1:9.   [30] Cf. 1 Cor. 6:19.

3. Paul urges us to love one another (4:9–12)

Now about brotherly love we do not need to write to you, for you yourselves have been taught by God to love each other. [10]*And in fact, you do love all the brothers throughout Macedonia. Yet we urge you, brothers, to do so more and more.*

[11]*Make it your ambition to lead a quiet life, to mind your own business and to work with your hands, just as we told you,* [12]*so that your daily life may win the respect of outsiders and so that you will not be dependent on anybody.*

Paul moves on in this section from chastity to charity, from the control of sex to the importance of work, from the need to 'help the weak' to the need to 'warn those who are idle' (5:14).

It seems clear that there was a group in the Thessalonian church who needed a very different kind of instruction and exhortation. They are identified in 5:14 as the *ataktoi*, and Paul says they are to be 'warned' rather than 'helped'. In classical Greek the word *ataktos* was applied to an army in disarray, and to undisciplined soldiers who either broke rank instead of marching properly or were insubordinate. It then came to describe any kind of irregular or undisciplined behaviour. The AV therefore translated the word 'unruly' or 'disorderly', and for centuries people wondered what kind of rebellious group this was which was causing the apostle so much anxiety. But discoveries earlier this century of secular papyri, dating from the first century, which had been well preserved in the dry sands of Egypt, showed that the word *ataktos* had developed another meaning in non-literary Greek. MM gives an example from an apprenticeship contract with a weaver which a father signed for his son in AD 66. In it he undertook that if the boy played truant and missed any workdays, he would make them up. And the verb for 'play truant' is *atakteō*.[31] The RSV and NIV therefore translate *ataktos* 'idle', although *TDNT* draws attention to its 'attested breadth of meaning' and states that outside Christianity, in relation to work, its emphasis is 'not in the first instance . . .

---

[31] The full text of the contract is given by George Milligan in *Selections from the Greek Papyri* (CUP, 1910), pp. 54–58.

on sloth but rather on an irresponsible attitude to the obli-gation to work'.[32] Paul uses the word (as adjective, adverb or verb) four times in his letters to the Thessalonians (1 Thes. 5:14; 2 Thes. 3:6–7, 11), and here in 4:11 the same group of people are evidently referred to, although the word *ataktos* is not used. The context in each case makes it plain that the *ataktoi* had given up their work and needed to be exhorted to go back to it.

But why had some Thessalonian Christians abandoned their jobs? What was the cause of their *ataxia*? Several sugges-tions have been made. Some think there was a scarcity of work in the city. But Paul implies that the idle are unwilling, not unable, to work (2 Thes. 3:10). Others believe that they had adopted either the Greek disdain for manual crafts or the super-spiritual idea that Christians ought to be preaching, not labouring. More recently, Dr Bruce Winter has proposed that Thessalonian *ataxia* was due to the social convention of patron-client relationships, whereby a wealthy patron would gather a large clientele of dependents. He points out that AD 51 was a famine year, so that many may have been on the 'corn dole'. Paul's purpose then was to persuade clients to work and patrons to stop acting as benefactors. Only in this way would dependence be overcome.[33] Even if this back-ground is correct, however, the traditional explanation remains cogent. It still seems probable that the *ataktoi* had misunderstood Paul's teaching about the Parousia and had stopped working in the mistaken belief that it was imminent. Their idleness was due to their 'eschatological excitement'[34] or 'Parousia hysteria'.[35]

Paul frames his appeal to them in terms of brotherly love. His argument is that to work for one's own living is a mark of love, because then we do not need to depend on the support of fellow Christians, while deliberately to give up work is a breach of love because then we become parasites on the body of Christ. Underlying this reasoning is the fact that a special kind of love binds the members of God's family together. The word for this *brotherly love* is *philadelphia*. In

[32] See article on *tasso* by Gerhard Delling, vol. 8, p. 48.

[33] From an essay by Bruce W. Winter entitled, ' "If a man does not wish to work . . .": A cultural and historical setting for 2 Thessalonians 3:6–16' (*Tyndale Bulletin*, 40:2, 1989), pp. 303–315.

[34] Best, pp. 175, 178; Bruce, p. 92.   [35] Hendriksen, p. 107.

secular Greek and LXX it was used in relation to blood brothers and sisters, but in the New Testament it is applied to the fraternity of faith not blood.[36] It is natural that those who know God as their Father should love one another as sisters and brothers in his family. So Paul writes that *about brotherly love* he does *not need to write* to them, since they themselves *have been taught by God to love each other* (9). *And in fact*, he goes on, *you do love all the brothers throughout Macedonia* (10a). In what sense were they *theodidaktoi*, 'God-taught'? Of course God had taught his people in the Old Testament to love their neighbour, and Jesus had given his disciples his 'new command' to 'love one another'.[37] But Paul's reference seems to be to teaching given neither by the Father in the Old Testament, nor by the Son during his public ministry, but rather by the Holy Spirit dwelling in our hearts. The prophets had promised that in the Messianic age all God's people would receive the Spirit, be 'taught by the Lord' and know him,[38] and in the New Testament it was believed that this promise had been fulfilled.[39] In consequence, strictly speaking, beyond the 'anointing from the Holy One' (probably a reference to the Holy Spirit) no human teachers are essential.[40] To love our brothers is an indispensable sign that 'we have passed from death to life'.[41] Nevertheless, although the Thessalonians did not need further instruction from Paul about brotherly love, he proceeded to give it to them all the same: *Yet we urge you, brothers, to do so more and more* (10).

From this general teaching about brotherly love, Paul goes on to the particular manifestation of it which he sees to be missing in the *ataktoi*, who have given up working. He evidently has them in mind when he addresses three admonitions to the whole church. The first is this: *Make it your ambition to lead a quiet life* (11a). This is a striking oxymoron, or contradiction of terms, which could be rendered into English 'make it your ambition to have no ambition!'[42] The idleness of the Thessalonians was apparently accompanied by a feverish

---

[36] *E.g.* Rom. 12:10; Heb. 13:1; 1 Pet. 1:22; 2 Pet. 1:7.   [37] Jn. 13:34.
[38] Is. 54:13; Je. 31:34.   [39] Jn. 6:45.
[40] 1 Jn. 2:20, 27; *cf.* Gal. 5:22.   [41] 1 Jn. 3:14.
[42] This rendering was first used by G. G. Findlay in his Greek commentary (1904), p. 92. But later commentators and translators have also used it, including JBP.

excitement, which Paul wanted to damp down. As their second ambition they were to *mind* their *own business* (11b). As Paul was to write in his second letter, because they were 'not busy' with their own business, they had become 'busybodies' (2 Thes. 3:11), meddling in other people's matters. Thirdly, they were to *work with* their own *hands*, just as Paul had told them when he was with them (11c). It was the Greeks who despised manual work as degrading to free men and fit only for slaves. Christianity came into direct collision with this view. Paul the tentmaker reinforced the example of Jesus the carpenter and gave dignity to all honest human labour.[43]

The apostle had two particular reasons for this threefold appeal to the Thessalonians to be quiet, non-interfering and hard-working. The first was that their *daily life* might *win the respect of outsiders* (12a),[44] and the second that they might *not be dependent on anybody* (12b; *cf.* 2:9), but rather enjoy 'an honourable independence' (JBP). In this way Paul brings together the two communities to which all Christians belong – the world and the church, 'outsiders' and the Christian brotherhood. He is concerned about the Thessalonians' relationship with both. He wants them to command the respect of unbelievers and not to be a burden on their fellow-believers.

We have no liberty to apply Paul's teaching about work to the unwaged who are drawing unemployment benefit or living on welfare. The contemporary problem of unemployment is both a symptom of economic recession and a traumatic personal experience. What Paul is condemning here is not unemployment as such (when people want work but cannot find it) but idleness (when work is available but people do not want it). He is emphasizing that we should be keen to earn our own living, in order to support ourselves and our family, and so not need to rely on others. True, it is an expression of love to support others who are in need; but it is also an expression of love to support ourselves, so as not to need to be supported by others.

[43] *E.g.* 2 Thes. 3:8–10; 1 Cor. 4:12; Eph. 4:28.
[44] *Cf.* Col. 4:5; 1 Pet. 2:12.

Conclusion

In 1 Thessalonians 4:1–12 Paul has addressed himself to the two areas of sex / marriage and work. Both are creation gifts, having been instituted by God in Genesis 2. Both are still parts of everyday human experience. And Paul gives us here a Christian perspective from which to view them. Two aspects of this perspective are particularly noteworthy.

The first is the call to *unselfishness*. We are to please God (1) and to love one another (9). To these fundamental simplicities the apostle reduces our ethical obligation. Christian morality is not primarily rules and regulations, but relationships. On the one hand, the more we know and love God, the more we shall want to please him. Children quickly learn what pleases or displeases their parents. Husband and wife understand each other so well that they know instinctively what to do and what to avoid. Similarly we are to develop a spiritual sensitivity towards God, through his Word and Spirit, until in every dilemma it becomes safe and practical to ask ourselves 'Would it please him?' On the other hand, love for others leads us to serve them. Whatever we wish others would do to us, we shall want to do to them. It is a wonderfully liberating experience when the desire to please God overtakes the desire to please ourselves, and when love for others displaces self-love. True freedom is not freedom from responsibility to God and others in order to live for ourselves, but freedom from ourselves in order to live for God and others.

Secondly, Paul issues a call to *growth*. We are to please God 'more and more' (1), and we are to love one another 'more and more' (10). Christian complacency is a particularly horrid condition. We have constantly to be on our guard against vanity and apathy. In this life we never finally arrive. We only 'press on towards the goal'.[45] Our justification is indeed *hapax* ('once and for all'); but our sanctification is always *mallon* ('more and more').

[45] Phil. 3:14.

4. CHRISTIAN HOPE
or HOW THE GOSPEL SHOULD INSPIRE THE CHURCH

Having sought by his teaching to 'admonish the idle' and 'help the weak', Paul now sets out to 'encourage the faint-hearted' (5:14, RSV). If we enquire into the cause of their faint-heartedness, the context supplies the answer. Their anxiety related first to the problem of bereavement (they were apprehensive about their Christian friends who had died) and secondly to the problem of judgment (they were apprehensive about themselves and their own readiness for the day of reckoning). Paul is once again clear that the solution to the church's problems is to be found in the gospel. So, in order to embolden the faint heart of the Thessalonians, he aims to stimulate their Christian hope by developing the theology on which it rests. This hope is the confident expectation of the Parousia, and this theology is the truth that the Christ who is coming is the same Christ who died and rose again, in whom they had put their trust. Paul applies this doctrine to both their problems. And in so doing he addresses them affectionately as 'brothers' (4:13; 5:1, 4). He sees no need to rebuke them for their anxieties; he prefers to issue a sympathetic, fraternal exhortation.

1. The problem of bereavement (4:13–18)

Bereavement is a very poignant human experience. However firm our Christian faith may be, the loss of a close relative or friend causes a profound emotional shock. To lose a loved one is to lose a part of oneself. It calls for radical and painful adjustments, which may take many months. Dr Leighton Ford, the Canadian evangelist and mission leader, put it well when his elder son Sandy died in 1982 at the age of 21. 'The struggle is to bring our faith and our emotions together', he wrote.[1]

Bereavement also occasions anguished questions about those who have died. What has happened to them? Are they all right? Shall we see them again? Such questions arise partly from a natural curiosity, partly from Christian concern for the dead, and partly because their death reminds us of our own mortality and undermines our security. In addition, the Thessalonians had a theological question to put to Paul. He had evidently taught them that the Lord Jesus was going to reappear, in order to take his people home to himself. I do not myself believe that he had dogmatized about the time of the Parousia, or led them to expect that Christ would come within their lifetime. It seems to me more probable that he would teach what Jesus had taught, namely that he might come at any time, on account of which they must be ready. At all events, they seem to have been expecting him so soon that some had given up their jobs, while others were totally unprepared for the experience of bereavement. Relatives or friends of theirs had now died before Christ's advent. They had not anticipated this; it took them by surprise and greatly disturbed them. How would the Christian dead fare when Jesus came for his own? Would they stand at a disadvantage? Would they miss the blessing of the Parousia? Were they even lost? It seems clear that the Thessalonians had addressed such questions as these to Paul, either directly or through Timothy.

a. A negative introduction (4:13)

Brothers, we do not want you to be ignorant about those who fall asleep, or to grieve like the rest of men, who have no hope.

Before the apostle responds to their enquiries with positive

[1] Leighton Ford tells the full story in *Sandy: A heart for God* (IVP, 1985). It is moving in its honesty, especially about the combination of 'tears, questions and silence' (p. 164), for 'when you love deeply, you hurt deeply' (p. 173).

instruction about the Lord's return, he makes two preliminary and negative points. First, he writes, *we do not want you to be ignorant about those who fall asleep* (13a), that is, 'who sleep in death' (REB). The description of death as sleep we will consider in a moment. Meanwhile, we note Paul's antipathy to ignorance. Expressions like 'I want you to know' and 'I do not want you to be ignorant' occur a number of times in his letters. Sometimes he is referring to his personal circumstances;[2] he realizes that the deepening of fellowship and trust between himself and his readers depends on their having accurate information about him. At other times, he says he wants them to understand about the mystery of Israel,[3] the solemnity of God's judgment,[4] the relations between the sexes,[5] and spiritual gifts.[6] He traces many problems of Christian faith and life to ignorance, and regards knowledge as the key to many blessings.

Secondly, *we do not want you ... to grieve like the rest of men, who have no hope* (13b). We observe that Paul does not forbid us to grieve altogether. Mourning is natural, even for a while emotionally necessary. It would be very unnatural, indeed inhuman, not to mourn when we lose somebody near and dear to us. To be sure, it is appropriate at Christian funerals joyfully to celebrate Christ's decisive victory over death, but we do so only through tears of personal sorrow. If Jesus wept at the graveside of his beloved friend Lazarus, his disciples are surely at liberty to do the same. What Paul prohibits is not grief but hopeless grief, not all mourning but mourning *like the rest of men, who have no hope*, that is, like the pagans of his day (for he does not take the Jews into consideration here).

But was the ancient world absolutely devoid of hope in relation to death and the hereafter? No. Ernest Best correctly writes: 'It is wrong to say that the rest of men had no hope whatsoever.'[7] The fact is that a few Greek philosophers speculated about the immortality of the soul, and there was a vague popular concept of the dead as 'shades' enduring a flimsy existence in a dismal Hades. But such notions could not possibly be graced with the Christian word 'hope' (*elpis*), which means 'a joyful and confident expectation of eternal

---

[2] *E.g.* Rom. 1:13; 2 Cor. 1:8; Phil. 1:12; Col. 2:1.   [3] Rom. 11:25.
[4] 1 Cor. 10:1.   [5] 1 Cor. 11:3.   [6] 1 Cor. 12:1.   [7] Best, p. 185.

life through Jesus Christ' (GT). On the contrary, there was in antiquity, in the face of death, neither joy nor triumph nor celebration, nor any defiant challenge like 'O death, where is your victory?'[8] Instead, there was a 'general hopelessness'.[9] F. F. Bruce quotes Theocritus as writing 'hopes are for the living; the dead are without hope'.[10] And Bishop Lightfoot eloquently presented Christian and pagan attitudes in a sharp antithesis:

> The contrast between the gloomy despair of the heathen and the triumphant hope of the Christian mourner is nowhere more forcibly brought out than by their monumental inscriptions. The contrast of the tombs, for instance, in the Appian Way, above and below ground, has often been dwelt upon. On the one hand, there is the dreary wail of despair, the effect of which is only heightened by the pomp of outward splendour from which it issues. On the other, the exulting psalm of hope, shining the more brightly in all ill-written, ill-spelt records amidst the darkness of subterranean caverns (*i.e.* Roman catacombs).[11]

This, then, was Paul's introduction to his answer to the Thessalonians' question. He wanted them neither *to be ignorant* about the Christian dead, nor *to grieve* over them in hopelessness. Indeed, he saw that these two things were closely related. Sub-Christian mourning was due to ignorance; only knowledge could inspire true Christian hope.

Why, however, does the apostle refer to death as 'sleep'? In three successive verses he describes people who have 'died' as having 'fallen asleep' (13, 14, 15). Is he implying that the dead enter a state of unconsciousness? We begin our response by pointing out that sleep has been a regular euphemism for death in many cultures. Bicknell was probably right to explain that 'the metaphor is suggested by the stillness of the body'.[12] A second thought, that death is a rest after labour, seems to have been conveyed by the Old Testament statement that certain patriarchs and kings 'slept with their fathers'.[13] But in Christian contexts a third idea is introduced, namely

[8] 1 Cor. 15:55.   [9] Milligan, p. 56.   [10] Bruce, p. 96.
[11] Lightfoot, *Notes*, p. 63.   [12] Bicknell, p. 44.
[13] *Cf.* also Rev. 14:13.

that death is only temporary. As sleep is followed by an awakening, so death will be followed by resurrection. Already in Daniel 12:2 we read that 'Multitudes who sleep in the dust of the earth will awake: some to everlasting life, others to shame and everlasting contempt.' Similarly, Jesus seems to have had resurrection in mind when he said: 'Our friend Lazarus has fallen asleep; but I am going there to wake him up.'[14]

It is, then, because a human corpse lies in the grave still, as it were resting, and awaiting resurrection, that it is appropriate to call death 'sleep' and a graveyard a 'cemetery' (*koimētērion*, a sleeping place). Cemeteries are dormitories of the dead. But these metaphorical (indeed theological) allusions to a dead body are not intended to teach that the condition of the soul during the interim period between death and resurrection will be one of unconsciousness. Calvin, whose first Christian book entitled *Psychopannychia* or 'Soulsleep' (1534) was an attack on this notion, wrote in his commentary on verse 13: 'The reference . . . is not to the soul but to the body, for the dead body rests in the tomb as on a bed, until God raises the person up.'[15] Certainly Jesus' own references to what happens after death suggest a conscious awareness of bliss or pain.[16] And Paul, in contrasting this world and the next, wrote that for him life meant 'Christ' and death meant 'gain'. He could hardly regard death as 'gain', however, still less as 'better by far', unless he believed that it would bring him a closer, richer, fuller experience of Christ than he was already enjoying on earth.[17]

What, then, is the Christian hope, in contrast to pagan hopelessness, for those who have died in Christ, which does not eliminate mourning altogether, but which comforts and fortifies us in the midst of grief?

b. A fundamental creed (4:14–15)

We believe that Jesus died and rose again and so we believe that God will bring with Jesus those who have fallen asleep in him. [15]*According to the Lord's own word, we tell you that we who are still alive, who are left till the coming of the*

---

[14] Jn. 11:11; *cf.* Mk. 5:39; 1 Cor. 15:20. [15] Calvin, p. 363.
[16] Lk. 16:19ff.; 23:43. [17] Phil. 1:21–23; *cf.* 2 Cor. 5:8.

Lord, will certainly not precede those who have fallen asleep.

It is immediately clear that the Christian hope focuses on *the coming of the Lord* (15), which Paul here calls the *Parousia*. Although this word's usual meaning is simply either a 'presence' or a 'coming', BAGD explains that it was used 'in a special technical sense' of Christ, and that this use had a double background.

> On the one hand, the word served as a cult expression for the coming of a hidden divinity, who makes his presence felt by a revelation of his power . . . On the other hand, *parousia* became the official term for a visit of a person of high rank, especially of kings and emperors visiting a province . . . These two technical expressions can approach each other closely in meaning, can shade off into one another, or even coincide. . . .

Thus the coming of Jesus, Paul seems to be hinting by the mere adoption of this word, will be a revelation of God and a personal, powerful visitation by Jesus, the King. It can hardly be fortuitous that he is writing this to the Thessalonians among whom, at least according to his critics, he had defied Claudius Caesar's decrees by announcing 'that there is another king, one called Jesus'.[18]

The Christian hope, however, is more than the expectation that the King is coming; it is also the belief that when he comes, the Christian dead will come with him and the Christian living will join them. For it is the separation which death causes (or seems to cause) which is so painful, both separation from Christ, since the dead have died before he comes, and separation from those who survive them, since they have gone ahead and left the living behind. It is these two bitter separations which the apostle solemnly assures his readers are neither real nor permanent. For the dead will come with Jesus, and the living will not precede them. He expresses his assurance in the form of a creed: *We believe that . . . and so we believe that . . . we tell you that . . .* (14–15). Thus, the creed has three clauses. The first relates to Jesus (he *died and rose again*, 14a), the second to the Christian dead (*God will*

[18] Acts 17:7.

bring them *with Jesus*, 14b), and the third to the Christian living (they *will certainly not precede* the Christian dead, 15).

First, *Jesus died and rose again*. This is the irreducible core of the gospel, which the apostles preached and which the church believes. Paul elaborates it later.[19] In this letter he gives it only in embryo, with a minimum of explanation. He writes only that Christ 'died for us' (5:10), in order to deal with our sins and so secure our 'salvation' (5:9). But he did not remain in death; he rose again, which implies that in some sense he triumphed over it.

Secondly, Jesus did not die and rise alone, for those who have died in him will rise with him. 'God will bring them to life with Jesus' (NEB). True, in spite of NEB, Paul does not explicitly say this. He says rather *that God will bring with Jesus those who have fallen asleep in him* (14b). That is, he is referring to the Parousia, not the resurrection. Nevertheless, the resurrection is implied, for there is in Paul's mind 'an unexpressed inner connection'[20] between the death and the resurrection of believers in Christ.[21] If God did not abandon Jesus to death, he will not abandon the Christian dead either. On the contrary, he will raise them as he raised him, and he will then bring them with him, so that when he comes, they will come too.

Thirdly, Paul addresses himself to the Christian living: *we tell you that we who are still alive, who are left till the coming of the Lord, will certainly not precede those who have fallen asleep* (15).

What Paul is affirming, then, is that neither the Christian dead nor the Christian living will be left behind or excluded or disadvantaged in any way. On the contrary, God will observe 'the most absolute impartiality' between them.[22] Neither group will take precedence over, nor have the advantage over, the other. In particular, there is no possibility that the Christian dead (about whom the Thessalonians were anxious) will be separated either from Christ (for they will come with him) or from the Christian living (for they will be joined by them). The apostle's emphasis is on the unbreakable solidarity which the people of Christ enjoy with him and with each other, and which death is utterly unable to destroy.[23]

[19] *E.g.* 1 Cor. 15:1–4.   [20] Best, p. 188.
[21] *E.g.* Rom. 6:4–10; 2 Cor. 4:14.   [22] Hendriksen, p. 115.
[23] *Cf.* Rom. 8:35–39.

Two further questions arise from verse 15, to which we must give some attention. First, Paul makes his declaration about the Christian living *according to the Lord's own word*; to what 'word' was he referring? Secondly, he associates himself with the Christian living by using the first person plural (*we who are still alive, who are left till the coming of the Lord*, verses 15 and 17); was he asserting that the Parousia would take place during his life-time?

First, what is this 'word of the Lord' to whose authority Paul appealed for his statement about the Parousia, whether it is thought to refer only to verse 15 or to cover verses 16 and 17 as well? Broadly speaking, there are two possibilities. Either it was a saying of the historical Jesus, or it was a pronouncement of the contemporary Lord, now ascended and glorified, speaking through one of his prophets or apostles. That there were a number of Christian prophets in those days is well known. Since, however, the authority of the prophets was inferior to that of the apostles,[24] it would be odd for an apostle to appeal to a prophet's authority. Was Paul then alluding to his own apostolic authority, claiming that the word of the Lord had come to him as it had kept coming to God's messengers in the Old Testament? Some notable commentators have held this view. J. B. Lightfoot thought it probable 'that St Paul refers to a direct revelation, which he had himself received from the Lord'.[25] Henry Alford similarly explained the phrase 'by the word of the Lord' (AV) as meaning 'by direct revelation from him made to me'.[26] And Milligan concluded his discussion: 'On the whole, therefore, it is better to fall back upon the thought of a direct revelation granted to the Apostles to meet the special circumstances that had arisen.'[27] But the problem with this interpretation is that Paul was accustomed to making a broad and general claim that Christ was speaking through him and that his words were God's words;[28] it would be anomalous for him to single out one or two sentences as being in a special sense *the Lord's own word*. It seems more probable, therefore, that Paul was quoting a remembered *logion* or saying of the historic Jesus. There are other examples of his

[24] *Cf.* Acts 21:10–14; 1 Cor. 14:37–38; 1 Thes. 5:20–22, 27.
[25] Lightfoot, *Notes*, p. 65. [26] Alford, p. 274. [27] Milligan, p. 58.
[28] *E.g.* 1 Cor. 2:12–16; 7:40; 2 Cor. 13:3; Gal. 4:14; 1 Thes. 2:13.

doing this, for example on divorce[29] and on the payment of evangelists and teachers.[30] Since, however, there is no saying of Jesus recorded in the Four Gospels which Paul can be shown to be quoting here, either he was making an allusion rather than a citation,[31] or he was quoting an otherwise unknown word of Jesus, a so-called *agraphon* or unwritten saying, as he did later to the Ephesian elders.[32]

The second question which is raised by verse 15 (as also by verse 17) concerns Paul's use of the first person plural ('we'). It seems to imply that he expected to be *still alive* when the Parousia took place, in which case he was of course mistaken. His error is confidently asserted by liberal scholars while those who query their conclusion and suggest an alternative are accused of reprehensible manipulation. What case for the defence of Paul can be made? First, since Jesus himself stated that the day of the Parousia was known only to the Father,[33] and since Paul virtually said the same thing in this very letter (5:1), it is antecedently improbable that the apostle would assert what neither he nor anybody else knew. Secondly, he continued to hold together in his later letters two apparently incompatible perspectives, namely his expectation both of the Lord's coming and of his own death and resurrection. In Philippians, for example, he combined his confident affirmations that 'the Lord is near' (Phil. 4:5) and that when he comes he will transform our bodies (3:20–21), with a longing to die (1:20–23) and 'to attain to the resurrection from the dead' (3:10–11). The case is similar in his Corinthian correspondence. On the one hand he could cry *Maranatha* ('Come, O Lord')[34] and again use the first person plural that 'We will not all sleep, but we will all be changed',[35] while on the other hand he could elaborate considerably on death and resurrection.[36]

Thirdly, Paul's major practical emphasis in 1 Thessalonians 5:1–11 is on the need for watchfulness because the Parousia

---

[29] 1 Cor. 7:10–11.   [30] 1 Cor. 9:14; 1 Tim. 5:18.
[31] *E.g.* to Mt. 24:31.
[32] Acts 20:35. See Jeremias: 'it is hard to resist the conclusion that 1 Thes. 4:16f. is an independent dominical saying, and that it has just as much claim to a place in our list as the saying preserved in Acts 20:35' (p. 5; *cf.* pp. 64–66).
[33] Mk. 13:32; *cf.* Acts 1:6–7.   [34] 1 Cor. 16:22.   [35] 1 Cor. 15:51.
[36] *E.g.* 1 Cor. 6:14; 15:12ff.; 2 Cor. 4:1 – 5:10.

will come unexpectedly like a thief in the night. This was also the thrust of the teaching of Jesus, who said, 'Therefore keep watch, because you do not know on what day your Lord will come.'[37] Again, 'Therefore keep watch, because you do not know the day or the hour.'[38] Now the call for watchfulness does not necessarily mean that the Parousia *will* come in our life-time, but only that it *may*. This was Paul's position. G. C. Berkouwer rightly wrote of 'the brilliant glow of Paul's expectation', which is evident in his letters.[39] He knew that after the death, resurrection, exaltation and Spirit-gift of Jesus there was no further saving event on God's calendar before the Parousia. The Parousia would be the next and the last. For that reason Paul was eagerly expecting it, and it came naturally to him to say 'we who are still alive', meaning 'those of us who are alive'.[40] It should be equally natural for us to use the same language. So JB is right to say that Paul included himself 'more by aspiration . . . than by conviction'.[41] He was certainly not dogmatizing; in 5:10 he envisaged the possibility of his death before the Lord's coming.

c. An eschatological programme (4:16–17)

For the Lord himself will come down from heaven, with a loud command, with the voice of the archangel and with the trumpet call of God, and the dead in Christ will rise first. [17]After that, we who are still alive and are left will be caught up together with them in the clouds to meet the Lord in the air. And so we will be with the Lord for ever.

Having outlined the Christian creed in relation to Christ, the Christian dead and the Christian living (14–15), in which he has emphasized the negative truth that those who are alive at Christ's coming will emphatically *not precede*, or 'have no advantage over' (REB), those who have died, Paul goes on to make four positive affirmations, relating to four great eschatological events.

---

[37] Mt. 24:42.   [38] Mt. 25:13.   [39] Berkouwer, p. 109.
[40] Marshall, p. 127.   [41] JB, 1 Thes. 4:15, note i.

(i) The Return: The Lord himself will come down from heaven (4:16a)

We note that it is *the Lord himself* who will 'descend' (RSV), not one of his deputies or representatives. The Parousia will be a personal coming, a visit in person, of *the Lord*, that is, Jesus. Accompanying his return there will be a universal, authoritative, divine proclamation which presumably will both announce the end and summon the dead to rise. For the Parousia and the resurrection are inseparable. As at the creation God 'spoke and it came to be',[42] and as at the tomb Jesus called in a loud voice 'Lazarus, come out!' and he came out,[43] so on the last day the dead will hear the creative, commanding voice of God and will obey.[44] JBP captures the drama well: 'One word of command, one shout from the archangel, one blast from the trumpet of God and the Lord himself will come down from Heaven!' We are probably not meant to imagine three distinct noises (the *command*, the *voice* and the *trumpet*) but rather to understand the variety and repetition as indicating the overwhelming, irresistible nature of the summons.

(ii) The Resurrection: And the dead in Christ will rise first (4:16b)

Already in verse 14 Paul has assured the Thessalonians that when Jesus comes God will bring the Christian dead with him. But he did not explain how or in what form they would accompany him, although the reference to Jesus dying and rising gave us a clear hint. Now, however, Paul is explicit in supplying the missing information. Their resurrection will precede their coming. *The dead in Christ will rise first*. This sequence is appropriate. Since the Christ who comes will be the Christ who himself *died and rose again* (14), so those who have died in him will now rise with him, and the resurrected Christ will be accompanied at his coming by his resurrected people.[45] Again we observe the gist of Paul's argument. There is no possibility that those who have died in Christ will ever be separated from Christ. They died 'through' him (14); they sleep 'in' him (16); they will rise 'with' him; and they will come 'with' him too (14). Christ and his people

---

[42] Ps. 33:9.   [43] Jn. 11:43–44.   [44] Jn. 5:25–28.
[5] *Cf.* 1 Cor. 15:20–23.

belong to each other inseparably and indissolubly.

(iii) The Rapture: We who are still alive . . . will be caught up together with them . . . (4:17a)
When I was a new convert, I used to imagine that 'the Rapture' referred to that moment when, seeing Christ face to face, we would be 'enraptured' with his presence, in other words overwhelmed with ecstatic joy. And we do indeed use the word in this sense in some of our hymns:

Oh then what raptured greetings
    On Canaan's happy shore!
What knitting severed friendships up
    Where partings are no more![46]

Great things he hath taught us, great things he hath done,
    And great our rejoicing through Jesus the Son;
But purer and higher and greater will be
    Our rapture, our transport, when Jesus we see.[47]

Father of Jesus, love's reward,
    What rapture will it be,
Prostrate before thy throne to lie,
    And gaze and gaze on thee.[48]

In our text the meaning is different, however. The English word 'rapture' is derived from the Latin *rapere*, meaning to seize. It corresponds to the Greek verb *harpazō*, which Paul uses here, and which expresses suddenness and violence, as when the centurion ordered his troops to take Paul by force in order to rescue him from a possible lynching.[49] Just so those still alive at the Parousia will be 'swept up' (JBP) or 'snatched up'[50] *together with them in the clouds*. The parallel between verse 15b and verse 17 is impressive. According to verse 15b 'we who are still alive, who are left . . .' will not precede the Christian dead. According to verse 17 'we who are still alive and are left' will be caught up together with them. The negative and positive statements dovetail. So far

[46] Henry Alford, *Ten thousand times ten thousand*.
[47] Fanny J. Crosby, *To God be the glory*.
[48] Frederick William Faber, *My God how wonderful thou art*.
[49] Acts 23:10.   [50] Best, pp. 180, 197–199.

103

from forestalling them, we shall join them. The purpose of this violent action (whose agency is not identified) will be not only to unite the Christian living with the Christian dead (*together with them*), but also to unite them with Christ (*to meet the Lord*). Once more Paul's concern is revealed, namely that the living, the dead and the Lord will be together. The truth that the redeemed will *meet the Lord* is expressed by another technical term (*apantēsis*). 'When a dignitary paid an official visit (*parousia*) to a city in Hellenistic times, the action of the leading citizens in going out to meet him and escort him back on the final stage of his journey was called the *apantēsis*.'[51]

Many details of this heavenly 'meeting' are omitted. For example, there is no reference in verse 17 to the Christian living being 'changed' (as in 1 Cor. 15:51–52), any more than there was in verse 14 to the Christian dead being 'raised'. Both are assumed. Further, it is not clear how literally we are to understand our being *caught up . . . in the clouds*. We know from Jesus himself that his coming will be personal, visible and glorious, but we also know from him that it will not be local ('There he is!' 'Here he is!') but universal ('like the lightning, which flashes and lights up the sky from one end to the other').[52] Presumably, therefore, our going to meet him will also transcend space. As for *the clouds*, they are to every Bible reader a familiar and easily recognized symbol of the immediate presence of God – at the Exodus,[53] on Mount Sinai,[54] filling the tabernacle,[55] during the wilderness wanderings,[56] at the transfiguration of Jesus,[57] at his ascension,[58] and at his glorious appearing.[59] The reference to *the air* may be equally symbolic, for it was thought of as the dwelling-place of the devil and his demons.[60] 'The fact that the Lord chooses to meet his saints there, on the demons' home ground so to speak, shows something of his complete mastery over them.'[61]

(iv) The Reunion: And so we will be with the Lord for ever (4:17b)

Having been caught up to *meet the Lord*, we shall now *be*

[51] Bruce, p. 102. [52] Lk. 17:23–24. [53] Ex. 13:21; 14:19.
[54] Ex. 19:16; 24:15. [55] Ex. 40:34–35. [56] Ex. 40:36–38.
[57] Mk. 9:7. [58] Acts 1:9. [59] Dn. 7:13; Mk. 13:26; 14:62; Rev. 1:7
[60] *Cf.* Eph. 2:2. [61] Morris, NICNT, p. 146.

with the Lord for ever. The momentary encounter will lead to an everlasting fellowship. Thus the descending Lord and the ascending saints, heaven and earth, will be united. For this is Paul's theme. The Christian dead (about whom the Thessalonians were worrying) will be separated neither from Christ (since God will bring them *with him*, 14) nor from the Christian living (who will be caught up *with them*, 17a). On the contrary, we will all be always *with the Lord* (17b). We cannot miss this threefold repetition of the preposition *syn*, 'together with'. This is the ultimate reunion, the *synagōgē* or 'our being gathered to him', to which the apostle will allude in his second letter (2 Thes. 2:1).

Paul has been content to refer in the barest, briefest way to the four great eschatological events which we have called the Return, the Resurrection, the Rapture and the Reunion. How are we in the twentieth century to react to his teaching which comes to us from the first? We must resist three temptations. First, we have no liberty to embroider his instruction with fanciful speculations of our own, or even to stretch the text beyond what the apostle intended to say. To be sure, it is tantalizing that he says nothing here about the nature of the resurrection body, the resurrection of unbelievers, the judgment day, the new heaven and the new earth, hell, or the final reign of God. And there is a place, of course, for supplementing what Paul writes here with what he teaches elsewhere in the New Testament. Yet even in this we must be cautious and allow these five verses to retain their own integrity. Secondly, we must resist the temptation of sophisticated 'modernists' to de-bunk Paul, to dismiss him as a child of his age, to deny that he was an inspired apostle, and to strip his statements of their 'mythological' clothing. We must insist that, however much imagery he may have used, he was referring to real events which belong to history, not myth. Thirdly, we must avoid the total literalism which denies that the passage contains any figures of speech at all. For the sleep of the dead, the spatial 'descent' of the Lord, the archangel's voice and the trumpet blast, the clouds and the air all belong to the realm of symbolic and apocalyptic imagery. Resisting these three temptations, we will be wise to combine affirmation (we are eagerly expecting a cosmic event which will include the personal, visible appearing of Jesus Christ and the gathering to him of all his people, whether dead or alive at the time) with agnosticism about the full reality behind the imagery.

d. A practical conclusion (4:18)

Therefore encourage each other with these words.

It is important to remember that Paul is addressing himself to a group of 'faint-hearted' Thessalonians. His purpose in this passage is to fortify them in their bereavement, not answer academic questions about the last things. 'There is absolutely nothing in it for curiosity', wrote James Denney, 'though everything that is necessary for comfort.'[62]

Most contemporary commentators compare Paul's message with a second-century letter of condolence, which was discovered in one of the Oxyrhynchus papyri and first published in 1907 by Adolf Deissmann. It was written by an Egyptian lady named Irene to a bereaved couple whose son had died. She is very sorry, she says. She weeps over her friends' lost relative, as she has herself recently wept over the loss of her own dear one, Didymas (her husband perhaps, or more probably her son). She and her family have done everything they can in the circumstances (perhaps funeral offerings and prayers). 'But nevertheless', she concludes in despair, 'against such things one can do nothing. Therefore, comfort one another. Farewell.'[63]

In contrast to the 'comfort one another' of Irene, who acknowledged that she had 'nothing' to offer as its basis, Paul's 'comfort one another' (RSV) is built upon *these words*. Nothing comforts and sustains the bereaved like words of Christian truth. In saying this, we must not forget one of the lessons of the Book of Job. Job's already appalling condition was aggravated, not ameliorated, by his mindless and heartless so-called 'comforters'. They began well, in that for seven days they sat beside him in silent sympathy. One wishes that, when this first week was over, they had kept their mouths shut. Instead, they drowned poor Job in a torrent of cold, conventional, false verbiage to the effect that he was being punished for his sins, until in the end God himself contradicted them in anger, and accused them of not speaking about

---

[62] Denney, p. 180.   [63] Deissmann, pp. 176–178.

him what was right.[64] Their mistake, however, was not that they had talked, but that they had talked 'folly'. Generally speaking, words can and do comfort, if they are true and gentle, and if they are spoken at the right time. In the case of the Thessalonians, to compensate for their ignorance (13), Paul taught them the great truths of the return of the Lord, the resurrection of the Christian dead, the rapture of the Christian living and the reunion of all three with each other. With these words they could indeed comfort one another.

2. The problem of judgment (5:1–11)

Two distinct problems have always fascinated (and often perplexed) human minds, not least Christian minds, and continue to do so. The first relates to what happens after death. Where are our loved ones, and shall we see them again? The second relates to what will happen at the end of the world. Is there going to be a day of reckoning, and if so how can we prepare for it? The first is the problem of bereavement, and concerns others who have died. The second is the problem of judgment, and concerns us as well.

It is evident that the Thessalonians in their 'faint-heartedness' were apprehensive on both counts. They were worried about their friends who had died, and whether they would suffer any disadvantages at the Parousia; and they were worried about themselves, and whether they were ready to stand before Christ at his coming. Both are modern anxieties too.

So the apostle Paul, being the realistic and caring pastor that he was, addressed himself to both fears and relieved them by the application of appropriate truths. In 4:13–18, as we have seen, his topic was bereavement and the Christian dead. Now in 5:1–11 it is judgment and the Christian living.

The problem was straightforward. During his visit Paul had evidently taught the Thessalonians about *the day of the Lord* (2). He had no doubt explained from the Old Testament that it would be a day of judgment. Amos, the first of the great eighth-century BC prophets, had made that plain. 'Woe to you who long for the day of the LORD!' he had fulminated. 'Why do you long for the day of the LORD? That day will be darkness, not light ... pitch-dark, without a ray of

[64] Job 42:7–8.

brightness'.[65] Joel had called it 'the great and terrible day of the LORD'.[66] How, then, can we sinners get ready for it?

The Thessalonians were proposing their solution to the problem, and wanted Paul's help; but Paul rejected their solution as false, and proposed the true solution in its place. He begins his reference to their solution with 'Now, brothers' (1) and his exposition of his solution with 'But you, brothers' (4).

a. The wrong solution: knowing the date (5:1–3)

Now, brothers, about times and dates we do not need to write to you, [2]for you know very well that the day of the Lord will come like a thief in the night. [3]While people are saying, 'Peace and safety', destruction will come on them suddenly, as labour pains on a pregnant woman, and they will not escape.

The Thessalonians were asking Paul *about times* (*chronoi*) and *dates* (*kairoi*), as the apostles had asked Jesus before them.[67] Usually *chronos* means a period of time and *kairos* a point of time, a crisis or opportunity. But it does not seem that Paul is making this distinction here. Why, however, were the Thessalonians asking their question? Not, it seems, out of idle curiosity, but rather for a very practical reason: they wanted to make suitable preparations for the day of judgment. They thought they could most easily get ready for Christ's coming in judgment if they could know when he would arrive. It was naïve, to be sure, but perfectly understandable.

Paul responds, however, that the solution to their problem does not lie in knowing the date. To begin with, nobody knew or could know it. Jesus had said that he did not even know it himself, and that only the Father knew it.[68] And later he told the apostles, 'It is not for you to know the times or dates the Father has set by his own authority.'[69] In consequence of this universal ignorance of the date, Jesus said, 'the Son of Man will come at an hour when you do not expect him.'[70] The Thessalonians knew this too, because Paul had already told them so. That is why he said, *we do not need*

---

[65] Am. 5:18–20; *cf.* Is. 13:6.　　[66] Joel 2:31; *cf.* 1:15; Mal. 4:5.
[67] Mk. 13:4; Acts 1:6.　　[68] Mk. 13:32.　　[69] Acts 1:7.　　[70] Mt. 24:44.

to write to you (1). It would be pointless to do so, *for you know very well* (2) that the day will come unexpectedly. It is as if Paul wrote: 'You know that nobody knows the date, and that therefore you cannot know it either.'

Paul now uses two metaphors to illustrate how the Lord will come. First, *the day of the Lord will come like a thief in the night* (2). Jesus had used the same analogy,[71] and it also occurs elsewhere in the New Testament.[72] The trouble with burglars is that they do not tell us when they are coming. They make no advance announcement of their arrival. It is not their habit to send a warning postcard. The same unexpectedness will characterize the day of the Lord. Secondly, *While people are saying, 'Peace and safety'* (that is, they imagine they are entirely secure), *destruction will come on them suddenly, as labour pains on a pregnant woman, and they will not escape* (3).

Here, then, are two affirmations about judgment, each enforced by a vivid simile. First, the day of the Lord will come like a thief (2). Secondly, destruction will come like labour pains. Both illustrations teach that Christ's coming will be sudden. Suddenly, in the middle of the night, a burglar breaks in. Suddenly, in the pregnancy of an expectant mother, labour begins. At the same time, there is an obvious difference between them. For although both are sudden, the burglar is unexpected, whereas labour (once pregnancy has begun) is expected. So, putting the two metaphors together, we may say that Christ's coming will be (1) sudden and unexpected (like a burglar in the night), and (2) sudden and unavoidable (like labour at the end of pregnancy). In the first case there will be no warning, and in the second no escape.

The Thessalonians' hope that they will solve their problem by finding out the date of the Parousia has been disappointed, therefore. What alternative solution is there? If Christ is going to come suddenly, unexpectedly and unavoidably, how can we get ready? Paul tells us.

b. The right solution: staying alert (5:4–8)

But you, brothers, are not in darkness so that this day should surprise you like a thief. [5]*You are all sons of the light and*

---

[71] Mt. 24:43.   [72] *E.g.* 2 Pet. 3:10; Rev. 3:3; 16:15.

sons of the day. We do not belong to the night or to the darkness. ⁶So then, let us not be like others, who are asleep, but let us be alert and self-controlled. ⁷For those who sleep, sleep at night, and those who get drunk, get drunk at night. ⁸But since we belong to the day, let us be self-controlled, putting on faith and love as a breastplate, and the hope of salvation as a helmet.

The apostle explains that there is no need for us to be alarmed by the prospect of the Lord's coming, because there is no need for it to take us by surprise. 'Surprise' is the key word in Paul's argument. There are two reasons why people are taken by surprise when a burglar breaks in. The first is that he comes unexpectedly during the night, and the second is that the householder is asleep. We can do nothing about the first reason, but we can about the second. Similarly, Christ's coming is definitely going to be unexpected. The solution to our problem lies not in knowing when he will come, but in staying awake and alert. For then, even if his Parousia is totally unexpected, we will be ready for him and not taken by surprise. *But you, brothers, are not in darkness so that this day should surprise you like a thief* (4).

Let me enlarge on Paul's argument about day and night, light and darkness. Burglars take people by surprise because they come at night. To begin with, it is dark, so that we do not see them coming. In addition, most people are fast asleep. Or if they are awake, they are probably out at a party and may even be drunk. *For those who sleep, sleep at night, and those who get drunk, get drunk at night* (7).⁷³ So darkness, sleep and drunkenness are three reasons why people are unprepared for a night visit by a burglar. If only he would oblige us by coming in the daytime! Then we would be ready for him. It would be light, and we could see him. We would ourselves be wide awake, and we would be alert and sober.

Just so with the coming of Christ. Will he come in the darkness or in the light? Spiritually speaking, will he come at night-time or at day-time? The answer to this vital question is 'Both; it depends who we are'. In the case of unbelievers, he will come in the night because they belong to the night and live in darkness. *But you, brothers, are not in darkness*

---

⁷³ *Cf.* Job 24:13–17.

... (4). *You are all sons of the light and sons of the day. We do not belong to the night or to the darkness* (5).

This truth needs further elaboration. The Bible divides history into two ages or 'aeons'. From the Old Testament perspective they were called 'the present age' (which was evil) and 'the age to come' (which would be the time of the Messiah). Moreover, the two ages were sometimes portrayed in terms of the night and the day. The present age was like a long dark night, but when the Messiah came, the sun would rise, the day would break, and the world would be flooded with light.[74]

The Bible also teaches that Jesus Christ is that long-awaited Messiah, and that therefore the new age began when he came. He was the dawn of the new era. He ushered in the day. He proclaimed the break-in of the kingdom of God.[75] At the same time, the old age has not yet come to an end. As John put it, 'the darkness is passing and the true light is already shining'.[76] So, for the time being, the two ages overlap. Unbelievers belong to the old age, and are still in the darkness. But those who belong to Jesus Christ have been transferred into the new age, into the light. Already in Christ we have 'tasted ... the powers of the coming age'.[77] Already, God has brought us 'out of darkness into his wonderful light'.[78] Only when Christ comes in glory will the present overlap the end. The transition period will be over. The old age will finally vanish, and those who belong to it will be destroyed. The new age will be consummated, and those who belong to it will be fully and finally redeemed.

So then (and this is the point which we have been working up to), whether we are ready for Christ's coming or not depends on which age we belong to, on whether we are still in the darkness or already belong to the light. It is only if we are in the light that we will not be taken by surprise.

Imagine that you and your family are enjoying your summer holiday. One evening the sun goes down, you draw the curtains, and everybody goes to bed. You sleep well too, because the following day you are expecting a visit from the family's favourite Uncle Bill. But because you are tired, you oversleep. In the morning the sun rises as usual, but you

[74] Cf. Lk. 1:78–79.   [75] Mk. 1:14–15.   [76] 1 Jn. 2:8.
[77] Heb. 6:5.   [78] 1 Pet. 2:9.

know nothing about it because you are still fast asleep and the curtains are still drawn. Only one member of the family wakes early, your eldest daughter. She gets up and flings back the curtains of her room, so that the sun streams in. Suddenly, there is a loud knock on the front door, and Uncle Bill stands outside. Your daughter is ready to welcome him. She is not taken by surprise, for she is awake, alert and in the light. But the rest of you are covered with confusion because you are still asleep and still in the darkness.

So the question which Paul's teaching presses upon us is this: to which age do we belong, the old or the new? Do we belong to the night or to the day? Are we asleep or awake? Are our curtains still drawn, or has the light of Jesus Christ shone in upon us? Verses 4 to 8 become quite clear, once we have grasped the biblical teaching on the two ages – the old age of darkness and the new age of light. For the imagery of day and night, light and darkness, is continued throughout.

Moreover, Paul begins with an affirmation as to who we are, and continues with an exhortation as to what we should be. Indeed, he repeats this pattern for emphasis. First, he declares: *But you . . . are not in darkness* (4), because *you are all sons of the light and sons of the day* (5a). In consequence (associating himself with them), *we do not belong to the night or to the darkness* (5b). *So then*, because of who we are, *let us not be like others* (literally, 'the rest of humankind', as in 4:13), *who are asleep, but let us be alert and self-controlled* (6). In other words, if we belong to the day (the new day which dawned with Christ), our behaviour must be daytime behaviour. Let's not sleep or even yawn our way through life, or live in our pyjamas. Let's stay awake and alert. For then we shall be ready when Christ comes and we will not be taken by surprise.

The second time Paul affirms who we are and urges us to live appropriately, he goes beyond watchfulness and self-control to the need for us to be properly armed for the Christian warfare: *But since we belong to the day, let us be self-controlled, putting on faith and love as a breastplate, and the hope of salvation as a helmet* (8). Several times in his letters Paul likens Christians to soldiers and refers to our necessary armour and equipment.[79] At the same time, he feels

[79] *E.g.* Rom. 13:12; 2 Cor. 6:7; 10:4; Eph. 6:10–18.

free to vary the symbolism. For example, in Ephesians 6 the breastplate is 'righteousness' and the helmet 'salvation', whereas here the breastplate and helmet together represent the triad of graces we considered in 1:3, namely 'faith, love and hope'.

c. Foundations for Christian hope: God's appointment and Christ's death (5:9–10)

How is it possible for us to put on as our helmet *the hope of salvation*? On what foundation is our Christian hope built? Some of the Thessalonians were afraid of the Parousia, because to them it spelled judgment; how could they be confident that it would bring them salvation instead? It was to answer these questions that Paul wrote verses 9 and 10.

For God did not appoint us to suffer wrath but to receive salvation through our Lord Jesus Christ. *[10]He died for us so that, whether we are awake or asleep, we may live together with him.*

So far Paul has based how we should behave (awake, alert, self-controlled, well-armed) on who we are (children of the day and of the light). Now he goes on to base who we are on who God is and on what he has done for us. He makes two great statements.

First, *God did not appoint* (or 'destine') us to suffer wrath (to endure the fearful condemnation our sins deserve) *but to receive salvation* (a rescue from God's wrath and judgment, and the corresponding gift of a free forgiveness) *through our Lord Jesus Christ* (9).

Secondly, this Lord Jesus Christ *died for us so that . . . we may live together with him* (10). There is no developed doctrine of the Atonement here. Nevertheless, some important truths are taught. To begin with, he died *for us*, on our behalf and for our benefit. This must mean 'for our sins', the phraseology Paul used later, since throughout Scripture death is the penalty for sin.[80] He died that we might live. Thus his death and our life are deliberately contrasted and inseparably connected. Our life is due entirely to his death, and the kind

---

[80] *E.g.* Rom. 6:23.

of life he has won for us is a life lived *together with him*. So he died our death that we might live his life. Through his death we have been not only reprieved but reconciled. And the fullness of this life with him will be ours *whether* at the Parousia *we are awake or asleep* (10). The metaphor here must refer to our physical condition (whether we are alive when Jesus comes or have died beforehand, as in 4:13–15), and not to our spiritual and moral state (whether we are self-controlled or self-indulgent, as in verses 6–8). That is, the time of our death is irrelevant. At the Parousia the Christian living will have no advantage over the Christian dead, and *vice versa*. Both groups will equally receive the fullness of salvation and life.

It is helpful to bring the apostle's two statements together. First, God appointed us to receive salvation (9). Secondly, Christ died for us that we might live (10). Thus our future salvation depends on God's purpose, and our future life on Christ's death. Our 'hope of salvation' is well founded, therefore. It stands firmly on the solid rock of God's will and Christ's death, and not on the shifting sands of our own performance or feelings. The ultimate reason why we should be bold rather than faint-hearted in anticipation of the Parousia lies not in who we are (children of the day and of the light) but on who God is, as revealed in the cross (the giver of salvation and life).

d. Conclusion: a community of mutual support (5:11)

Therefore encourage one another and build each other up, just as in fact you are doing.

Paul uses the same verb *parakaleō* here as he has done in 4:18. It was a true instinct, however, which led some English translations (*e.g.* RSV) to render it 'comfort' in 4:18, where the context is consolation for the bereaved, and 'encourage' in 5:11, where the context is faint-heartedness in anticipation of the Parousia.

The world can be a tough and unfriendly place, as we all know to our cost. It is easy to get hurt by it. In addition, bereavement can be a very painful experience. We are also prone to fear when we think of Christ's coming to judge. These emotions can tear us apart. We can become dispirited and depressed. But God means his church to be a community of mutual support. 'Comfort one another', Paul writes (4:18, RSV); *encourage one another*, and *build each other up* (5:11). All three are, of course, expressions of that yet more basic command to *love each other* (4:9). Moreover, the word 'one another' or 'each other' (*allēloi*) emphasizes the reciprocity of Christian care. We are not to leave it to an élite of professional comforters or counsellors. These have an important role to fulfil, of course, but supporting, caring, encouraging and comforting are ministries which belong to all members of the Body of Christ. They were already being exercised in Thessalonica. Paul was able to add to his call for mutual love the acknowledgment that 'in fact, you do love all the brothers throughout Macedonia' (4:10), and similarly to his call for mutual encouragement and upbuilding he added the clause *just as in fact you are doing* (5:11). No community could call itself Christian if it is not characterized by reciprocal love. Yet equally no community is such a paradise of love that its members do not need to hear Paul urging them 'to do so more and more' (4:10).

How, then, is this fundamental ministry of comfort, encouragement and upbuilding to be exercised? Doubtless in many ways, ranging from the simplicities of a smile, a hug or a squeeze of the hand to the costliness of patient listening, sympathy and friendship. Yet here in 1 Thessalonians we need to come back to Paul's emphasis on 'these words' (4:18). True, the Thessalonians' problem of anxiety in the face of bereavement and judgment was a personal and pastoral one. But the solution Paul gave them was theological. The true pastor is always a good theologian, and what makes a pastoral counsellor 'Christian' is his or her skilled application of the Word of God.

Looking back over this chapter, which doctrine is it which Paul applies to the Thessalonians' need? He refers to many, but one stands out. It is not just that Christ is coming. That fact can cause anxiety rather than reassurance. No, it is the further truth that the Christ who is coming to us is the very same Christ who died for us and rose again. In both sections of our text Paul emphasizes that Christ's cross, resurrection and Parousia must be held together, and that their ultimate objective is that we may live *with him*. 'We believe that Jesus died and rose again ... and that God will bring *with Jesus* those who have fallen asleep in him' (4:14). Again, 'He died for us so that, whether we are awake or asleep [*i.e.* when he comes], we may live together *with him*' (5:10). The foundation of Christian faith and hope, indeed the essence of the good news, is that Jesus died and rose in order to bring us into union with him, and that when he comes he will take us to be with him for ever. Our coming King is none other than our crucified and risen Saviour. We therefore have absolutely nothing to fear. On the contrary, we may be certain that nothing (neither death, nor bereavement, nor judgment) can separate us from him who died to bring us to himself. Therefore comfort, encourage and upbuild one another with these words!

5. CHRISTIAN COMMUNITY
or HOW TO BE A GOSPEL CHURCH

The apostle Paul cherished high ideals for the Christian church. According to his characterization of it at the beginning of his letter (1:1–4), it is a community loved and chosen by God, drawing its life from him, and manifesting this divine life in the basic Christian graces of faith, love and hope. Such a community could justly be called a 'gospel church', both because it has been brought into being by the gospel and because it is continuously shaped by the gospel.

One New Testament picture of a gospel church portrays it as the family of God, whose members recognize and treat one another as sisters and brothers. This seems to be the key concept in the second half of 1 Thessalonians 5, since the word *adelphoi*, 'brothers' (which includes the *adelphai*, 'sisters', in the one *adelphotēs*, 'brotherhood'),[1] occurs five times (verses 12, 13, 25, 26 and 27). It bears witness to the truth that if through Christ God is our Father, then *ipso facto* our fellow believers are our sisters and brothers. We not only belong to 'the day' (5:1–11); we also belong to 'the family' (5:12–28). Moreover, this fact of our mutual relationships profoundly affects our mutual behaviour. Paul has already urged the Thessalonians to 'love one another' with *philadelphia* or 'brotherly love' (4:9–10), to 'comfort one another' (4:18, RSV), to 'encourage one another and build each other up' (5:11). Now he develops further his vision for the church family, and for the 'one anotherness' of its members.

[1] 1 Pet. 2:17; 5:9.

117

He takes up one by one three essential aspects of the life of the local church (all of which are items of contemporary debate or concern), and gives apostolic instruction about them. First, he addresses himself to the leadership or pastorate (verses 12–13) and tells us how pastors and people, 'clergy' and 'laity', should regard and relate to each other. Secondly, he writes about the fellowship of the local church (verses 14–15)and about the responsibilities of church members to care for each other. Thirdly, he comes to the church's public worship (verses 16–28), what should be included in it, and in particular how the Word of God evokes the worship of God.

1. The pastorate (5:12–13)

Now we ask you, brothers, to respect those who work hard among you, who are over you in the Lord and who admonish you. [13]*Hold them in the highest regard in love because of their work. Live in peace with each other.*

Historically speaking, the church of Jesus Christ has oscillated unsteadily between the equally unbiblical extremes of 'clericalism' and 'anti-clericalism'. Clericalism is a situation in which the clergy keep the reins of power in their own hands, monopolize all pastoral leadership and ministry, and, having been put on a pedestal, receive an exaggerated deference, while the so-called 'laity' are well and truly sat upon. Then able men and women are allowed no space in which to develop their God-given gifts or exercise them in appropriate ministries. On the contrary, the only contributions from them which are welcomed are their presence on Sundays to occupy otherwise empty pews, some administrative and practical assistance, and (of course) their cash. At the opposite extreme is the over-reaction called anti-clericalism. This sometimes begins with the recovery of Paul's model of 'the body of Christ', in which every member of the local church, like every member of the human body, has a particular and distinctive function. Some Christians overpress the analogy, however, and deduce from it that clergy in any shape or form are redundant. 'The church is better off without them', they cry; 'let's found a Society for the Abolition of the Clergy!' But this extreme position overlooks the fact that, according to the New Testament, the Chief Shepherd delegates to under-shepherds or 'pastors' the privileged oversight of the flock which he has purchased with his own blood.[2]

We know that the Thessalonian church had responsible leaders, since Luke mentions Aristarchus[3] and Secundus[4] by name. But we do not know (because we are not told) what prompted Paul to write verses 12 and 13. Probably some church members had been disrespectful towards their leaders. On the other hand, some leaders may have provoked this reaction by their heavy-handed or autocratic behaviour. Paul rejected both attitudes. For it is God's will, he taught, that every local church should enjoy pastoral oversight, but not his will that pastors should dominate and organize every-thing. They are not meant to monopolize ministries, but rather to multiply them.

Notice now how Paul describes local church leaders. He uses three expressions in verse 12. Since these are participles, introduced by a single definite article, it is evident that the same people are in mind, although they are portrayed from three distinct perspectives.

First, Christian leaders are those *who work hard among you*. It is a significant phrase because some people regard the pastorate as a Sundays-only occupation, in fact a sinecure (*i.e.* a paid job involving little or no work). And, to be sure, some clergy have been known to be lazy. But true pastoral work is hard work. The verb Paul uses (*kopiaō*) normally re-fers to manual occupations. It means to 'toil, strive, struggle' (BAGD), and to grow weary in doing so. It conjures up pictures of rippling muscles and pouring sweat. Paul applied it to farm labourers[5] and to the physical exertions of his own tent-making (2:9; 2 Thes. 3:8). But he also used it in relation to his apostolic labours,[6] to the hard work of his colleagues,[7] and to those who 'labour in preaching and teaching'.[8] Whether it is study and the preparation of sermons, or visit-ing the sick and counselling the disturbed, or instructing people for baptism or marriage, or being diligent in inter-cession – these things demand that we 'toil, striving with all the energy which he [*sc.* Christ] mightily inspires within' us.[9]

Secondly, Christian leaders are those *who are over you in*

---

[2] Acts 20:28.   [3] Acts 19:29; 20:4; 27:2; *cf.* Col. 4:10; Phm. 24.
[4] Acts 20:4.   [5] *E.g.* 2 Tim. 2:6.   [6] *E.g.* 1 Cor. 15:10; 1 Tim. 4:10.
[7] *E.g.* Rom. 16:12.   [8] 1 Tim. 5:17, RSV.   [9] Col. 1:29, RSV.

the Lord. True, the very first thing which needs to be said about Christian ministers of all kinds is that they are 'under' people (as their servants) rather than 'over' them (as their leaders, let alone their lords). Jesus made this absolutely plain.[10] The chief characteristic of Christian leaders, he insisted, is humility not authority, and gentleness not power. Nevertheless, authentic servant-leadership still carries an element of authority.[11] Bo Reicke writes in *TDNT* that *proïstēmi* in the intransitive middle meant originally to 'put oneself at the head' or 'go first'. Then metaphorically it came to signify either to 'preside' in the sense of to direct or rule, or to 'protect' or 'care for'. MM shows from the papyri how it was applied to a variety of officials, superintendents, village heads or chiefs, landlords, estate managers and guardians of children, in all of which the notions of 'leading' and 'caring' seem to be combined. The same combination is suggested in the New Testament, in which the 'leadership' of Romans 12:8 (*ho proïstamenos*) comes in the middle of three other caring ministries, and the same verb is used of a father 'managing' his own home and children.[12] It was natural, therefore, to use the verb of Christian elders, for 'If anyone does not know how to manage his own family, how can he take care of God's church?'[13] We see again, as we did in 1 Thessalonians 2 and 3, that pastoral care is parental care. The element of 'management' cannot be eliminated, yet here in relation to the leaders of the Thessalonian church 'the emphasis is not on their rank or authority but on their efforts for the eternal salvation of believers' (*TDNT*). This is in keeping with the startling originality of Jesus, who taught that in God's kingdom the first are last, the leaders servants and the chiefs slaves. Those who are 'over' others *in the Lord* (that is, in the Christian community, whose members are bound together by their common allegiance to Jesus) must never forget their Lord's teaching on leadership.

Thirdly, Christian leaders are those *who admonish you*. The verb *noutheteō* is almost invariably used in an ethical context. It means to warn against bad behaviour and its consequences,[14] and to reprove, even discipline, those who have done wrong. Being a negative word, it is often coupled

[10] Especially in Mk. 10:42–45.   [11] *Cf.* Heb. 13:7, 17, 24.
[12] 1 Tim. 3:4–5, 12.   [13] 1 Tim. 3:5; *cf.* 5:17.
[14] *E.g.* Acts 20:31; 1 Cor. 4:14.

with 'teaching', *e.g.* 'admonishing and teaching everyone'.[15] Both activities belong to the responsibility of pastors. Moreover *noutheteō* does not denote a harsh ministry. As Leon Morris has put it, 'while its tone is brotherly, it is big-brotherly'.[16]

Here, then, are three parallel expressions, which indicate that Paul envisages a distinct group of leaders, who are 'over' the congregation in the Lord, to whom has been entrusted their pastoral oversight and care, including admonition, and who are expected to work hard in serving them. It is true that 'they are identified by their activities rather than by a name'.[17] Does it necessarily follow, however, that at this time 'they did not have a name'?[18] Unless Luke was guilty of an anachronism, they were already during Paul's first missionary journey called 'elders' (*presbyteroi*).[19] A few years later they were also called 'pastors' and 'overseers' or 'bishops' (*episkopoi*).[20] Their ministry may take different forms, and has developed different patterns in the history of the church, but in each case it must give the Christian community the pastoral care (*episkopē*) which God intends it to enjoy, especially by teaching.

What attitude should the local congregation adopt towards its pastors? They are neither to despise them, as if they were dispensable, nor to flatter or fawn on them as if they were popes or princes, but rather to *respect* them (12), and to *Hold them in the highest regard* (NEB 'in the highest possible esteem') *in love because of their work* (13a). This combination of appreciation and affection will enable pastors and people to *Live in peace with each other* (13b). Yet in too many churches they are at loggerheads, which is painful to those involved, inhibiting to the church's life and growth, and damaging to its public image. By contrast, happy is the church family in which pastors and people recognize that God calls different believers to different ministries, exercise their own ministries with diligence and humility, and give to others the respect and love which their God-appointed labour demands! They will *live in peace with each other*.

---

[15] Col. 1:28; 3:16.   [16] Morris, NICNT, p. 166.   [17] Best, p. 226.
[18] *Ibid.*   [19] Acts 14:23.   [20] Acts 20:17, 28.

2. The fellowship (5:14–15)

And we urge you, brothers, warn those who are idle, encourage the timid, help the weak, be patient with everyone. [15]*Make sure that nobody pays back wrong for wrong, but always try to be kind to each other and to everyone else.*

These two verses begin with the words *And we urge you, brothers*, much as verses 12 and 13 were introduced by the words 'Now we ask you, brothers.' The formula is identical except for the change of verb. It is probable, therefore, that the 'brothers' addressed are the same people. In verse 12 these were clearly the rank and file members of the Thessalonian church, because they were distinguished from their leaders whom they were told to respect. The 'brothers' of verse 14 must surely, therefore, be the same church members. It is they and not the leaders whom Paul now urges to give pastoral care to specially needy people in the congregation, and indeed to each other. The existence of pastors does not relieve members of their responsibilities to care for one another.

First, the apostle singles out for mention three particular groups whom the *brothers* are to care for. They must *warn those who are idle* (the *ataktoi* who were playing truant from work), *encourage the timid* (the *oligopsychoi* or 'fainthearted', those anxious either about their friends who had died or about their own salvation), and *help the weak* (those finding sexual self-control difficult, who were addressed in 4:3–8). The verb for *help* (*antechomai*) presents a graphic picture of the support which *the weak* needed. It is as if Paul wrote to the stronger Christians: 'Hold on to them', 'cling to them', even 'put your arm round' them.[21] He then continued: *be patient with everyone* or, as perhaps it should in the context be translated, be very patient 'with them all' (RSV). One might say that the idle, the anxious and the weak were the 'problem children' of the church family, plagued respectively with problems of understanding, faith and conduct. Every church has members of this kind. We have no excuse for becoming impatient with them on the ground that they are difficult, demanding, disappointing, argumentative or rude. On the contrary, we are to be *patient* with all of them.

[21] Moffatt, p. 41.

Makrothymia, often translated 'long-suffering', is an attribute of God,[22] a fruit of the Spirit and a characteristic of love.[23] Since God has been infinitely patient with us, as he was (for example) with Saul of Tarsus,[24] we too must be patient with others.

Secondly, Paul moves on from particular groups needing help to general Christian behaviour. *Make sure*, he writes, or 'See to it' (REB), *that nobody* (or 'none of you', RSV) *pays back wrong for wrong*. Here is an allusion both to the teaching of Jesus in the Sermon on the Mount[25] and to his own remembered refusal to hit back.[26] All personal revenge and retaliation are forbidden to the followers of Jesus. And in place of these negative attitudes and actions, we are enjoined: *always try to be kind* (RSV 'seek to do good', NEB 'aim at doing the best you can') *to each other* within the fellowship of God's children *and* indeed *to everyone else*, including (as Jesus specifically taught) our enemies. Perhaps Paul had in mind the slanderers and persecutors of Thessalonica.

'See to it', the apostle writes.[27] We recall that he is not addressing the church's leaders, although they of course have a vital role in pastoral oversight. Instead, he is laying on the whole congregation the responsibility to care for each other as sisters and brothers, to give appropriate support, encouragement or admonition to the church's problem children, and to ensure that all its members follow the teaching of Jesus, cultivating patience, renouncing retaliation and pursuing kindness. It is a beautiful vision of the local church as a community not only of mutual comfort and encouragement (4:18; 5:11) but of mutual forbearance and service as well.

3. The worship (5:16–22, 27)

Be joyful always; [17]*pray continually;* [18]*give thanks in all circumstances, for this is God's will for you in Christ Jesus.*

[19]*Do not put out the Spirit's fire;* [20]*do not treat prophecies with contempt.* [21]*Test everything. Hold on to the good.* [22]*Avoid every kind of evil. . . .* [27]*I charge you before the Lord to have this letter read to all the brothers.*

---

[22] Ex. 34:6; Ps. 103:8.   [23] Gal. 5:22; 1 Cor. 13:4.   [24] 1 Tim. 1:16.
[25] Mt. 5:39, 44; *cf.* Rom. 12:17–21.   [26] 1 Pet. 2:20ff.; 3:9.
[27] *Cf.* Dt. 29:18.

At first reading one might not think that this section relates to the nature and conduct of public worship. But there are clear indications that this is primarily what Paul has in mind. To begin with, all the verbs are plural, so that they seem to describe our collective and public, rather than individual and private, Christian duties. The prophesying of verse 20 is obviously public. The holy kiss of verse 26 presupposes a meeting (you cannot kiss people at a distance!). And verse 27 envisages the reading of the letter when 'all the brothers' are present. It is this context, then, which suggests that the rejoicing, the praying and the thanksgiving of verses 16–18 (like Eph. 5:19–20 and Col. 3:15–17) are also meant to be expressed when the congregation assembles. Dr Ralph Martin goes further and considers that these short, sharp commands read like 'the "headings" of a Church service'.[28]

Now public worship is a vital part of the life of the local church. It is even essential to its identity. Yet in the interests of 'spontaneity' worship services often lack both content and form, and so become slovenly, mindless, irreverent or dull. Most churches could afford to give more time and trouble to the preparation of their worship. It is a mistake to imagine either that freedom and form exclude one another, or that the Holy Spirit is the friend of freedom in such a way as to be the enemy of form. This is demonstrated both by the early church's use of the Psalms, and by the many fragments of Christian hymns, psalms, creeds and confessions which are imbedded in the New Testament itself.[29]

The apostle Paul issues four instructions with regard to public worship, which lay down four of its essential ingredients.

a. Rejoice always! (5:16, RSV)

This injunction can hardly be interpreted as a general exhortation to Christians to 'be joyful always' (NIV) or 'be happy in your faith at all times' (JBP), for joy and happiness are not at our command, and cannot be turned on and off like a tap. We would be wiser to understand this instruction as meaning

---

[28] Martin, p. 136.
[29] Notable examples are 1 Cor. 15:3–5; Phil. 2:6–11; 1 Tim. 3:16; Rev. 4:8, 11; 15:3–4. For a thorough treatment of this topic see R. P. Martin's *Worship in the Early Church*.

'Rejoice in the Lord always'.[30] Then at once it becomes reminiscent of many Old Testament commands like those which introduce the *Venite*, 'Come, let us sing for joy to the LORD', and the *Jubilate*, 'Shout for joy to the LORD'.[31] In other words, Paul is issuing not an order to be happy but an invitation to worship, and to joyful worship at that. Yet many church services are unforgivably gloomy and boring. Although, to be sure, it is always appropriate to worship Almighty God with awe and humility, yet every service should also be a celebration, a joyful rehearsal of what God has done and given through Christ. So let there be organs and trumpets and drums and singing!

b. Pray continually! (5:17)

The disciples of Jesus, he said, 'should always pray and not give up', and he added his parable of the wicked judge and the persistent widow in order to enforce his dictum.[32] His teaching did not relate, however, to private individual prayer only (entering our room, closing the door and speaking to the Father in secret),[33] for he went on in the Sermon on the Mount to give us the 'Our Father', which can only be prayed with others.[34] So, if praise is one indispensable element of public worship, prayer is another, especially in the form of intercession. Each congregation should accept the responsibility to engage in serious intercession, not only during the Sunday services but at a midweek prayer meeting as well. We should be praying for our own church members, far and near; for the church throughout the world, its leaders, its adherence to the truth of God's revelation, its holiness, unity and mission; for our nation, parliament and government, and for a just, free, compassionate and participatory society; for world mission, especially for places and peoples resistant to the gospel; for peace, justice and environmental stewardship; and for the poor, the oppressed, the hungry, the homeless and the sick. I sometimes wonder if the comparatively slow progress towards world peace, world equity and world evangelization is not due, more than anything else, to the prayerlessness of the people of God.

[30] Phil. 4:4.   [31] Ps. 95:1; 100:1.   [32] Lk. 18:1–8.
[33] Mt. 6:6.   [34] Mt. 6:9.

c. Give thanks in all circumstances! (5:18a)

Thankfulness ought always to characterize the people of God, as they say to themselves: 'Praise the LORD, O my soul, and forget not all his benefits'.[35] Indeed, 'the Christian's life is to be an unceasing eucharist'.[36] Thanksgiving also belongs, side by side with rejoicing and praying, to our public worship.[37] In it there is a place for a 'general thanksgiving' in which we express our gratitude both for the material blessings of the creation and above all for God's priceless love in redeeming the world through Jesus Christ, which we celebrate at the Lord's Supper, the Holy Communion or, as it soon came to be called in the early church, the Eucharist (*eucharistia* meaning simply 'thanksgiving'). Alongside a 'general thanksgiving' and regular Eucharists, most churches have a Harvest Thanksgiving and perhaps a Thanksgiving Sunday, Patronal Festival or Anniversary Service, in order to thank God for particular blessings. We cannot of course thank God 'for all circumstances', including those which are evil and displeasing to him; but we can and should thank him *in all circumstances* or 'whatever happens' (REB).

We may not always feel like praising, praying or giving God thanks. Our circumstances may not be conducive to these things. Yet we are to do so all the same. Why? Because *this is God's will for you in Christ Jesus* (18b). This statement almost certainly belongs to all three commands which precede it. It is God's will, as expressed and seen in Jesus Christ, whenever his people meet together for worship, and whatever their feelings and circumstances may be, that there should be rejoicing in him, praying to him and giving him thanks for his mercies.

d. Listen to the Word of God!

This exhortation, although not to be found in so many words in Paul's text, seems to me a legitimate heading to cover his references to prophecy in verses 20–22 (we will come back to verse 19 later) and to the public reading of his letter in verse 27.

Do not treat prophecies with contempt (20). Here is a clear

---

[35] Ps. 103:2.   [36] Bicknell, p. 61.   [37] *Cf.* Eph. 5:20.

command to the church to listen to whatever messages purport to come from God, and not to 'despise' (RSV, REB) or reject them unheard and untested.

In the post-Pentecost era all God's people receive the Holy Spirit and all may therefore 'prophesy',[38] that is, know and speak God's mind and will. Nevertheless, in the early church a number of people were called in a more specific way 'prophets' or 'prophetesses', e.g. Agabus, Judas and Silas, Philip's four daughters, and others.[39] In our day pentecostal and charismatic Christians believe that God is again giving the gift of prophecy to his church in the same way and measure as he did at the beginning. Although this is a controversial question, there are some aspects of it on which all biblical Christians should be able to agree.[40]

Because we affirm the supremacy and sufficiency of Scripture, we naturally recognize a major difference between Paul's time and our own, namely that we have the completed canon of Scripture, the written Word of God. Certainly, therefore, there are today no apostles comparable to the apostles of Christ like Peter, John and Paul, and no prophets comparable to the biblical prophets, whether the Old Testament authors or John who called his book (the *Revelation*) a 'prophecy'.[41] Otherwise, if there were such inspired people in the church today, we would have to add their words to Scripture, and the whole church would have to listen and obey. But no, it should not be difficult for us to agree that in the *primary* sense in which 'apostles and prophets' appear in Scripture (namely as organs of direct revelation and infallible teachers) there are no more. Paul refers to them (*i.e.* their teaching) as the 'foundation' on which the church is built,[42] and nobody has the right to tamper with, add to or subtract from that foundation; it has been

[38] Acts 2:17ff.; *cf.* Nu. 11:29.

[39] Acts 11:27–28; 21:10–11; 15:32; 21:8–9; *e.g.* 1 Cor. 14:1ff.

[40] For recent studies on 'prophecy', from different points of view, see the essay by E. Earle Ellis, 'The Role of the Christian Prophet in Acts', in *Apostolic History and the Gospel*, ed. W. Ward Gasque and Ralph P. Martin (Paternoster, 1970); *Prophecy* by David Atkinson (Grove, 1977); *New Testament Prophecy* by David Hill (John Knox, 1979); *Keep in Step with the Spirit* by J. I. Packer (IVP, 1984), pp. 214–217; *Prophecy Past and Present* by Clifford Hill (Highland, 1989); and *The Gift of Prophecy in the New Testament Today* by Wayne Grudem (Kingsway, 1988).

[41] Rev. 1:3; 22:7ff., 18–19.   [42] Eph. 2:20.

laid once and for all.

Nevertheless, once the uniqueness of the biblical prophets (and apostles) has been conceded, we should be ready to add that there are today secondary and subsidiary kinds of prophetic gift and ministry. For God undoubtedly gives to some a remarkable degree of insight either into Scripture itself and its meaning, or into its application to the contemporary world, or into his particular will for particular people in particular situations. It seems to be quite legitimate to call this insight 'prophetic' insight and this gift a 'prophetic' gift. Speaking personally, I think we would be wise to limit ourselves to this adjectival use ('prophetic' gifts and ministries), in order to reserve the nouns ('prophet' and 'prophecy') for the inspired biblical authors. I recognize that the New Testament itself does not draw this neat distinction, and calls both kinds of people 'prophets'. Nevertheless, we live in different days, in which, in order to preserve our doctrine of the unique inspiration of Scripture, and in order to avoid confusion, to make this distinction would be helpfully clarifying.

Be that as it may, Paul's injunction to us is to treat with respect and not with contempt any utterance which claims to come from God. Indeed, we are neither to reject it outright, nor to accept it outright. We are rather to listen to it, and as we do so to *test everything* (21a), to sift it, to 'weigh carefully what is said'.[43] How are we to evaluate it, however? Paul does not answer this question here, but we can do so from the teaching of Jesus and his apostles elsewhere. Although discernment is a spiritual gift,[44] we are nevertheless given certain tests to apply to teachers. The first test is the plain truth of Scripture. Like the inhabitants of Berea, we are to 'examine the Scriptures' to see if what any Christian teacher says is true.[45] The second test is the divine-human person of Jesus. If we are to 'test the spirits to see whether they are from God, because many false prophets have gone out into the world', this is how we are to discern between the true and the false: 'Every spirit [*i.e.* prophet claiming inspiration] that acknowledges that Jesus Christ has come in the flesh is from God, but every spirit that does not acknow-

---

[43] 1 Cor. 14:29.　　[44] 1 Cor. 2:13–16; 12:10.
[45] Acts 17:11; *cf.* Dt. 13:1ff.

ledge Jesus is not from God. This is the spirit of the antichrist
. . .'.[46] The third test is the gospel of God's free and saving
grace through Christ. Anybody who perverts this gospel
(whether preacher, prophet, apostle or even angel) deserves
to be 'eternally condemned'.[47] The fourth test is the known
character of the speaker. When Jesus told us 'Watch out for
false prophets', warning us that they are wolves disguised as
sheep, he added: 'By their fruit you will recognise them'.[48]
Just as a tree may be identified by its fruit, so a teacher may
be identified by his character and conduct. This is an argument against listening to strangers, for the congregation
cannot apply this test to them. The fifth test is the degree to
which what is said 'edifies', that is, builds up and benefits,
the church. An authentic prophetic message will 'strengthen,
encourage and comfort' the hearers, 'edify the church', bring
a conviction of sin and an awareness of God, and be conducive to peace and order, and above all to love.[49]

Once these tests have been applied to the words spoken,
the Thessalonians would be in a position to *hold on to [kate-
chō] the good* (21b) and to *avoid [apechomai] every kind of
evil* (22). The verbs point the alternatives. And the word
kalos ('good') was used of what was '*genuine* as opposed to
counterfeit coin'.[50] It is Paul's apparent use of the imagery of
testing coins which led many of the early Greek fathers to
associate with his instruction Jesus' otherwise unrecorded
saying: 'Become approved money changers' (or 'bankers'),
that is, people who know how to distinguish true coinage
from false.[51]

Having considered Paul's instruction to the Thessalonians
to test 'prophecies' (20–22), we are ready to consider the
further instruction he gave them to have this letter of his read
publicly to the whole congregation (27). It is illuminating to
compare and contrast this appeal to them to listen to his
letter with his previous injunction to listen to prophets. *I
charge you*, he writes. The sudden change to the first person
singular may indicate that he now took the pen from his

[46] 1 Jn. 4:1–3; *cf.* 1 Cor. 12:3; 2 Jn. 9–10.   [47] Gal. 1:6–9.
[48] Mt. 7:15ff.
[49] 1 Cor. 14:3; 14:4, 31; 14:24–25; 14:33, 40; 1 Cor. 13.
[50] Milligan, p. 76.
[51] *Cf.* Lightfoot, *Notes*, p. 85; Denney, pp. 244–245; Morris, NICNT,
pp. 177–178; and especially Jeremias, pp. 89–93.

amanuensis, as he usually did near a letter's conclusion,[52] and/or that he felt the need to assert his apostolic authority in making this important demand. Whether he feared the neglect or even the suppression of his letter by a particular group we do not know. But he certainly used extremely strong terms in order to ensure that everybody without exception would have the chance to hear it. 'I put you on oath', he wrote, and solemnly added a reference to the presence and/or authority of *the Lord, to have this letter read to all the brothers.* He was later to make the same charge to the Colossians, with the supplementary requirement that they and the Laodiceans (referring perhaps to *Ephesians*) exchange their letters. It is a quite extraordinary instruction. Already the Old Testament was read in the Christian assemblies, for the custom had been taken over from the synagogues. But now the apostles' letters were also to be read aloud during the worship service, so that each local church would gradually make its own collection of their letters and memoirs. This was the origin of the tradition of having both an Old and a New Testament lesson in church. The clear implication is that these apostolic documents were to be regarded as being on a level with the Old Testament Scriptures. Paul saw nothing incongruous in this.

Further, he gave the Thessalonians no command to test his teaching, as they were to test the words of the prophets, in order to sift the wheat from the chaff, the good from the evil, the genuine from the spurious. They were to weigh prophetic utterances, because not all of them were from God; but they were to listen to everything the apostle wrote, and were expected to believe and obey it all. Thus Paul unequivocally put his authority as an apostle above that of the prophets.[53] Just so today, granted that a subsidiary prophetic gift exists, Scripture has supreme authority in the church. It is God's Word which the church, for its own health and growth, needs to hear read and expounded.

Looking back now over Paul's teaching about public worship, we see that it should always include two complementary elements. On the one hand, there should be rejoicing in the Lord, praying, and giving of thanks, and on the other

[52] *E.g.* 2 Thes. 3:17; 1 Cor. 16:21; Gal. 6:11.
[53] See also 1 Cor. 14:36–38. And note that apostles are named above prophets in two of Paul's lists of *charismata* (1 Cor. 12:28–29; Eph. 4:11).

listening to God's Word read, expounded and applied. For God speaks to his people through his Word, and they respond to him in praise, prayer and thanksgiving. As the Book of Common Prayer puts it, we assemble in God's presence both 'to hear his most holy Word' and 'to set forth his most worthy praise'. Indeed, in every well-constructed worship service the pendulum should swing rhythmically between God addressing his people through Scripture and his people responding to him in confession, faith, adoration or prayer.

Moreover, in both these aspects of corporate worship (the listening and the responding) we are to acknowledge the sovereignty and freedom of the Holy Spirit. 'Do not quench the Spirit' (19, RSV), the apostle writes. This prohibition comes right in the middle of the other exhortations. It could therefore apply either to those which precede it or to those which follow it. We might read, 'Rejoice in the Lord, pray continually, give thanks in all circumstances, do not quench the Spirit.' Or we could read, 'Do not quench the Spirit, do not despise prophecies, but test everything, cling to the good, abstain from the evil.' In fact, I see no reason why we should not do both. In that case, Paul is saying 'Let the Holy Spirit speak to you through his word, and listen to his voice; do not quench him', and also 'Let the Holy Spirit move you to respond to the word in praise, prayer and thanksgiving; do not quench him.'

The word for 'quench' (*sbennumi*) was used of extinguishing both lights and fires, although commentators tend to opt for the latter here and translate *Do not put out the Spirit's fire*. But the Holy Spirit is light as well as fire and, far from extinguishing him, we must let him both shine and burn within us. As for his role in public worship, we should expect him to speak to us with a living, contemporary voice through the ancient Scriptures and then to move us to respond to God appropriately with all our being. This does not mean that he cannot use set forms, since (as we have seen) they are found in the New Testament text itself. But perhaps the best way to avoid Spirit-quenching traditions in public worship is to develop a flexible combination of liturgy and spontaneity, form and freedom.

4. Conclusion (5:23–28)

*May God himself, the God of peace, sanctify you through
and through. May your whole spirit, soul and body be kept
blameless at the coming of our Lord Jesus Christ.* [24]*The one
who calls you is faithful and he will do it.*

[25]*Brothers, pray for us.* [26]*Greet all the brothers with a holy
kiss.* [27]*I charge you before the Lord to have this letter read
to all the brothers.*

[28]*The grace of our Lord Jesus Christ be with you.*

Paul has given us towards the end of his letter an idyllic
picture of the local church. In referring to the pastorate, the
fellowship and the worship he has touched on the three main
relationships of church members – to their pastors (respect
and love), to each other (mutual care and support) and to
God (both listening and responding to him). Moreover, all
three are transformed when we remember that we are 'brethren' (the key word of the section, I have suggested), brothers
and sisters in the family of God. Yet this living out of *philadelphia* in the local church is possible only by the gracious
work of God, which Paul specially highlights in several of
his six final sentences.

a. Paul prays for their sanctification (5:23)

He refers to *God himself*, whom he describes as *the God of
peace*,[54] either because he is the author of harmony, or
because he is himself the only perfectly integrated personality
who exists. He then frames a double petition. He prays
first that God will *sanctify* them through and through, and
secondly that their whole spirit, soul and body may *be kept
blameless* at the Parousia. Although on the surface one prayer
is for their 'sanctification'; and the other for their 'preser-
vation', there is no substantial difference between them if, as
seems probable, the second should be paraphrased 'be kept
so as to be blameless at the Parousia'. Certainly the emphasis
in both prayers is on the thoroughness of God's sanctifying
work, 'through and through' translating *holotelēs* and 'whole'

---

[54] The same title occurs in Rom. 15:33; 16:20; Phil. 4:9 and Heb. 13:20.
Cf. 'the Lord of peace' in 2 Thes. 3:16.

translating *holoklēros*. If these words can be distinguished, then probably the former implies 'a totality from which no part is excluded' and the latter 'an integrity in which each part has its due place and proportion'.[55]

This 'wholeness' is further emphasized in the expression *spirit, soul and body*. 'Over this passage', Findlay writes, 'the Trichotomists and Dichotomists wage war',[56] that is, those who think that human beings have three parts (spirit, soul and body) and those who think we have only two (whether 'soul and body' as in Mt. 10:28 or 'spirit and flesh' as in 2 Cor. 7:1). It must certainly be agreed that usually the New Testament describes us as having two parts, the one material and the other immaterial. Moreover, 'spirit' and 'soul' are often synonymous in Scripture as when Mary said 'My soul glorifies the Lord, and my spirit rejoices in God my Saviour'.[57] In fact, only twice, apart from this verse in 1 Thessalonians, are 'spirit' and 'soul' clearly distinguished in the New Testament.[58]

If, on the other hand, Paul is here affirming a tripartite view of our humanness, as the early fathers mostly believed, then Lightfoot's explanation seems best. The spirit is 'the ruling faculty in man . . . through which he holds communication with the unseen world'; the soul is 'the seat of all his impulses and affections, the centre of his personality'; while the body 'links him to the material world and is the instrument of all his outward deeds'.[59] But we should not press Paul's formulation into a precise scientific or theological statement of human beings; it surely has a rhetorical element, as when we are to love the Lord our God with all our heart, soul, mind and strength.[60]

b. Paul affirms God's faithfulness (5:24)

Having expressed his double prayer for the thorough sanctification of the Thessalonians, he feels the need to remind both himself and them of the ground of his bold request. It is the call of God, which is a call to holiness (4:7; *cf.* 2:12) and the faithfulness of God to his called, covenant people.

---

[55] Findlay, *Greek*, p. 132.   [56] *Ibid.*, p. 133.   [57] Lk. 1:46–47.
[58] In Heb. 4:12 *psychē* (soul) and *pneuma* (spirit) are distinguished, as are the adjectives *psychikos* and *pneumatikos* in 1 Cor. 2:14–15.
[59] Lightfoot, *Notes*, p. 89.   [60] Mk. 12:30.

God upholds those whom he calls, and fulfils that which he has promised. We can rely on his steadfast love, which never fails but endures for ever.

c. Paul asks for their prayers (5:25)

Three times in this letter Paul has told the Thessalonians of his prayers for them. He mentions them continually in his prayers, he says (1:2). He prays both for the overflowing of their love and for the strengthening of their hearts in holiness (3:12–13). And he prays for their complete sanctification (23). Now he asks them to pray for him. It is a touching example of his personal humility and of the reciprocity of Christian fellowship.[61]

d. Paul tells them to greet each other (5:26)

Indeed, he is explicit in urging them to *greet all the brothers*, in other words to avoid discrimination and favouritism. He also bids them add a physical gesture to their verbal greeting, namely *a holy kiss*.[62] The form which kissing takes varies considerably from culture to culture. It may involve the use of our hands, arms, mouths, cheeks or noses. Or the custom of our country may be to stand back and bow, without any bodily contact. Yet the apostle's instruction is clear that when Christians meet each other they should greet each other, and that their verbal greeting should be made stronger, warmer and more personal by a culturally appropriate sign. Originally the 'holy kiss' was a social gesture. But already by the time of Justin Martyr (in the middle of the second century) it had become a liturgical practice during Holy Communion.[63] It is being helpfully revived in many churches today.

e. Paul insists that his letter be read publicly (5:27)

We have already noted this requirement, the strong terms in which it is framed, the emphasis on everybody hearing the

---

[61] *Cf.* 2 Thes. 3:1–2; Rom. 15:30–32; Eph. 6:19.
[62] *Cf.* Rom. 16:16; 1 Cor. 16:20; 2 Cor. 13:12; 1 Pet. 5:14 ('a kiss of love').
[63] Justin Martyr, *First Apology*, chapter 65.

reading, and its implications for Paul's selfconscious authority as an apostle and for the church's spiritual well-being.

f. Paul wishes them the grace of Christ (5:28)

Whether Paul took the pen from his amanuensis in order to write the previous verse or not, it seems extremely probable that he wrote this final benediction with his own hand. A concluding reference to grace was almost his signature, so central was it to his whole theology. He had begun by wishing them grace (1:1); he now ends in the same way. It is no empty, conventional formula, however; for grace is the heart of the gospel, indeed the heart of God.

If a local church is to become a gospel church, it must not only receive the gospel and pass it on, but also embody it in a community life of mutual love. Nothing but the grace of Christ can accomplish this.

B. THE MESSAGE OF 2 THESSALONIANS

A CHRISTIAN PERSPECTIVE ON HISTORY

INTRODUCTION TO 2 THESSALONIANS

It was Henry Ford in the witness box, during his libel suit against the *Chicago Tribune* in July 1919, who declared 'History is bunk'. Somebody else once suggested that 'the most accurate chart of the meaning of history is the set of tracks made by a drunken fly with feet wet with ink, staggering across a piece of white paper. They lead nowhere and reflect no pattern of meaning'. Similarly, Rudolf Bultmann wrote that 'the question of meaning in history has become meaningless'.[1]

Christians who look to Scripture as their authority profoundly disagree with these gloomy assessments. For the God of the Bible is the God of history. He has entitled himself 'the God of Abraham, Isaac and Jacob'.[2] He chose Israel out of the nations to be his covenant people and took about two thousand years to prepare them for the fulfilment of his promise to Abraham in the coming of their Messiah. Above all, he came to us in Jesus Christ when Augustus was emperor of Rome, and 'suffered under Pontius Pilate, was crucified, died and was buried'. Then on the third day he rose again and, having sent his Spirit, has for two further millennia been pushing his church out into the world to take the good news to its furthest extremities. One day (known only to the Father), when the gospel has been 'preached in the whole

---

[1] Quoted from Bultmann's *History and Eschatology* by George Eldon Ladd in *The Gospel of the Kingdom* (1959; Eerdmans, 1973), p. 131.
[2] *E.g.* Ex. 3:6.

world as a testimony to all nations',[3] the end will come. For Christ will return in glory, terminate the historical process and perfect his reign.

The Christian view of history, therefore, is linear, and neither circular nor cyclical. We believe that it will come to a planned end, a grand finale, consisting of the Parousia, the Resurrection, the Judgment and the Kingdom. That these events are history's goal is plain in both Paul's letters to the Thessalonians. They contain between them four of the most important New Testament passages about eschatology, the culmination of all things. In particular, the vivid descriptions in the second letter of the coming of Christ (2 Thes. 1) and of the previous appearance of Antichrist (2 Thes. 2) justify the sub-title of this exposition *A Christian perspective on history*.

This is not to claim, of course, that the apostle sat down with the deliberate intention of writing an essay on 'Christianity and History'. No, 2 Thessalonians, like all his other letters, is an *ad hoc* document, which was called forth by special, local circumstances to which he was responding. He mentions three groups of people, who were disturbing the peace of the Thessalonian church, and he addresses himself consecutively to the situations which they had created.

First, there were the persecutors. Already three times in his first letter Paul has alluded to the opposition which the Thessalonians were having to endure (1 Thes. 1:6; 2:14; 3:3). Since then, probably only a few weeks or months later, news reached him in Corinth that matters had got worse. So in chapter 1 we read of their 'persecutions and trials' (2 Thes. 1:4). They seem moreover to have been asking questions about the rationale of their afflictions. Why were they having to suffer so much? In his answer Paul does more than comfort them. He offers them a theodicy, a vindication of the justice of God. In fact, the emphasis of his first chapter is on 'the righteous judgment of God' (1:5, RSV).

Secondly, there were some false teachers, who seem to have been responsible for circulating a forged document (a 'prophecy, report or letter supposed to have come from us', 2:2), to the effect that 'the day of the Lord' had 'already come'. Paul has a head-on collision with this serious error.

---

[3] Mt. 24:14.

'Don't let anyone deceive you in any way', he writes (2:3). He then proceeds to explain how the Parousia cannot come until 'the Rebellion' has taken place, and that the Rebellion will not happen until what is holding it back has been removed. Meanwhile, the Thessalonians must stand firm in the teaching they have previously received from the apostle. That is the focus of chapter two.

Thirdly, there were the idlers, the *ataktoi*, whom we met in the first letter, and whom some commentators dub 'loafers'. Their profile becomes clearer in chapter 3 than it has been before. These irresponsible 'busybodies' were ignoring the teaching Paul had already given, both in person and by letter. So he is obliged now to issue some sharp, authoritative instructions, which border on excommunication.

It would be a mistake, however, to understand Paul's second letter in terms merely of confronting the persecutors (chapter 1), contradicting the false teachers (chapter 2) and rebuking the idlers (chapter 3). For he turns these negative situations to positive advantage. He focuses on the Parousia, when wrongs will be righted and Christ's judgment and salvation will be fulfilled; on the Antichrist, called here 'the man of lawlessness' (2:3), whose appearing is anticipated by 'the secret power of lawlessness . . . already at work' (2:7) and who will be decisively overthrown by Jesus Christ; and meanwhile, before these two 'comings' or 'appearings' take place, on our Christian responsibility to live according to the teaching of Christ's apostles, not least in relation to earning our own living. Here, then, is a straightforward analysis of Paul's second letter, his 'Christian perspective on history':

1. The revelation of Christ (2 Thes. 1)

2. The rebellion of Antichrist (2 Thes. 2)

3. The responsibility of Christians (2 Thes. 3)

6. THE REVELATION OF CHRIST

Paul's epistolary greeting need not delay us, since it is almost identical with the opening words of his first letter.

Paul, Silas and Timothy,

To the church of the Thessalonians in God our Father and the Lord Jesus Christ:

²Grace and peace to you from God the Father and the Lord Jesus Christ.

Paul associates the same missionaries with him, for they were well known in Thessalonica, having shared in the original evangelization of the city: *Paul, Silas and Timothy.* He describes the church there in the same way as before, indicating that it owes its existence to and draws its life from God the Father and the Son. It is *the church of the Thessalonians in God our Father and the Lord Jesus Christ,* although three verses later he is able to reverse the order and write of 'the churches of God' (4, RSV) in various places. And he sends them the same greeting, more theological than conventional, wishing them those greatest of all gifts, *grace and peace,* although this time adding a reference to the single source of these two blessings, and thus repeating the words *God the Father and the Lord Jesus Christ.*

The NIV rightly divides the rest of 2 Thessalonians 1 into three paragraphs, which I am calling (1) a thanksgiving for God's grace (1:3–4), (2) a defence of God's justice (1:5–10), and (3) a prayer for God's power (1:11–12).

1. A thanksgiving for God's grace (1:3–4)

We ought always to thank God for you, brothers, and rightly so, because your faith is growing more and more, and the love every one of you has for each other is increasing. ⁴*Therefore, among God's churches we boast about your perseverance and faith in all the persecutions and trials you are enduring.*

Both letters begin with an expression of heartfelt thanksgiving to God for his blessing on the Thessalonian church; they therefore invite comparison. Both thank God for the same triad of Christian graces, and both see in these qualities evidence of God's activity in and among his people. But three differences, although minor, are noteworthy.

First, in 1 Thessalonians 1 Paul wrote simply 'we always thank God for all of you', while here he expresses his sense both of obligation and of propriety in doing so: *We ought always to thank God for you, brothers, and rightly so* (3a), or 'as is fitting' (RSV). Perhaps Paul's stronger language of thanksgiving and his sense of its propriety express his recognition of the Thessalonians' spiritual growth, while his sense of obligation attributes their growth to God's grace.

Secondly, in 1 Thessalonians 1 Paul remembered gratefully that their faith, love and hope were productive (their 'work produced by faith', 'labour prompted by love' and 'endurance inspired by hope', 1:3); now, however, he emphasizes rather that these qualities are progressive: *your faith is growing more and more*, luxuriating like a tropical plant, *and the love every one of you has for each other* (NEB, 'each for all and all for each') *is increasing* (3b). It is evident that his earlier prayer that their love might 'increase and overflow' (1 Thes. 3:12) and his vision that they would love each other 'more and more' (1 Thes. 4:10) were being fulfilled. It is the two verbs in verse 3 which are emphatic. 'The words *hyperauxanei* and *pleonazei* are carefully chosen', wrote Bishop Lightfoot; 'the former implying an internal, organic growth, as of a tree; the other a diffusive or expansive character, as of a flood irrigating the land'.[1] Although Paul does not go on to mention

[1] Lightfoot, *Notes*, p. 98.

'hope', the third grace, he does refer to the *perseverance* or 'endurance' (*hypomonē*) which in 1 Thessalonians 1:3 he had written was 'inspired by hope'. Again, although he does not say that their perseverance is growing like their faith and love, he seems to imply it because he could *boast* about it *among God's churches*, and it was flourishing even *in all the persecutions and trials* which they were *enduring* (4).

Yet this idea of spiritual growth is foreign to many people, not least in the areas of faith and love. We tend to speak of faith in static terms as something we either have or have not. 'I wish I had your faith', we say, like 'I wish I had your complexion', as if it were a genetic endowment. Or we complain 'I've lost my faith' like 'I've lost my spectacles', as if it were a commodity. But faith is a relationship of trust in God, and like all relationships is a living, dynamic, growing thing. There are degrees of faith, as Jesus implied when he said 'You of little faith' and 'I have not found anyone in Israel with such great faith'.[2] It is similar with love. We assume rather helplessly that we either love somebody or we do not, and that we can do nothing about it. But love also, like faith, is a living relationship, whose growth we can take steps to nurture.

Thirdly, in 1 Thessalonians 1 Paul saw their faith, love and hope as evidence of God's love and election ('For we know, brothers loved by God, that he has chosen you', 1:4); here he implies that their progress is due to God's active grace within them.[3] True, he does not use the word 'grace'. Yet he attributes their spiritual health to God. For, instead of congratulating them on their faith, love and perseverance, he thanks God for these things, and indeed acknowledges that he *ought always* to do so. True again, he admits candidly that he was 'boasting' about them, which at first hearing introduces a jarring note. For 'thanksgiving' and 'boasting' appear incompatible, since thanksgiving gives the credit to God, while boasting gives it to human beings. Yet there is one kind of boasting which is perfectly compatible with thanksgiving, because in reality it is a synonym; it is 'boasting in the Lord'.[4] In that sense thanking and boasting are two sides of the same coin. When talking to God, we *thank* him for his grace; when talking to human beings, we *boast* of his

---

[2] Mt. 8:26, 10.   [3] *Cf.* 2 Cor. 8:1.   [4] *E.g.* 1 Cor. 1:31.

grace (*cf.* 1 Thes. 2:19).

There is an important practical lesson to learn here. What should our attitude be to Christians who are doing well in some aspect of their discipleship? Some people resort to congratulations: 'Well done! I think you're marvellous. I'm proud of you.' Others are uncomfortable with this and see its incongruity. It borders on flattery, promotes pride and robs God of his glory. So, although they may thank God privately in their prayers, they say nothing to the person concerned. They replace flattery with silence, which leaves him or her discouraged. Is there a third way, which affirms people without spoiling them? There is. Paul exemplifies it here. He not only thanks God for the Thessalonians; he also tells them that he is doing so: 'we ought always to thank God for you ... we boast about you'. If we follow his example, we will avoid both congratulation (which corrupts) and silence (which discourages). Instead, we can affirm and encourage people in the most Christian of all ways: 'I thank God for you, brother or sister. I thank him for the gifts he has given you, for his grace in your life, for what I see in you of the love and gentleness of Christ'. This way affirms without flattering, and encourages without puffing up.

2. A defence of God's justice (1:5–10)

All this is evidence that God's judgment is right, and as a result you will be counted worthy of the kingdom of God, for which you are suffering. *[6]God is just: He will pay back trouble to those who trouble you [7]and give relief to you who are troubled, and to us as well. This will happen when the Lord Jesus is revealed from heaven in blazing fire with his powerful angels. [8]He will punish those who do not know God and do not obey the gospel of our Lord Jesus. [9]They will be punished with everlasting destruction and shut out from the presence of the Lord and from the majesty of his power [10]on the day he comes to be glorified in his holy people and to be marvelled at among all those who have believed. This includes you, because you believed our testimony to you.*

Paul sees in the Thessalonians, he says, not only evidence of God's grace in their lives, but also 'evidence of the righteous judgment of God' (5, RSV). But what is it in the Thessalonian situation which Paul perceives as an *endeigma*, a 'manifest token' (AV), a 'plain indication' (BAGD), *that God's judgment is right* or 'just'? Is it the very fact that the Thessalonians are suffering for Christ? Or is it the faith, love and endurance which they are displaying in the midst of their sufferings? I think it is both.

On the one hand, Jesus had taught that suffering was the unavoidable path to glory, both for himself and for his followers.[5] Similarly, Paul had insisted that it is only through many tribulations that we can enter God's kingdom,[6] and that only if we share in Christ's sufferings will we ever share in his glory.[7] So suffering and glory, tribulation and the kingdom, belong inseparably to one another. Therefore, since God was allowing the Thessalonians to suffer, they could know that he was preparing them for glory. Their suffering was itself evidence of the justice of God, because it was the first part of the equation which guaranteed that the second part (glory) would follow.

On the other hand, although God was allowing the persecutors some rope, it was evidently in the Thessalonians that he was especially at work. He was on their side, sustaining and sanctifying them.[8] He was using their persecutions as a means through which to develop their faith, love and perseverance, in contrast to the prejudice, anger and bitterness of their persecutors, and so was preparing them for his eternal kingdom. By these qualities they were not 'made worthy' (RSV) of the kingdom, in the sense of deserving it, but they were *counted worthy of the kingdom of God, for which* they were *suffering* (5). As Bishop Lightfoot wrote, the verb *axioō* 'never signifies "to make worthy", but always "to account worthy"'.[9] Similarly, according to Leon Morris, 'the meaning is declaratory'; they were 'deemed' or perhaps 'shown to be' worthy.[10] God's transforming grace was fitting them for their heavenly inheritance.

Indeed, because *God is just*, he will vindicate them publicly one day. He will reverse the fortunes of both groups, the persecutors and the persecuted, when Christ comes. *He will pay back trouble* to the trouble-makers (6), and will *give relief* (from affliction) to those who have been afflicted,

[5] *E.g.* Mk. 8:31ff.; Lk. 24:26; Jn. 12:24ff.
[6] Acts 14:22.   [7] Rom. 8:17.   [8] *Cf.* Phil. 1:28.
[9] Lightfoot, *Notes*, p. 105.   [10] Morris, NICNT, pp. 198–199.

including the apostles (7a). Of course it takes spiritual discernment to see in a situation of injustice (like the persecution of the innocent) evidence of the just judgment of God. Our habit is to see only the surface appearance, and so make only superficial comments. We see the malice, cruelty, power and arrogance of the evil men who persecute. We see also the sufferings of the people of God, who are opposed, ridiculed, boycotted, harassed, imprisoned, tortured and killed. In other words, what we see is injustice – the wicked flourishing and the righteous suffering. It seems completely topsy-turvy. We are tempted to inveigh against God and against the miscarriage of justice. 'Why doesn't God do something?' we complain indignantly. And the answer is that he *is* doing something and will go on doing it. He is allowing his people to suffer, in order to qualify them for his heavenly kingdom. He is allowing the wicked to triumph temporarily, but his just judgment will fall upon them in the end. Thus Paul sees *evidence that God's judgment is right* in the very situation in which we might see nothing but injustice.

We need the same spiritual discernment and godly perspective as Paul had. In the Thessalonians' success, instead of flattering them, he thanked God for the evidence of his grace. In their sufferings, instead of complaining, he thanked God for the evidence of his justice.

Paul's assurance of the righteousness of God's future judgment naturally prompts three questions: (1) When will it happen? (2) Who will be punished? (3) What form will the punishment take?

First, *when* will God vindicate his justice and redress the present imbalance of human experience? Answer: *This will happen when the Lord Jesus is revealed from heaven in blazing fire with his powerful angels* (7b). The *parousia* (official visit) has now become the *apokalypsis* (unveiling) of Jesus Christ. The basic affirmation of his coming is almost identical in both letters:

1 Thes. 4:16 'the Lord himself will come down from heaven'.

2 Thes. 1:7 'the Lord Jesus is revealed from heaven'.

According to both statements his coming will be personal

147

(the same Lord Jesus, he himself and no other, who lived, died, rose and ascended, will come again), visible (having disappeared from sight at the ascension, he will reappear) and glorious (his first coming having been in weakness and obscurity, his second will be in power and public magnificence). Different details of his appearing are selected for mention, however. Instead of the loud command, the voice of the archangel and the trumpet call of God, we now read of *blazing fire*, a regular biblical symbol of the holy, consuming nature of God's presence.[11] And the retinue which will accompany the descending Lord, which in 1 Thessalonians was the Christian dead (4:14), is now *his powerful angels*, although both saints and angels may well be included in the expression 'all his holy ones' (1 Thes. 3:13).

The second question relates to *who* will be punished when our Lord comes as judge. Paul writes: *He will punish those who do not know God and do not obey the gospel of our Lord Jesus* (8). Since in the first letter the heathen were described as people 'who do not know God' (4:5), while the Jews were accused of both driving out the evangelists and hindering their spread of the gospel (2:15–16), some commentators have concluded that the two categories of people Paul mentions in verse 8 are pagans and Jews respectively. His readers could not have been expected to pick up this distinction, however. It seems more probable that both expressions describe unbelievers in general, indeed their wilful rejection of both the knowledge of God[12] and the gospel of Christ. The REB brings out their wilfulness by calling them 'those who refuse to acknowledge God and who will not obey the gospel . . .'.

Thirdly, *what* will their judgment be? *They will be punished with everlasting destruction and shut out from the presence of the Lord and from the majesty of his power* (9). The Greek sentence reads 'eternal destruction away from [*apo*] the presence of the Lord'. But most translators, recognizing that Paul's emphasis is not so much on the destruction of the wicked as on the separation from God which their destruction will involve, feel the need to elaborate the preposition *apo*, 'away from'. For example, the punishment will be 'eternal destruction and exclusion from the presence of the Lord'

---

[11] *E.g.* Ex. 3:2; 13:22; 19:18. [12] *Cf.* Rom. 1:28.

(RSV); they will be *shut out* (NIV) or 'cut off' (REB) from his presence. Do these words throw any light on the debate between biblical Christians about the nature of hell? That the final state of those who reject God and Christ will be awful and eternal is not in dispute. But the question whether their exclusion-destruction means conscious torment or ultimate annihilation cannot be settled by an appeal to this verse and its vocabulary, since the apostle does not here clearly allude to either.

In contrast to the appalling nature of hell, Paul goes on to portray the glory of heaven. For when Christ *comes*, he will not only judge those who reject the gospel, but he will also *be glorified in his holy people and . . . be marvelled at among all those who have believed*, which *includes* the Thessalonians who, on hearing the apostle's *testimony* to them (the gospel), had *believed* (10). That is to say, not only will the Lord Jesus be 'revealed' objectively in his own splendour (7), so that we see it, but his splendour will be revealed in us, his redeemed people, so that we will be transformed by it and will become vehicles by which it is displayed. The exact purport of this depends on how we understand the repeated preposition *en*, which NIV translates first *in his holy people* and secondly *among all* believers. *En* could also be translated 'by' or 'through'. So how will the coming Lord Jesus be glorified in relation to his people? Not 'among' them, as if they will be the theatre or stadium in which he appears; nor 'by' them, as if they will be the spectators, the audience who watch and worship; nor 'through' or 'by means of' them, as if they will be mirrors which reflect his image and glory; but rather 'in' them, as if they will be a filament, which itself glows with light and heat when the electric current passes through it.

The distinction between these models is important. A theatre is not changed by the play which is performed in it. An audience is not necessarily moved by the drama enacted before it. A mirror is certainly not affected by the images it reflects. But a filament is changed. For when the current is switched on, it becomes incandescent. So when Jesus is revealed in his glory, he will be glorified in his people. We will not only see, but share, his glory. We will be more than a filament which glows temporarily, only to become dark and cold again when the current is switched off. We will be radically and permanently changed, being transformed into his likeness. And in our transformation his glory will be seen in us, for we will glow for ever with the glory of Christ, as indeed he glowed with the glory of his Father.[13]

Take the Transfiguration as an illustration. On that occasion Jesus was glorified in his physical body. His face shone like the sun, while his skin and clothing glistened and became as white as light. In other words, his body became a vehicle for his glory. So will it be with his spiritual body, the church. The Body of Christ will be transfigured by the glory of Christ, not temporarily as at the Transfiguration, but eternally.

3. A prayer for God's power (1:11–12)

With this in mind, we constantly pray for you, that our God may count you worthy of his calling, and that by his power he may fulfil every good purpose of yours and every act prompted by your faith. [12]*We pray this so that the name of our Lord Jesus may be glorified in you, and you in him, according to the grace of our God and the Lord Jesus Christ.*

Although the future of God's people is secure, Paul does not presume upon it. On the contrary, the prospect of our final transformation is an incentive to the pursuit of holiness now. So Paul's eschatological vision leads him to earnest prayer.

With this in mind, he writes, namely the future glorification of Christ in his people, *we constantly pray for you*. It is prayer which links the future to the present, the vision of what is to come with the reality of what is. Paul's prayer consists of two parallel petitions. The first is that *our God may count you worthy of his calling* (11a). We have already noted, in relation to verse 5, that *axioō* does not mean to 'make worthy' (in spite of the RSV). There is no possibility of our establishing or accumulating merit in such a way as to deserve God's favour. No, when God called us to himself through Christ, he did it in his free grace to the unworthy and the undeserving. Since then, he has been summoning us to 'live a life worthy of the calling' with which we have been called.[14] He has also been working in us in order to narrow the gap between what we were when he called us and what

[13] *E.g.* Jn. 14:13.   [14] Eph. 4:1.

we should be and shall be. Only so may we be 'counted worthy' of his call and so of entry into his kingdom (5).

Paul's second petition is this: *that by his power he* [*sc.* God] *may fulfil every good purpose of yours and every act prompted by your faith* (11b). The Greek refers literally to 'every purpose of goodness and every act of faith', without specifying whose purpose and whose activity are in mind. Since *eudokia* ('purpose') in the New Testament nearly always refers to God, whereas 'faith' must be ours not his, some commentators accept the combination of 'all that *his* goodness desires to do and that *your* faith makes possible' (JBP). Others, because the two phrases are most naturally taken as parallels, apply them both to the Thessalonians, their 'delight in well-doing' on the one hand[15] and the activity prompted by their faith on the other. Paul's point is that 'purpose' and 'faith' are both attitudes of the mind and heart; he therefore prays that God will *fulfil* both by *his power*, so that they issue in good deeds.

Even the translation of thoughts into actions is not, however, the ultimate goal of Paul's prayers. He has a higher and nobler motive still, namely the glory of Jesus Christ. *We pray this*, he writes, *so that the name of our Lord Jesus may be glorified in you, and you in him, according to the grace of our God and the Lord Jesus Christ* (12). That is, when by God's power God's people live a life worthy of his call, and when their resolve issues in goodness and their faith in works, then Jesus himself is seen and honoured in them, and they through union with him are seen in their true humanness as the image of God. It is a breath-taking concept that even now, before the end, this double glorification can take place – though only according to God's grace. As always, grace and glory go together. Glory is the end; grace is the means to it. There can be no glory without grace.

Conclusion: the glory of Jesus Christ

The most striking feature of this chapter is its recurring references to the glory of Christ. Paul unfolds his theme in four stages, which all relate directly or indirectly to the Parousia.

---

[15] Lightfoot, *Notes*, p. 106.

a. The Lord Jesus will be revealed in his glory (1:7)

It is true that the word 'glory' does not occur in this verse. Yet it is quite evident that his coming will be glorious. For when the veil which now hides him from our sight is removed, what will be 'revealed' to us, but his glory? He is coming 'from heaven' (by divine not human decision), 'in blazing fire' (the consuming fire of his judgment) and 'with his powerful angels' (as a spectacular retinue). These are traditional apocalyptic symbols, but the reality will transcend the imagery. The Parousia will be no petty, local sideshow ('Look, here he is! Look, there he is!'); it will be an event of awe-inspiring, cosmic splendour (like lightning flashing across the whole sky, Jesus said). Then at last Isaiah's prophecy will be completely fulfilled: 'And the glory of the LORD will be revealed, and all mankind together will see it.'[16]

b. The Lord Jesus will be glorified in his people (1:10)

The RSV translates in his people as 'in his saints', but this does not of course refer to a small minority of particularly saintly Christians. Rather, it refers to all his redeemed people, who have fled to him for refuge, without exception.

As we saw in the exposition of verse 10, the revelation of the glory of Jesus Christ will not be objective only (so that we see it), but also in his people (so that we share it). We ourselves will be glorified. This will entail a complete transformation into Christ's image. Our bodies will become at the Resurrection 'like his glorious body'.[17] Our characters will become Christ-like. 'What we will be has not yet been made known. But we know that when he appears, we shall be like him.'[18] Finally delivered from all sin and selfishness, we shall instead be filled to capacity with love for God and others. In consequence, we shall discover our true human identity. We, who all our lives have been pathetic apologies for human beings, will at last be fully human and fully free because fully Christ-like.

And by thus transforming us into his own image, Christ himself will be seen, admired and adored in us. Moreover, the two glorifications – his and ours – will take place simul-

---

[16] Is. 40:5.　　[17] Phil. 3:21.　　[18] 1 Jn. 3:2.

taneously.[19] He will be glorified in us, and we will be glorified in him. For 'the glory of God does not exclude but includes the glory of man', as G. C. Berkouwer has written. 'This human glory, so prominent in the pages of Scripture, is not in competition with God's glory. . . . Rather, the glory of God is revealed in the glory of man, in the "glory that is to be revealed in us" (Rom. 8:18).' This does not mean, of course, that our human creatureliness will ever be abolished. Yet it does indicate that the final, eschatological glory of human beings will be more than a *restoration*; it will *transcend* their original created state.[20]

Notice, however, that the apostle's emphasis is not so much on the glorification of the saved as on the glorification of the Saviour in the saved. For it is he who is coming to be glorified in his saints and to be marvelled at in believers (10). This revelation of glory (of the glory of Christ displayed to us and in us) is very different from many popular notions of heaven. Some of these are grossly selfish and materialistic. For example, Sydney Smith, the nineteenth-century Anglican wit and divine, Canon of St Paul's Cathedral, once said (doubtless with his tongue in his cheek) that his idea of heaven was 'eating *patés de foie gras* to the sound of trumpets'.[21] Or take, more seriously, the famous Moody and Sankey hymn 'Oh that will be glory for me'. The words are formally correct, yet the impression they convey is false. For the 'glory' they promise sounds extremely selfish, as if we will be revelling only in the good things *we* will receive and the good times *we* will enjoy, whereas the very essence of heaven is the eradication of our selfishness, our transformation into Christ's image, and our preoccupation with his glory.

I wish we could stop with this double revelation of Jesus Christ to and in his people. It is with considerable reluctance that we now turn back to verses 8 and 9.

---

[19] *Cf.* Rom. 8:17.   [20] Berkouwer, p. 448.
[21] Attributed to Sydney Smith in the first edition of *The Oxford Book of Quotations*, this witticism was in later editions attributed to Samuel Rogers, as recollected by Sydney Smith.

c. Those who reject Christ will be excluded from his glory (1:8–9)

'Vengeance' in verse 8 is an unfortunate translation, whether 'taking vengeance' (AV) or 'inflicting vengeance' (RSV). For the English word sounds harsh and vindictive, whereas the Greek original (*ekdikēsis*) has no such overtones. It speaks only of justice, and of a judicial punishment.

What, then, will be the fate of Christ-rejectors? It is not meant to be understood as twofold ('eternal destruction and exclusion', RSV), but as a single destiny of being destroyed by being excluded and disqualified from 'the presence of the Lord and the glory of his might' (RSV). For the horror of this end will not be so much the pain which may accompany it as the tragedy which is inherent in it, namely that human beings made by God, like God, and for God, should spend eternity without God, irrevocably banished from his presence. Jesus himself had spoken of this dreadful expulsion, and of the 'weeping and gnashing of teeth' which would accompany it.[22] Moreover, by being separated from the glory of Christ, the condemned will be alienated from their own true identity as human beings. Instead of being fulfilled or 'glorified', their humanity will shrink and shrivel and be destroyed. Instead of shining with the glory of Christ, their light will be extinguished in outer darkness.

Here, then, is the solemn alternative which Paul once set before the Thessalonians and now sets before us. Heaven is to be 'with the Lord for ever' (1 Thes. 4:17); hell is to be excluded from the Lord for ever (9). Heaven is sharing in Christ's glory as he is glorified in us; hell is a total non-participation in his transforming glory. Those in whom Christ is glorified thereby find themselves and the fullness of their humanity; those excluded from the glory of Christ thereby lose themselves in total, irrecoverable ruin.

d. Meanwhile Jesus Christ must begin to be glorified in us (1:12)

We have seen how Paul, immediately after stating the stark alternative between participation and non-participation in the

---

[22] *E.g.* Mt. 7:23; 8:12; 22:13; 25:30, 41, 46.

glory of Christ, went on to pray that through God's powerful work within the Thessalonians 'the name of our Lord Jesus may be glorified in' them, and they in him (12). The very same word for 'glorified' is used in verse 12 as in verse 10. For the glorification of Jesus in his people, and their consequent glorification, are not a transformation which is entirely reserved for the last day. The process begins now. Indeed, it *must* begin now if it is to be brought to its proper end when Christ comes. That day will not suddenly reverse the processes which are going on now; it will rather confirm and complete them.

Jesus seems to have taught this same progression in the Upper Room. He prayed that he might be glorified by means of his death and resurrection and that his own people might see his glory in heaven.[23] But between these two termini he could make the astonishing statement 'I am glorified in them'.[24]

[23] Jn. 17:5, 24.   [24] Jn. 17:10, RSV; *cf.* 17:22.

7. THE REBELLION OF ANTICHRIST

It was not only persecutors who were disturbing the peace of the Thessalonian church; it was false teachers as well. In fact, the intellectual assault on Christianity is often fiercer than the physical. To be sure, both kinds of challenge can be beneficial, like the refining of precious metals in the fire. But both can also be painful and cause havoc. So Paul first identified the nature of the error (2:1–3), then contradicted it by a full exposition of appropriate truth (2:4–12) and thirdly expressed his confidence in the Thessalonians' stability (13–17).

1. Paul's warning against the error of the false teachers (2:1–3)

Concerning the coming of our Lord Jesus Christ and our being gathered to him, we ask you, brothers, ²not to become easily unsettled or alarmed by some prophecy, report or letter supposed to have come from us, saying that the day of the Lord has already come. ³Don't let anyone deceive you in any way, for that day will not come until the rebellion occurs and the man of lawlessness is revealed, the man doomed to destruction.

The particular false teaching which had been making headway in Thessalonica related to *the coming [parousia] of our Lord Jesus Christ and our being gathered to him* (our *episynagōgē* to him, the cognate verb describing how the angels will 'assemble' God's people on the last day[1]). Both topics, Christ's coming to us and our going to him, the unity of heaven and earth, had featured in Paul's first letter (1 Thes. 4:13 – 5:11). At that time, the Thessalonians were troubled that the Parousia had not come quickly enough, since some of their friends had died before it had taken place; now their problem was that it had come too quickly, for some teachers were *saying that the day of the Lord has already come* (2), or *is already here* (REB). Perhaps they had got hold of Paul's emphasis that Christians are 'children of the day' (1 Thes. 5:5, AV) and 'belong to the day' (1 Thes. 5:8), and were deducing from this that the day must therefore have arrived. Otherwise how could they belong to it?

A modern version of the belief that Christ has already come is found among Jehovah's Witnesses. Their founder, Pastor Charles T. Russell, first taught that the world would end in 1874, and then revised his calculations to 1914. After this year had passed, his successor Judge J. F. Rutherford asserted that Christ did in fact come on 1 October 1914, but invisibly. On that day he exchanged an ordinary seat at the Father's right hand for the throne of his kingdom. So no parousia of Christ is to be expected; it has already taken place.[2]

It was in response to some similarly bizarre notion that Paul wrote this paragraph. He begs the Thessalonians with strong affection, as his *brothers, not to become easily unsettled or alarmed* (1c–2a). The single word *unsettled* translates a phrase meaning 'shaken from your mind', that is, from your conviction or composure. The verb (*saleuthēnai*) is an aorist infinitive, referring to their initial upset, and was used of 'ships being forced from their moorings by the pressure of a storm'.[3] The second verb (*throeisthai*) is a present imperative and seems therefore to describe their continuing state of anxiety. They were 'in a constant state of nervous excitement'[4] or, as we might say, 'in a flap'. The source of their confusion was *some prophecy* (literally, 'spirit'), *report* (verbal message or statement) *or letter supposed to have come from us* (2b). The last words, indicating that the false teachers

---

[1] Mk. 13:27.

[2] See A. A. Hoekema, *Jehovah's Witnesses* (Paternoster, 1973), especially pp. 90–91.

[3] Plummer, II, p. 40.   [4] Frame, p. 245.

were claiming Paul's authority for their particular view, are probably meant to cover all three possible media of communication. The mention of a letter might refer to a forgery, and would explain why Paul adopted the custom of signing his letters personally (*e.g.* 2 Thes. 3:17). But it could equally refer to his first letter to them and to the heretics' claim to have its correct interpretation.

At all events, Paul denies that their teaching has his imprimatur. Indeed, he contradicts it. *Don't let anyone deceive you in any way* (3a), he writes. It is bad enough for them to be unsettled or alarmed; it would be worse for them to be deceived. What he does is to clarify the order of future events. *The day of the Lord* (2b) cannot be here already, he says, because *that day will not come until* two other things have happened. A certain event must take place, and a certain person must appear. The event he calls *the rebellion* (*apostasia*, 'the Great Revolt' JB; 'the final rebellion against God' REB) and the person *the man of lawlessness*, the rebel. Although Paul does not call him the 'Antichrist', this is evidently who he is. John writes of the expectation of his coming.[5] He will be in the world before he emerges into public view. But only when the rebel *is revealed* (3b) will the rebellion break out. Paul had told them this, and more, about the man of lawlessness, when he was with them. He chides them for their forgetfulness. *Don't you remember that when I was with you I used to tell you these things?* (5). The safeguard against deception and the remedy against false teaching were to hold on to the original teaching of the apostle. The Thessalonians must neither imagine that he had changed his mind, nor swallow ideas that were incompatible with what he had taught them, even if it was claimed that these ideas emanated from him. Loyalty to apostolic teaching, now permanently enshrined in the New Testament, is still the test of truth and the shield against error.

In countering the false teaching that the day of the Lord had already arrived, Paul's essential point was that the rebellion will precede the Parousia. He does not deny that the Parousia will still be sudden and, to those unprepared for it, unexpected. But, as he argued in his first letter, it will not take believers by surprise. For one thing they already belong

[5] 1 Jn. 2:18.

to the day; for another they know that the rebellion will herald its arrival.

2. Paul's teaching about the rebellion of Antichrist (2:4–12)

He will oppose and will exalt himself over everything that is called God or is worshipped, so that he sets himself up in God's temple, proclaiming himself to be God.
⁵Don't you remember that when I was with you I used to tell you these things? ⁶And now you know what is holding him back, so that he may be revealed at the proper time. ⁷For the secret power of lawlessness is already at work; but the one who now holds it back will continue to do so till he is taken out of the way. ⁸And then the lawless one will be revealed, whom the Lord Jesus will overthrow with the breath of his mouth and destroy by the splendour of his coming. ⁹The coming of the lawless one will be in accordance with the work of Satan displayed in all kinds of counterfeit miracles, signs and wonders, ¹⁰and in every sort of evil that deceives those who are perishing. They perish because they refused to love the truth and so be saved. ¹¹For this reason God sends them a powerful delusion so that they will believe the lie ¹²and so that all will be condemned who have not believed the truth but have delighted in wickedness.

In this paragraph the apostle goes on to elaborate some details of the rebellion – in particular its leader (3b–5), its outbreak (6–8a) and its dynamics (8b–12).

a. The leader of the rebellion (2:3b–5)

In verses 3b and 4 the apostle introduces the chief rebel, the leader of the rebellion, by four names or titles, each with the definite article either supplied or assumed. One might render them 'the Antinomian' (*the man of lawlessness,* uncompromisingly hostile to the rule of law), 'the Doomed' (*the man doomed to destruction,* literally 'the son of destruction', a Hebraism meaning that his destiny is ruin), 'the Enemy' (who *will oppose . . . everything that is called God . . .,* being committed to godlessness) and 'the Climber' (who *will . . . exalt himself over . . . God,* in blatant self-aggrandisement).

It seems to be the first and the last two of these which Paul emphasizes. They characterize Antichrist in relation to God and the law, and declare him to be implacably opposed to both.

First, there will be his opposition to law. Paul calls him both 'the man of lawlessness' (3) and 'the lawless one' (8). Presumably this means that he will be defiant of all law, both the moral law (asserting that there are no such things as moral absolutes) and the civil law (advocating anarchy in the name of freedom). Antichrist will be the ultimate antinomian. Jesus himself predicted that, in the future, 'Because of the increase of wickedness [*anomia*, 'lawlessness'], the love of most will grow cold'.[6]

Secondly, there will be his opposition to God. Verse 4: *He will oppose and will exalt himself over everything that is called God or is worshipped, so that he sets himself up in God's temple, proclaiming himself to be God*. All commentators have been puzzled by the mention of God's temple. Is it a reference to the temple in Jerusalem, or to the church, or to neither? Although, before its destruction in AD 70, there were several desecrations of the Jerusalem temple, yet it would seem a gross anachronism to make Jerusalem (even if it had a temple) the centre of Antichrist's global movement. Alternatively, Paul may be referring to the church, for he several times described it as the temple in which God dwells,[7] and may be indicating that Antichrist will infiltrate and capture Christendom. Yet it is doubtful if the Thessalonians would have picked up this allusion. I think I. H. Marshall is right: 'No specific temple is in mind, but the motif of sitting in the temple and claiming to be God is used to express the opposition of evil to God.'[8] In addition, *sets himself up* means 'takes his seat' (RSV) or 'enthrones himself' (REB). It has overtones of brazen effrontery. 'To *sit*', writes Ernest Best, '. . . is to display the minimum of respect and to make the maximum claim to deity, for God sits; it is not to sit alongside other gods in a pantheon but to take a unique place'.[9] Antichrist will thus dethrone God in order to enthrone himself. He will even commit the ultimate blasphemy of *proclaiming himself to be God*, the verb *apodeiknymi* being often used to

---

[6] Mt. 24:12.   [7] *E.g.* Eph. 2:21.   [8] Marshall, p. 192.
[9] Best, p. 286.

denote 'the proclamation of a sovereign on his accession'.[10] Having set himself against every object of worship, he will demand for himself the worship which he has forbidden to everybody and everything else.

Here, then, are the two principal targets of Antichrist's venom. Yet God and law, religion and ethics, are the two essential ingredients of culture, which act as a glue to bond a community together, and are therefore two authorities which humankind have normally recognized. To oppose them is to undermine the foundations of society. More than that, Antichrist's godlessness and lawlessness will go beyond a denial of these basic authorities to a demand that worship and obedience be given to him alone. Not anarchy, but totalitarianism is his goal.

But who is he? Who will he be? Is there any possibility that we, nineteen and a half centuries after Paul was writing, can positively identify the person he had in mind?[11] We will be wise, for at least two reasons, to approach the interpretative task with humility. The first reason is that, as the text indicates, Paul had taught the Thessalonians about the man of lawlessness by word of mouth. Consequently, he introduces him without explanation and sees no need to repeat what he has already taught them. 'You remember . . . you know . . .', he writes (5–6). So there was a background knowledge common to Paul and the Thessalonians which we do not share. The result, writes Dr Leon Morris, is that 'This passage is probably the most obscure and difficult in the whole of the Pauline writings and the many gaps in our knowledge have given rise to extravagant speculations.'[12]

This brings us to the second need for humility. Church history is littered with incautious, self-confident but mistaken attempts to find in Paul's text a reference to some contemporary person and event. Let this be a warning to us to be more cautious and tentative than some others have been. At the

[10] Lightfoot, *Notes*, p. 113.
[11] For a full and reverent enquiry into what Paul meant by 2 Thes. 2:1–12, see chapter 5, 'The Man of Sin', in Geerhardus Vos' thorough work *The Pauline Eschatology* (pp. 94–135). A good historical summary of the church's attempts to identify the Antichrist may be found in F. F. Bruce, pp. 179–188 ('Excursus on Antichrist'). See also George Milligan, pp. 158–165 (Note I, 'The Biblical Doctrine of Antichrist'), and pp. 166–173 (Note J, 'On the Interpretation of 2 Thes. 2:1–12').
[12] Morris, TNTC, p. 125.

same time, we have no liberty to abandon the task as hopeless, for 2 Thessalonians 2 is an important part of Scripture, which has been written and preserved for the church's instruction.

The fundamental theme of opposition to God has a long history, and the New Testament references to Antichrist have an Old Testament background. Although the Old Testament contains some imprecise allusions to the Babylonian creation myth, in which the chaos monster Tiamat struggles against the god Marduk, it is in the Garden of Eden that we are first made aware of human beings seduced by the devil into defying God. The prophets detected this arrogant spirit in the surrounding pagan emperors, so that in two passages their ambition to rival or replace God is deliberately portrayed in language which echoes Genesis 3. The King of Babylon fell because he said in his heart 'I will ascend to heaven; . . . I will sit enthroned . . . I will make myself like the Most High',[13] while the ruler of Tyre dared to say: 'I am a god [or God]; I sit on the throne of a god [or God] . . .'.[14]

It was during the second century BC, however, that the most notable embodiment of rebellion against God and his people took place. The Syrian King Antiochus IV, known as Epiphanes, was guilty of appalling desecrations of the temple in Jerusalem. In 169 BC he presumed to enter the Holy of Holies, and the following year he erected an altar to Zeus on the altar of burnt offering, probably placed a statue of Zeus over it, and sacrificed a pig on it. This was the 'abomination that causes desolation',[15] 'desolating sacrilege' (RSV) or 'The Awful Horror' (GNB) which is referred to historically in the First Book of the Maccabees[16] and prophetically in the Book of Daniel.[17] Antiochus Epiphanes can be recognized without difficulty in Daniel as the king who is represented as a 'little horn'. He had 'a mouth that spoke boastfully', and in the interpretation of Daniel's dream which follows, it is said that 'he will speak against the Most High and oppress his saints'.[18] In a later vision Antiochus Epiphanes is called 'the king of the North' who invades the south, violates the temple fortress, abolishes the daily sacrifice, and sets up the abomination that causes desolation.[19] Indeed, 'the king will do as he pleases. He will exalt and magnify himself above every god and will

---

[13] Is. 14:13–14.   [14] Ezk. 28:2.   [15] Mt. 24:15; Mk. 13:14.
[16] 1 Macc. 1:54ff.   [17] Dn. 8:13; 9:27; 11:31; 12:11.
[18] Dn. 7:8, 25.   [19] Dn. 11:28–31.

say unheard-of things against the God of gods'.[20] Since phraseology from these prophecies was picked up both by Jesus (in his Olivet discourse) and by Paul (in 2 Thes. 2), Antiochus Epiphanes became a prototype of Antichrist.

The Jews saw another example of 'the abomination of desolation' in the Roman general Pompey, who in 63 BC defeated their nation, captured Jerusalem and desecrated the temple by intruding into the Holy of Holies. The so-called *Psalms of Solomon*, which were written soon afterwards, refer to him as 'the sinner' and 'the lawless one'.[21]

Jesus himself was evidently clear that Daniel's prophecy had not been completely fulfilled either in Antiochus Epiphanes or in Pompey, but awaited a further fulfilment. For he repeated or confirmed the prophecy: 'When you see "the abomination that causes desolation" standing where it does not belong – let the reader understand – then let those who are in Judea flee to the mountains.'[22] Several details of this verse are important.

1. Matthew's text adds the explanatory phrase 'spoken of through the prophet Daniel'; indeed the injunction to the reader to understand is probably encouraging him to read and reapply Daniel's prophecy.

2. Matthew's reference to the abomination is in the neuter (which is grammatically correct), but Mark's participle 'standing' is masculine, which suggests that he expected the sacrilege to be committed by a person.

3. Matthew replaces Mark's 'standing where it does not belong' with 'standing in the holy place', alluding to the temple.

To what 'abomination' was Jesus referring? Some commentators wonder if he had the mad emperor Gaius (Caligula) in mind. Only about ten years later (in AD 40), claiming the worship of all his subjects and angered by what he saw as Jewish disloyalty, he gave instructions for a large statue or image of himself to be erected in the temple. His order was never carried out, however. For when huge numbers of Jews protested in horror, the diplomatic interventions of Petronius, governor of Syria, and of King Herod Agrippa I, prevailed on the emperor to withdraw the order. He was

---

[20] Dn. 11:36.   [21] See *Psalms of Solomon* ii, xvii and xviii.
[22] Mk. 13:14; *cf.* Mt. 24:15–16.

then himself assassinated in AD 41.[23]

It is much more likely that Jesus was referring to the Jewish war of AD 66–70. He had many times predicted God's coming judgment on the Jewish nation, and had clearly warned them of the destruction of the temple.[24] Luke certainly understood that the abomination of desolation related to the Roman siege of Jerusalem.[25] As for the temple, it was profaned first by Jewish zealots during the war and then by the Roman army in AD 70, who carried their ensigns (which bore the emperor's image) into the temple courts and then proceeded to offer sacrifices to them.[26]

We come now to the apostle Paul. It is possible that he had Caligula's crazy scheme at the back of his mind, since only ten years had passed since his death and it must have been well remembered. But the emperor's plan had been frustrated. So Paul knew that Daniel's prophecies were still partially unfulfilled. In consequence, he repeated them, borrowing phraseology from Daniel as he did so, and at the same time universalizing them. If we are right in suggesting that sitting in God's temple (2:4) is a symbol of arrogance and even blasphemy, rather than a specific reference to Herod's temple in Jerusalem, then the rest of the picture Paul paints is of a rebellion which is global rather than local, and of an Antichrist who is more an eschatological than a contemporary figure.

As the emperor cult developed, it became ever more clearly a form of Antichrist, as Christians were commanded to substitute the words *kyrios kaisar* ('Caesar is Lord') for their basic Christian confession *kyrios Jesus* ('Jesus is Lord'). Augustus had been the first emperor to claim divinity and solicit worship. Later, Nero's combination of personal vanity and hostility to Christians made him an object of great dislike and fear. But it was Domitian, who became emperor in AD 81 and demanded to be worshipped as *Dominus et Deus*, who persecuted those who denied him the divine homage he coveted. It was almost certainly during his reign that John was banished to Patmos and wrote the Revelation. The most satisfactory explanation of the two 'beasts', which appear in Revelation 13 as allies of the dragon (the devil), is that both

[23] See Josephus' *Antiquities*, xviii.8.2–9.
[24] *E.g.* Mt. 24:1–2; Mk. 13:1–2; Lk. 19:41ff.; 21:5–6.
[25] Lk. 21:20–24.   [26] Josephus, *Wars*, vi.6.1.

represent the Roman Empire under Domitian, the monster emerging from the sea symbolizing its persecuting power and the monster emerging from the earth (later called 'the false prophet') symbolizing the emperor cult.

One other use of the Antichrist motif needs to be mentioned before we leave the New Testament references. This occurs in John's letters. He is the only New Testament author who employs the word 'Antichrist'. He also assumes that his readers are familiar with the expectation of his coming: 'you have heard that the antichrist is coming'. But then he boldly reinterprets the coming of Antichrist in terms of the contemporary activity of false teachers: 'even now many antichrists have come'.[27] What facilitates their identification is their denial of the incarnation. For 'Who is the liar? It is the man who denies that Jesus is the Christ. Such a man is the antichrist'.[28] Twice more John uses the word, insisting that anybody who 'does not acknowledge Jesus', especially who does not 'acknowledge Jesus Christ as coming in the flesh', is 'the deceiver and the antichrist'.[29]

This process of reinterpretation and re-application within Scripture itself, from Daniel through Jesus to Paul and John, gives an important flexibility to our understanding. Of particular significance is John's explicit and authoritative statement that the expectation of a single Antichrist has been fulfilled (or at least partly so) in the numerous false teachers who were denying the Incarnation in his day. This prepares us for the conclusion that the biblical prediction of the Antichrist may during the course of church history have had (and still have) multiple fulfilments, and that we would be unwise to look for only one in such a way as to pronounce all the others false.

In the post-apostolic centuries of the church Christians have practised considerable ingenuity in trying to identify one of their contemporaries as the man of lawlessness. After the demise of the persecuting emperors and the conversion of Constantine, the Roman emperor no longer seemed a suitable candidate. At first one or other of the Vandal leaders, who raided Roman provinces and finally sacked Rome (AD 455), looked anti-Christian enough to be Antichrist. In the Middle Ages, especially at the time of the Crusades, the

---

[27] 1 Jn. 2:18.   [28] 1 Jn. 2:22.   [29] 1 Jn. 4:3; 2 Jn. 7.

Western church identified the man of lawlessness as Muhammad, because he had 'stolen' the Christian holy places and caused many eastern Christians to commit 'apostasy'. Towards the end of the Middle Ages some of the Franciscans saw in the corrupt popes and their proud pretensions an expression of the one who would 'exalt himself' and 'set himself up in God's sanctuary', while at the beginning of the thirteenth century Emperor Frederick II and Pope Gregory IX found satisfaction in calling each other the Antichrist. The early Reformers (Wycliffe in England, the Waldensians in Italy and John Hus in Bohemia) all referred the prophecy to the Pope, or rather to particular popes on account of their corruption, whereas – with greater exegetical insight – the sixteenth-century Reformers, including Luther, Calvin and Zwingli on the Continent, Knox in Scotland and Cranmer in England, believed that the papacy itself was Antichrist. The Roman Catholic leaders of the Counter-Reformation then returned the compliment by identifying Luther as 'the man of sin'. The identification of the Pope as Antichrist continued at least into the seventeenth century. The Westminster Confession (1646), for example, affirms that the Lord Jesus Christ is the head of the church, and not the Pope, who is rather 'that man of sin, and son of perdition, that exalteth himself, in the Church, against Christ and all that is called God'.[30]

During the last two centuries political rather than religious leaders have been put forward as possible Antichrists. Candidates have included Napoleon Bonaparte (because of his arrogant absolutism), Napoleon III, Kaiser Wilhelm, Hitler, Mussolini and Stalin, and certainly strong elements of both godlessness and lawlessness have been seen in these men.

How should we react to what F. W. Farrar called 'that vast limbo of exploded exegesis'?[31] Certainly not by a contemptuous dismissal of prophecy, of the 'legend' of Antichrist, which 'is now to be found only among the lower classes of the Christian community, among sects, eccentric individuals and fanatics'.[32] If that were the case, I for one would be happy to be numbered among the 'lower classes'

[30] Westminster Confession of Faith, xxv.6.

[31] F. W. Farrar, *The Life and Work of St Paul* (Cassell, popular edition, 1891), p. 350.

[32] W. Bousset, article 'Antichrist', in *The Encyclopaedia of Religion and Ethics*, vol. I, ed. James Hastings (T. & T. Clark, 1908).

of eccentrics and fanatics! Instead, we should take careful note of the development of the Antichrist expectation within Scripture itself, how Daniel referred to Antiochus Epiphanes, how Jesus, Paul and John in Revelation reapplied the prophecy of Daniel, that is, how they recognized successive embodiments of godlessness and lawlessness, and how John in his Letters saw the false teachers as 'many antichrists', spreading their heresy around, much as Jesus had talked about 'pseudo-Christs'.[33] As Hendriksen has put it, 'history ... repeats itself. Better, prophecy attains multiple fulfilment'.[34] Yet all these, together with other evil leaders down the centuries, have been forerunners or anticipations of the final 'man of lawlessness', an eschatological yet historical person, the decisive manifestation of lawlessness and godlessness, the leader of the ultimate rebellion, the precursor of and signal for the Parousia. I agree with Geerhardus Vos that 'we may take for granted ... that the Antichrist will be a human person'.[35] And whether we still believe in the coming of Antichrist will depend largely on whether we still believe in the coming of Christ.

b. The outbreak of the rebellion (2:6–8)

Paul does not specify what form the rebellion will take. But the word he uses for it, *apostasia* (3), meant in classical Greek either a military revolt or a political defection, whereas in the LXX it applied to religious apostasy, namely Israel's rebellion against God. Presumably Antichrist's revolt, therefore, being directed against God and Law, will even infiltrate and engulf the nominal church.

Not yet, however. For the rebellion will not take place until the chief rebel has emerged (3). And, Paul adds, *you know what is holding him back, so that he may be revealed at the proper time* (6). Paul's preoccupation here is with the time of the rebellion. He uses a series of time references, in order that the Thessalonians may grasp the order of events:

[33] Mt. 24:24.
[34] Hendriksen, p. 177. Berkouwer develops the concept of '*continuous reinterpretation*, in which nothing of the eschatological promise is sacrificed' and by which 'the continuing actuality of the eschatological promise' is preserved (pp. 246–252).
[35] Vos, p. 113.

'*Now* you know what is restraining him, so that he may be revealed *at the proper time*. For *already* the mystery of lawlessness is at work secretly; but the one who *now* restrains it will *continue* to do so *until* he is removed. And *then* the lawless one will be revealed' (6–8). Two processes are now already going on simultaneously. On the one hand *the secret power of lawlessness is . . . at work* surreptitiously and subversively. On the other hand, the restraining influence is also at work, preventing the secret rebelliousness from breaking out into open rebellion. Only when this control is lifted will first the revolt and then the Parousia take place.

The nature of *what is holding him back* (6), which is later personalized as *the one who now holds it back* (7), has caused commentators many headaches. Once again we stand at an initial disadvantage, because Paul's Thessalonian readers knew what the restraining influence was (6), since he had regularly taught them about these things (5), whereas we have not had the benefit of the apostle's initial instruction. It is not altogether surprising, then, that even the great Augustine, reacting against unprofitable conjectures, declared, 'I frankly confess I do not know what he means.'[36]

Before we are in a position to weigh the possible interpretations, it may be helpful to bring together the four facts about the 'restraint' which Paul clarifies. First, it is at work now and is effectively stopping the outbreak of the rebellion. Secondly, 'it' may also be referred to as 'he' (8). The restraint is both neuter and masculine, something and someone, a pressure and a person. Thirdly, at the right time this 'it' or 'he' will be removed, and the removal will trigger the final timetable, namely the revelation first of Antichrist and then of Christ. Fourthly, there must be some reason, in addition to the Thessalonians' knowledge, which prompts Paul to write about the restraint and its removal in such guarded, roundabout and even cryptic terms. Here, then, are our four guidelines. The 'restraint' must be socially effective, capable of a personal manifestation, historically removable and delicate enough to be talked about in whispers and enigmas.

---

[36] Augustine, *The City of God*, xx.19

Three main explanations have been proposed.[37]

First, the restraining power is *the Holy Spirit and the work of the church*. In this case, the 'he who restrains' would be the Spirit himself, while the 'it who restrains' would be the church he indwells. Certainly Jesus intended his people, like salt in meat, to exercise a restraining influence on society. But why should Paul write of the Spirit and the church in such enigmatic terms? And the concept of the church being 'removed' before the rebellion would mean that it would not be there to greet Christ on his return.

The second suggestion is that the restraint is *Paul and the preaching of the gospel*. One or two of the early fathers held this view, and Calvin wrote: 'Paul declared that the light of the gospel must first be spread through every part of the world . . .'. Again, 'I hear Paul speaking of the universal call of the Gentiles'.[38] The 'restraint' on this showing is the necessary 'delay' until the world is evangelized. Oscar Cullmann took up and developed this theme, emphasizing Paul's unique role as the apostle to the Gentiles. In this case the masculine 'restrainer' is 'a self-designation of the apostle' and the neuter 'restraint' is his 'missionary preaching'.[39] But if the reference is to himself and his evangelism, why should he need to be so cryptic about it? Besides, did he really see himself at the centre of the eschatological stage, so that the rebellion awaited his removal from the scene? And how could his removal (presumably by death) be reconciled with his apparent hope of surviving until the Parousia (1 Thes. 4:13ff.)?

The third and most widely held view is that the restraining

---

[37] Ernest Best follows C. H. Giblin in challenging the traditional understanding of the verb *katechō*. It is usually translated 'hold back' or 'hinder', but can also mean 'hold sway' or 'rule'. Taking it in the latter sense, Ernest Best thinks that *to katechon* is a figure hostile rather than friendly to God. He calls it a 'hostile occupying power' which holds sway at present but will later step aside for the major power to take over (pp. 290–302). Since I have not found this attempted reconstruction convincing, I have considered in the text only those interpretations which take *katechō* to mean 'hold back' or 'restrain'.

[38] Calvin, p. 403; *cf.* Mt. 24:14.

[39] Oscar Cullmann, *Christ and Time* (1946; ET 1951, revised edition SCM, 1962), pp. 164–166. He links this view with the word of Jesus that the end will not come until the world has been evangelized (Mt. 24:13ff.; Mk. 13:10ff.).

influence is *Rome and the power of the state*. Tertullian seems to have been the first church father to enunciate this: 'What obstacle is there but the Roman state . . .?'[40] Not that the reference need be limited to the Roman Empire; every state, being the guardian of law and order, public peace and justice, meets the case equally well. It is true that in Revelation 13 the state is portrayed as satanic, and that when it appears in this guise it can hardly be conceived as the restrainer of Antichrist. Indeed, it is this which led Cullmann to declare the interpretation of the state as the restrainer 'the least probable hypothesis'.[41] Nevertheless, Paul regarded the state as God's agent for the punishment of evil.[42] In fact, there are four main arguments in favour of this interpretation:

1. It makes good sense. As Plummer wrote, 'the natural restrainer of lawlessness is the law, and in the first century the great organizer and executor of the law was the Roman Empire'.[43] He even wrote that this explanation fits so well that 'it is almost a waste of time to look for any other'.[44]

2. It tallies with Paul's known view and experience of the state. He and Silas as Roman citizens had recently experienced Roman justice both in Philippi and at the hands of the politarchs in Thessalonica itself, and the proconsul Gallio's fair handling of a potentially ugly situation in Corinth might be fresh in Paul's mind.[45] Further, he would soon be expounding to the Romans his conviction that the state was God's servant to punish evil and promote good.[46]

3. The combination of the neuter and the masculine is easily explained. 'Think', wrote Hendriksen, 'of the empire and the emperor, of justice and the judge, of law and the one who enforces it.'[47]

4. The enigmatic reference would be explicable, since there were obvious prudential reasons for not openly and explicitly predicting that the state would be 'taken out of the way' or 'removed from the scene' (REB).

Meanwhile, even during the period of restraint, and before the lawless one is revealed, *the secret power of lawlessness is already at work* (7a). 'The secret power' translates *to mystērion*. It cannot here bear its usual meaning in Paul's writings

---

[40] Tertullian, *On the Resurrection of the Flesh*, ch. xxiv.
[41] Oscar Cullmann, *The State in the New Testament* (SCM, 1957), p. 64.
[42] Rom. 13:1ff. [43] Plummer, II, p. 61. [44] *Ibid.*, p. 60.
[45] Acts 18:12–16. [46] Rom. 13:1–5. [47] Hendriksen, p. 182.

of 'a truth once hidden but now revealed', since it is still secret and is contrasted with the coming 'revelation' of the man of lawlessness. Before he is revealed openly, however, the lawlessness he embodies is operating secretly. His anti-social, anti-law, anti-God movement is at present largely underground. We detect its subversive influence around us today – in the atheistic stance of secular humanism, in the totalitarian tendencies of extreme left-wing and right-wing ideologies, in the materialism of the consumer society which puts things in the place of God, in those so-called 'theologies' which proclaim the death of God and the end of moral absolutes, and in the social permissiveness which cheapens the sanctity of human life, sex, marriage and family, all of which God created or instituted.

Were it not for some remaining restraints (which preserve a measure of justice, freedom, order and decency) these things would break out much more virulently. And one day they will. For when the restraint is removed, then secret subversion will become open rebellion under the unscrupulous leadership of *the lawless one* who *will be revealed* (8a). Then we can expect a period (mercifully short) of political, social and moral chaos, in which both God and Law are impudently flouted, until suddenly *the Lord Jesus* will come and *overthrow* him *with the breath of his mouth and destroy* him *by the splendour of his coming* (8). 'There is no long battle', writes Ernest Best, 'victory comes at once.'[48]

c. The dynamics of the rebellion (2:9–12)

The rebellion will take place, according to Paul, publicly and visibly on the stage of history. It will be seen in a world-wide breakdown of the rule of law, of the administration of justice and of the practice of true religion. But Paul also introduces us to its invisible dynamics, to what is going on behind the scenes. He writes of the two major protagonists – Satan (9) and God (11), and uses the word *energeia* ('working', 'operation') in relation to both. Both God and Satan are at work in relation to the coming of Antichrist.

Paul begins with the devil, asserting that *The coming of the lawless one will be in accordance with the work [energeia]*

[48] Best, p. 304.

of Satan (9a). It would be an exaggeration to say that Antichrist will be an incarnation of Satan, as Christ is the incarnation of God. It would be more accurate to think of the coming of Antichrist as a deliberate and unscrupulous parody of the second coming of Christ. Paul shows this by using the same vocabulary of both. 'The systematic and . . . calculated adoption by Antichrist of the attributes of Christ is the most appalling feature in the whole presentation.'[49] Thus, in verses 1 and 8 (as in 1 Thes. 4:15) we read of the *parousia*, the personal and official coming of Jesus Christ; but at the beginning of verse 9 we read of the *parousia* of the lawless one, in direct juxtaposition to Christ's *parousia* at the end of the previous verse. Next, in 1:7 the Lord Jesus is going to be 'revealed' from heaven, whereas three times in chapter 2 (verses 3, 6 and 8) it is the lawless one who is going to be 'revealed' (it is not stated from where). Again, Christ is coming in power and glory (1:7), and in *splendour* (2:8), while the coming of the man of lawlessness will be accompanied by *all kinds of counterfeit miracles* [*en pasē dynamei*, 'in all power'], *signs and wonders* (9). Just as the ministry of Jesus was accredited by 'miracles, wonders and signs',[50] and also the ministry of the apostle Paul,[51] so the ministry of Antichrist will be accompanied by (though not authenticated by) miracles. For his will be *counterfeit miracles*, probably not in the sense that they will be fakes, but in the sense that they will deceive rather than enlighten. Thus both comings, of Antichrist and of Christ, will be personal (a *parousia*), visible (an *apokalypsis* or revelation) and powerful (with miracles). And tragically the coming of Antichrist will be such a clever parody of the coming of Christ that many will be taken in by the satanic deception. The reason for their being deceived is that *they refused to love the truth and so be saved* (10). Love of the truth (it is implied) was offered to them, but they rejected it. Behind the great deception there lay the great refusal.

For this reason God sends them a powerful delusion so that they will believe the lie (11). This 'lie' is 'the denial of the fundamental truth that God is God',[52] together with the blatant assertion by Antichrist that he is God. God will 'give them over' to their own wilful blindness.[53] And as a result

---

[49] Findlay, *Greek*, p. 181.   [50] Acts 2:22.
[51] Rom. 15:18–19; 2 Cor. 12:12.
[52] Bruce, p. 174.   [53] Rom. 1:24–25.

they *all will be condemned who have not believed the truth but have delighted in wickedness* (12). It is of great import- ance to observe that the opposite of 'believing the truth' is 'delighting in wickedness'. This is because the truth has moral implications and makes moral demands. Evil, not error, is the root problem. The whole process is grimly logical. First, they delight in wickedness, or 'make sinfulness their deliber- ate choice' (NEB). Secondly, they refuse to believe and love the truth (because it is impossible to love evil and truth simultaneously). Thirdly, Satan gets in and deceives them. Fourthly, God himself 'sends' them a strong delusion, giving them over to the lie they have chosen. Fifthly, they are condemned and perish. This is extremely solemn teaching. It tells us that the downward slippery path begins with a love for evil, and then leads successively to a rejection of truth, the deception of the devil, a judicial hardening by God, and final condemnation. The only way to be protected from being deceived is to love goodness and truth. These, then, are the dynamics (devilish and divine) which lie behind the final rebellion.

To sum up this whole paragraph, Paul has unfolded the historical process (present and future) in three stages. Now is the time of *restraint*, in which the secret power of lawless- ness is being held in check. Next will come the time of *rebellion*, in which the control of law will be removed and the lawless one will be revealed. Finally will come the time of *retribution*, in which the Lord Christ will defeat and destroy the Antichrist, and those who have believed the Antichrist-lie will be condemned. This is God's programme. History is not a random series of meaningless events. It is rather a succession of periods and happenings which are under the sovereign rule of God, who is the God of history.

3. Paul's confidence in the stability of the Thessalonians (2:13–17)

Stability is a coveted quality in every sphere of human life. Governments talk about stabilizing the economy. Builders endeavour to construct stable houses, and carpenters stable furniture. Aircraft and ships have 'stabilizers', to counteract turbulence and the ocean swell. And we admire people who have a stable personality, character and convictions.

The New Testament says much about Christian stability. In Paul's first Thessalonian letter he declared: 'now we really live, since you are standing firm in the Lord' (3:8). And here in his second letter, having urged them not to become 'easily unsettled' (2:2), he is about to issue the exhortation, *So then, brothers, stand firm . . .*' (15). In the words of Jesus we are not to be 'like reeds shaken by the wind',[54] but rather be rock-like and immovable. Moreover, the New Testament identifies the winds which threaten our stability, and against which we are to take our stand. The first is opposition or persecution (1 Thes. 1:4–6; 3:2–4), the second is false teaching (*e.g.* 2 Thes. 2:2–3),[55] and the third is temptation. Temptations are like strong gusts of wind which threaten to blow us over. That is why Paul prays that God will 'establish' the Thessalonians, so that they will be holy in God's presence (1 Thes. 3:13, RSV).

Behind these winds lurks the enemy of God and of the people of God, the devil, who is responsible for mounting this threefold attack, physical (persecution), intellectual (false teaching) and moral (temptation to sin). Moreover, this onslaught in its three dimensions will come to a crescendo and climax when Antichrist will be revealed. For he will inaugurate a time of unparalleled anarchy. Hell will break loose. And many will be swept away by the gale of error and evil. This is the background to the third section of 2 Thessalonians 2. It consists of a thanksgiving (13–14), an appeal (15) and a prayer (16–17). Paul turns from warning of Satan's activity to thanksgiving for God's, from history and its chaos to eternity and its security.

But we ought always to thank God for you, brothers loved by the Lord, because from the beginning God chose you to be saved through the sanctifying work of the Spirit and through belief in the truth. [14]He called you to this through our gospel, that you might share in the glory of our Lord Jesus Christ. [15]So then, brothers, stand firm and hold to the teachings we passed on to you, whether by word of mouth or by letter.

[16]May our Lord Jesus Christ himself and God our Father, who loved us and by his grace gave us eternal encouragement

---

[54] *Cf.* Mt. 11:7, RSV.   [55] *Cf.* Eph. 4:14.

and good hope, ¹⁷*encourage your hearts and strengthen you in every good deed and word.*

a. Paul begins with a thanksgiving (2:13–14)

The apostle repeats his own words at the beginning of the letter: *We ought always to thank God for you* (1:3; 2:13). He feels under this obligation because God is at work in their lives, because their faith, love and hope are abounding (1:3), and because God has chosen and called them, and will undoubtedly bring them safely home in the end. That is to say, in spite of present and future tribulation (ferocious, lawless and blasphemous), Paul feels no panic and adopts no panic measures. On the contrary, he expresses his assured thankfulness to God. His confidence in the stability of the Thessalonians is due entirely to his confidence in the stability of God's loving purpose for them. It is only because God is steadfast, that we can be steadfast too.

Paul now gives a marvellously comprehensive statement of God's saving purpose. As Denney rightly put it, here is 'a system of theology in miniature'.[56] In it the apostle alludes to the three persons of the Trinity, and in particular makes two parallel affirmations. The basic statements are as follows:

2:13 God chose you from the beginning to be saved through the sanctification of the Spirit.

2:14 God called you through the gospel to share in Christ's glory.

We notice that, in relation to both God's election and God's call, Paul specifies the end and the means. God chose us 'unto' (*eis*) salvation 'through' (*en*) the Spirit's sanctification, and God called us 'unto' (*eis*) the obtaining of Christ's glory 'through' (*dia*) the gospel. We had occasion, when commenting on 1 Thessalonians 1:4, to note that the biblical doctrine of divine election has always perplexed Christian people. Yet, although it perplexes our minds, it greatly comforts our hearts, and it is entirely consistent with our experience. We know the truth of Jesus' words 'You did not choose me, but I chose you'.[57] For we remember, before God laid hold of

---

[56] Denney, p. 342.   [57] Jn. 15:16.

us, how wilful, wayward and weak we were. There is, therefore, no option but to trace our salvation back beyond our 'decision' or 'commitment' (*i.e.* conversion) to the gracious initiative of God, and say 'God chose us ... God called us ...'.

First, *from the beginning God chose you.* 'From the beginning' translates *ap archēs*, which has strong manuscript support. Bruce Metzger explains that, nevertheless, the Editorial Committee of the United Bible Societies preferred the alternative reading *aparchēn* ('as firstfruits') mainly because Paul uses the word on six other occasions.[58] Yet 'as firstfruits' has no obvious meaning here, and the context seems to demand 'from the beginning'.[59] Next, he chose us *to be saved* (in contrast to those who are 'perishing', v. 10, and will be 'condemned', v. 12), our 'salvation' embracing the fullness of God's purpose to deliver us from the ravages and consequences of sin, culminating in our final, heavenly destiny. And the means by which he will accomplish this will be *the sanctifying work of the Spirit* (who indwells and transforms us) and our *belief in the truth* (13), for he opened our eyes to believe it, in contrast to those (10–12) who closed their minds to it and refused to believe.

Secondly, *he called you to this through our gospel.* Paul proceeds naturally from God's eternal choice to his historical call. *To this* must mean 'to this salvation just mentioned', and *through our gospel*, shows that the gospel is the means by which God's call comes to us and we respond to it. It is evident, then, that the doctrine of divine election, far from undermining evangelism, actually makes it essential, since it is through the preaching of the gospel that God calls us to himself. And the purpose of his call is *that you might share in the glory of our Lord Jesus Christ* (14), the glory which (as Paul has expounded in chapter 1) will be seen at the Parousia, by which Christ's people will themselves be glorified, and from which unbelievers will be excluded.

We need now to step back and survey this noble landscape. 'God chose you from the beginning for salvation. ... God called you through the gospel for glory.' There is nothing narrow-minded about the apostle Paul! His horizons are bounded by nothing less than the eternities of the past and

---

[58] Metzger, pp. 636–637.   [59] *Cf.* Eph. 1:4.

of the future. In the eternity of the past God chose us to be saved. Then he called us in time, causing us to hear the gospel, believe the truth and be sanctified by the Spirit, with a view to our sharing Christ's glory in the eternity of the future. In a single sentence the apostle's mind sweeps from 'the beginning' to 'the glory'. There is no room in such a conviction for fears about Christian instability. Let the devil mount his fiercest attack on the feeblest saint, let the Antichrist be revealed and the rebellion break out, yet over against the instability of our circumstances and our characters, we set the eternal stability of the purpose of God. We glance on to 2 Thessalonians 3:3 and declare with Paul, 'The Lord is faithful, and he will strengthen and protect you . . .'.

Nevertheless, Paul's confidence in God's stability of purpose did not prevent him from taking sensible precautions. He did not conclude that because God had chosen and called the Thessalonians, and would establish them and bring them to glory, he and they could sit back and do nothing. On the contrary, he had previously sent Timothy to 'establish' them (1 Thes. 3:2). Now he passes immediately from his confident thanksgiving first to an earnest exhortation to them to stand firm, and then to an equally earnest intercession that God will establish them.

b. Paul continues with an appeal (2:15)

So then, brothers, stand firm . . . We need to absorb the apostle's unexpected logic. For we would probably have drawn a different conclusion from what he has just written. We might have said: 'We are bound to give thanks for you . . . because God chose you . . . and God called you to share in Christ's eternal glory. So then, brothers, relax and take it easy!' But Paul's appeal is the opposite. Far from relaxing, they must brace themselves. Far from lying down and falling asleep, they must stand firm. That is, Paul's assurance regarding God's stable purpose for his people, instead of justifying irresponsible slackness, is the very basis on which he can urge them with confidence to be stable themselves.

The apostle's exhortation is a double one: 'Stand firm!' and 'hold to!' He seems to picture a gale, in which they are in danger both of being swept off their feet and of being

177

wrenched from their handhold. In face of this hurricane-force wind, he urges them to stand their ground, planting their feet firmly on *terra firma*, and to cling on to something solid and secure, clutching hold of it for dear life. Both verbs are present imperatives. Since the storm may rage for a long time, they must keep on standing firm and keep on holding fast.

Moreover, what they are to hold on to is specified. It is *the teachings* (*paradoseis*, 'traditions'). *Paradosis* means truth which, having been received, must be faithfully handed on. In this case it is Paul's own teaching, which he had received from God (*cf.* 1 Thes. 2:13) and which subsequently, he writes, *we passed on to you, whether by word of mouth* (his oral instruction when present with them) *or by letter* (his written instruction when absent). So these *paradoseis* are not the later traditions of the church, but the original teachings or traditions of the apostles. It is vital to preserve this distinction between the two kinds of tradition. The apostolic traditions are the foundation of Christian faith and life,[60] while subsequent ecclesiastical traditions are the superstructure which the church has erected on it. The primary traditions, to which we should hold fast, are those which the apostles received from Christ (either the historic Christ or the living Spirit of Christ), which they taught the early church by word or letter, and which are now preserved in the New Testament. To 'stand firm and hold to the teachings' means in our case to be biblical or evangelical Christians, to be uncompromisingly loyal to the teaching of Christ and his apostles. This is the road to stability. The only way to resist false teaching is to cling to the true teaching.

One other point may be made. Paul's appeal for stability is made to the Thessalonians as *brothers* (15). This is a recognition that the context within which they were to 'stand firm and hold to the teachings' was the Christian fellowship, the family of God. In other words, we need each other. The church is the fellowship of faith, the society for sacred study, the hermeneutical community. In it we receive teaching from pastors who are duly authorized to expound the tradition of the apostles, we wrestle together with its contemporary application, and we teach and admonish each other out of

[60] *Cf.* Eph. 2:20

the same Scriptures. To be sure, private and personal Bible study is essential, and the Reformers were correct to emphasize 'the right of private judgment'. Nevertheless, it also has its dangers. Left to ourselves, it is easy for us to misinterpret the Word of God, to put on it constructions it was never intended to bear, and even to manipulate it to suit our prejudices. So we need the checks and balances of the Christian family, in order to help restrain our rampant individualism and establish us in the truth. It is the Bible in the church which can develop our Christian stability, and so strengthen us to withstand the pressures of persecution, false teaching and temptation.

c. Paul concludes with a prayer (2:16–17)

It is instructive to observe that, having expressed his thanks to God for having chosen and called the Thessalonian Christians, he not only exhorts them to stand firm, but also now prays that God will establish them. We see, then, how Christian praise and Christian prayer belong together. The fact that God promises to do something (for which we praise him), far from discouraging prayer, actually encourages it, because God's promises are the only ground of our assurance that God will answer our prayers. Prayer is not a way of inducing God to do what he has said he will not do; it is the God-appointed way of enabling him to do what he has promised to do and enabling us to inherit his promises. God's promises and our prayers must not be separated.

Paul opens his prayer with these words: *May our Lord Jesus Christ himself and God our Father*. We notice how once again Paul couples the Father and the Son. He did it in 1 Thessalonians 1:1 and 3:11. But this time he startles us by even putting the Son before the Father. It is amazing enough, within twenty years of the resurrection, that Paul should have bracketed Jesus Christ with God; it is yet more amazing that now he brackets God with Jesus Christ. He also goes on, in spite of the plurality of the subject (Father and Son), to use the singular reflexive *who* and the singular verbs *loved* and *gave*. Paul is evidently quite clear, at least in the practice of prayer if not yet in theological formulation, about the equality and the unity of the Father and the Son.

Paul goes on to describe Father and Son by the reflexive

clause, *who loved us and by his grace gave us eternal encouragement and good hope* (16). His love, his grace and his gifts
are brought together, and his gifts ('eternal encouragement'
and 'good hope') seem to mean the same thing, since the
encouragement (*paraklēsis*) is specifically said to be 'eternal'
and our Christian hope looks forward to eternity also. The
apostle's two prayers are that God will *encourage your hearts*,
fortifying them inwardly, *and strengthen you* (*stērizai*, 'establish', as in 1 Thes. 3:13) *in every good deed and word* (17),
which is the outward and public evidence of the inward
strength. 'A good hope ought to work itself out in a good
life.'[61]

We have now looked at Paul's thanksgiving (13–14), exhortation (15) and prayer (16–17). The theme of all three has
been the same: Christian stability. He thanks God that he
has chosen and called the Thessalonians to salvation (that
most stable of all states); he appeals to them to stand firm;
and he prays that God will establish them. That is, his plea
to them to stand is sandwiched between his assurance that
they will and his prayer that they may. Yet still something
is missing, which I have so far deliberately omitted from the
exposition of the text. What is it that binds together Paul's
thanksgiving, exhortation and prayer? What is the ultimate
secret of Christian stability? It is the love of God. Three
times Paul alludes to it in 2 Thessalonians 2 and 3. First, he
describes the Thessalonians as 'brothers loved by the Lord'
(2:13; *cf.* 1 Thes. 1:4). Secondly, he describes the Father and
the Son as the God 'who loved us' (2:16). Thirdly, he prays
that the Lord will 'direct your hearts into God's love' (3:5).
Behind God's election, call and gifts there lies God's love.
That God is love, that he has set his love upon us, that he
loves us still, and that his love will never let us go, is the
foundation not only of all reality, but of Christian confidence
and Christian stability too. Our stability is not only impossible, but actually inconceivable, apart from the steadfastness
of the love of God.

> O give thanks to the LORD, for he is good,
> for his steadfast love endures for ever.
>
> (Ps. 136:1, RSV)

---

[61] Best, p. 322.

8. THE RESPONSIBILITY OF CHRISTIANS

Paul has been peering into the future. He has foreseen and foretold both the revelation of Christ on the last day and the rebellion of Antichrist which will precede and herald it. He has also indicated that meanwhile, although the final outbreak of lawlessness is being restrained, yet 'the secret power of lawlessness is already at work' in the world (2 Thes. 2:7). In this ambiguous situation, in which evil is both operative and held in check, what is the responsibility of Christian people? How should we behave, in view of the present tension and the final denouement?

1. Introduction: the centrality of the word

The apostle's answer concerns divine revelation. During the interim period between the two comings of Christ, while he is absent from the world, God has not left his people without a guiding light or a compass. On the contrary, he has given us both in Scripture. Already in chapter 2 Paul has written about the importance of believing the truth (2:1, 10–12) and holding fast to his teachings (2:13). Now in chapter 3 this becomes his preoccupation. He uses two expressions (*logos* and *paradosis*, 'word' and 'tradition') which, while not identical, overlap one another to a considerable extent, since both denote revealed truth.

The phrase *the message of the Lord* in 3:1 (literally 'the word of the Lord') has already occurred in 1 Thessalonians 1:8. There Paul says that it 'rang out'; here he longs that it

181

may 'spread rapidly'. In both cases he is referring to the propagation of the gospel. And in both cases too he is careful to define the gospel as 'the Lord's message'. Although it had been entrusted to him (1 Thes. 2:4), it had not originated with him, but with God. He knew this. So did the Thessalonians, for they had welcomed it 'not as the word of men, but as it actually is, the word of God' which was effectively at work in believers (1 Thes. 2:13).

The other word the apostle uses in this chapter is *paradosis* ('tradition'), that is to say, teaching which he had received, and passed on (6, *cf.* 2:15). Now the mere mention of the word 'tradition' is enough to raise a question in the minds of Protestants, who affirm the supremacy of Scripture and are resolved to subordinate tradition to it. Did not Jesus himself reject 'the traditions of the elders', in order that 'the word of God' might take precedence?[1] How then could Paul exalt what Jesus had abased? The answer must be that they were referring to different traditions, which had different origins. The Jewish oral traditions which Jesus rejected he called 'the traditions of men', whereas the traditions or teaching of the apostles had a divine origin. 'It is no contradiction', wrote Friedrich Büchsel, 'that Jesus repudiates tradition and Paul champions it. Paul's tradition agrees with Jesus' rejection, since they are both opposed to human tradition'.[2]

Another problem remains, however, in that at first sight Paul seems to contradict himself. On the one hand, he stoutly maintains the divine source of his teaching. He received it, he insists, 'not . . . from any man' but 'by revelation from Jesus Christ'.[3] He repeats this in his first letter to the Corinthians, asserting that he had 'received from the Lord' what he has passed on to them.[4] On the other hand, this particular tradition which he had received and handed on was the institution of the Lord's Supper. Are we to suppose that he received this information by direct revelation? Is it not more probable that human beings had given it to him? If so, how can he claim to have received it 'from the Lord'? Oscar Cullmann took up this very question in his essay entitled *The Tradition*. He developed a sustained argument concluding that:

[1] Mk. 7:1–13.   [2] Büchsel, *TDNT*, vol. II, p. 172.
[3] Gal. 1:12.   [4] 1 Cor. 11:23.

the designation *kurios* ('the Lord') can be understood as not only pointing to the historical Jesus as the chronological beginning and the first link of the chain of tradition, but to the exalted Lord as the real author of the whole tradition developing itself within the apostolic Church.[5]

Indeed, it was the apostles themselves who were given the unique privilege of receiving teaching from Jesus Christ and passing it on to the church:

> their essential function is to be bearers of direct revelation, one being concerned with one fact, another with another, so that they are dependent upon one another. But it is the united testimony of all the apostles which constitutes the Christian *paradosis*, in which the *Kurios* (Lord) himself is at work.[6]

Thus Paul can say that he has received 'from the Lord' a tradition which in reality he has received by way of other apostles. *Transmission by the apostles is not effected by men, but by Christ the Lord himself who thereby imparts this revelation.*[7]

By *paradosis*, then, Paul means not the tradition of the church but the teaching of the apostles and so of Christ the Lord himself. This distinction was clearly recognized by the early church. As Cullmann wrote, it *'distinguished between apostolic tradition and ecclesiastical tradition,* clearly subordinating the latter to the former, in other words, subordinating itself to the apostolic tradition'.[8]

So then, whether Paul is referring to 'the word' (1 Thes. 1:6, RSV), namely 'the word of the Lord', or to 'the tradition' (2 Thes. 3:6, RSV), namely the teaching of the apostles, it is divine revelation to which he is alluding. He sees the present period before the parousia of Christ as the era of the word, and that in two senses. First, the church must spread the word throughout the world. Secondly, the church must itself obey the word, conforming its own life to the teaching of the apostles. Paul's two longings, which he expresses in this

[5] Oscar Cullmann, ed. A. J. B. Higgins, *The Early Church* (SCM, 1956), p. 62.

[6] *Ibid.*, p. 68.   [7] *Ibid.*, p. 73.   [8] *Ibid.*, p. 87.

chapter, are that the word of the Lord may be 'honoured' both in the world (1) and in the church (4–15). Both are aspects of 'church growth', which is a fine expression so long as we remember that it has these two dimensions. God wants his church to grow both extensively (by its spread of the gospel) and intensively (by its own obedience to the gospel). Each is incomplete and unbalanced without the other. Both also demand time – world evangelization on the one hand and church formation on the other.

2. The word must be spread in the world (3:1–3)

Finally, brothers, pray for us that the message of the Lord may spread rapidly and be honoured, just as it was with you. ²And pray that we may be delivered from wicked and evil men, for not everyone has faith. ³But the Lord is faithful, and he will strengthen and protect you from the evil one.

By the words *Finally, brothers*, Paul indicates that he is about to take up his last topic and that 'the end of the letter is in view'.[9] But before he broaches his final theme he issues an emphatic appeal to his readers to *pray for* him and his mission team (indeed, to 'keep on praying' for them, the verb being a present imperative). That he asked for their prayers at the end of his first letter (1 Thes. 5:25), and now repeats his request, is a mark of his humility. That he also tells them of his intercession for them[10] is a mark of their rich reciprocal relationship. Christian fellowship is expressed in, and deepened by, our prayers for one another.

What does Paul ask the Thessalonians to pray for? He mentions two complementary items. First, *that the message of the Lord may spread rapidly and be honoured*, or literally, 'may run and be glorified'. The apostle loved to use vivid figures of speech. If in his first letter he likened the proclamation of the gospel to a trumpet blast or peal of thunder, which 'rang out' from Thessalonica (1 Thes. 1:8), he now personifies the word as a runner. Perhaps he is thinking of the Isthmian games, for which Corinth was famous, and in particular of the athletes who carried the Olympian torch.

[9] Best, p. 323.
[10] *E.g.* 1 Thes. 1:2; 3:11–13; 5:23; 2 Thes. 1:11–12; 2:16–17; 3:5, 16.

But the imagery also occurs in the Old Testament: 'his word runs swiftly'.[11] The Thessalonians are asked to pray that the gospel may run well, run fast, and that, wherever it goes, it may have 'a glorious reception'.[12] If Paul is still picturing the word as an athlete, he may now be seeing it 'crowned with glory' at the winning post.[13] On the other hand, the apostle may be making a more general allusion to the 'honour' which the word deserves to receive (as in Acts 13:48). In this case the prayer is that the Lord's message may 'speed on and triumph' (RSV) or may have a 'swift and glorious success' (REB), *just as* happened (Paul adds) *with you*. The word had come running into Thessalonica, and had been honoured by the reception it was given (1 Thes. 1:6). Now Paul asks them to pray that it may run on further, and may be received and glorified by others as it had been by them.

Without doubt the apostle is referring to the evangelization of the Roman empire. After leaving Thessalonica and then Berea, he evangelized Athens, the intellectual capital of the empire. He is now in Corinth, its commercial capital, and is experiencing some opposition to the word. Already he is beginning to dream of evangelizing Rome, the empire's administrative capital, for the main port of Corinth looked north-west across the Adriatic Sea to Italy. He urges his readers to pray that the gospel may run in every direction, and be welcomed.

Secondly, Paul asks for prayer that he and his missionary companions may be *delivered from wicked and evil men* (2).[14] It is one thing for the gospel to win friends who embrace it; it is another for the evangelists to be rescued from its enemies who oppose it. Since he uses the definite article, Paul seems to have a particular group in mind, perhaps the Jewish opponents of the gospel in Corinth.[15] He describes them not only as *evil* but as *atopoi*, literally 'out of place', and so 'unreasonable' (AV), 'wrong-headed' (REB), 'perverse',[16] and even 'bigoted' (JBP, JB). The reason why they reject the gospel is that *not everyone has faith* or (because of the definite article) 'the faith'. The latter is an objective body of belief, the former the faculty of believing it. *But,* Paul adds immediately, *the Lord (i.e.* Jesus) *is faithful* (3a, *cf.* 1 Thes. 5:24). In

---

[11] Ps. 147:15; *cf.* Ps. 19:4b–6 quoted in Rom. 10:18.
[12] Plummer, II, p. 86. [13] Frame, pp. 289, 291. [14] *Cf.* Rom. 15:31.
[15] Acts 18:6ff. [16] Milligan, pp. 109–110; Best, p. 326.

Greek, as in English, there is a deliberate play on the words *faith* and *faithful*. Indeed, by this contrast Paul is expressing his conviction that the faithlessness of human beings cannot possibly overturn the faithfulness of God, as shown in his covenant commitment to his people and his word.

God's faithfulness to his word is a recurring theme in the Old Testament. It was written of Samuel, for example: 'The LORD was with Samuel as he grew up, and he let none of his words fall to the ground.'[17] Again, God said to Jeremiah at the time of his call: 'I am watching to see that my word is fulfilled.'[18] He had made a similar promise to Isaiah: 'My word . . . will not return to me empty, but will accomplish what I desire and achieve the purpose for which I sent it.'[19] Paul shares this assurance. True, there was opposition from 'evil men' (2), and behind them from 'the evil one' himself (3). True also, they were engaged in spiritual warfare and so needed spiritual weapons: Paul had to preach and the Thessalonians had to pray. Yet behind his preaching and their prayers stood the faithful Lord himself, who watches over his word, and who confirms it by his Spirit in the hearers' hearts, so that it works in them effectively (1 Thes. 1:5; 2:13).[20]

Moreover, the same faithful Lord is faithful to his people as well as to his word. For *he will strengthen* (*stērizo*, 'establish', as in 1 Thes. 3:2, 13; 2 Thes. 2:17) *and protect you* (and 'us' too, indeed all his people) *from the evil one*. As in the Lord's Prayer ('rescue us from the evil one') so here, the reference is surely to the devil in person, and not to 'evil' in general. The context requires this. As Professor F. F. Bruce puts it, 'the personal "evil one" forms a more effective antithesis to the personal *Kurios* (*sc.* "Lord")'.[21] The great affirmation 'the Lord is faithful' is now seen to be pivotal. It looks back to the spread of the word and on to the strengthening of the church. God will not allow either his word or his church to fail. Hence Paul's 'confidence in the Lord' about both, and his sense of the propriety of praying for both.

What can we learn from these verses about mission? It is true that, in the Second Vatican Council's 'Dogmatic Constitution on Divine Revelation' (*Dei Verbum*), 2 Thessalonians

---

[17] 1 Sa. 3:19. [18] Je. 1:12. [19] Is. 55:11.
[20] *Cf.* 1 Cor. 2:5. [21] Bruce, p. 200.

3:1 is quoted with reference to the place of Scripture in the church. Lay people are to read it, scholars to interpret it, and clergy to preach it. 'In this way, therefore, through the reading and study of the sacred books, let "the word of the Lord run and be glorified" (2 Thes. 3:1)'.[22] But, although indeed an 'intensified veneration for God's word' should bring 'a new surge of spiritual vitality' to the church,[23] Paul's perspective in these verses is not the renewal of the church but the evangelization of the world. Three aspects of world mission are emphasized.

First, mission is concerned with the message which is being spread, and this message has a given and defined content. Astonishing as it may sound, by 'the message of the Lord' the apostle was alluding to his own preaching. 'Pray for *us*', he urged, 'that the message of the *Lord* may spread rapidly'. He knew himself to be the bearer of God's word (as in 1 Thes. 2:13). His gospel was God's gospel (1 Thes. 1:5, 8; 2:2, 4, 9). Today it is often the cultural elements of the message we preach which preoccupy people. And rightly so. We have to divest our gospel of the cultural clothing in which we have received it and sometimes even of the precise cultural garb in which Scripture presents it. We also have to reclothe it in cultural terms appropriate to the people to whom we proclaim it. 'Gospel' and 'culture' are two different entities; they must not be confused. Nevertheless, underneath its various cultural garments, the gospel remains a cluster of truths, which have been revealed by God, which may not be manipulated or edited by us, and which continue to be transcultural good news for everybody everywhere. This 'message of the Lord' must run throughout the world.

Secondly, mission is concerned with the reception as well as the proclamation of the message. This is why people who are committed to world evangelization pray that the evangel will *be honoured*, and that the evangelists will *be delivered from wicked and evil men*. There is in mission an interplay between four groups. The intercessors pray. The missionaries preach. Some hearers honour the word by believing it. Others refuse the message and oppose those who bring it.

Thirdly, mission is concerned with what John Mott at the

[22] *The Documents of Vatican II*, gen. ed. Walter M. Abbott (Geoffrey Chapman, 1966), pp. 125–128.

[23] *Ibid.*, p. 128.

1910 World Missionary Conference in Edinburgh called 'the superhuman factor'.[24] Evangelism is not a merely human activity undertaken by human energy and ingenuity. Unseen spiritual forces are also at work. Hence the call to prayer. Behind the evil men opposing the gospel stands the evil one. Behind the bearers of the Lord's message stands the faithful Lord. What encouragement Christian missionaries should draw from the affirmation that *the Lord is faithful*! Since some lack faith and are either unresponsive or actively resistant, how can we hope *that the message of the Lord may spread rapidly and be honoured*? Only because behind the word of the Lord is the faithfulness of the Lord. It is he who spoke the word in the first place and who speaks it still, who confirms its truth in human hearts, and who causes it to take root and bear fruit. He also stands faithfully by his covenant people, promising that he will never leave or forsake them.

3. The word must be obeyed in the church (3:4–15)

The apostle moves from the need to spread the word in the world to the need to obey the word in the church, from evangelism to obedience, and so from an affirmation of the Lord's faithfulness to his word to an affirmation of his authority in and through it. There is something fundamentally anomalous about Christians who share the word with others while disregarding it in their own lives.

The particular issue in relation to which Paul demanded obedience concerned the *ataktoi*, the idle. These 'loafers'[25] were the third group disturbing the Thessalonian church, after the persecutors (2 Thes. 1) and the false teachers (2 Thes. 2). We met them in Paul's first letter (1 Thes. 5:14, where the adjective *ataktos* occurs). In this chapter he uses the adverb *ataktōs* twice (verses 6 and 11) and the verb *atakteō* once (7, 'to live in idleness'). As we saw earlier, they were playing truant from work. Although some commentators have held that they were temperamentally lazy and sponging on the generous members of the church, and others that they had imbibed the Greek disdain for manual labour, a majority consider that it was their belief in the imminence of the

---

[24] John R. Mott, *The Decisive Hour of Christian Missions* (Methodist Missionary Society, 1910), p. 193.
[25] Best, pp. 331–345.

Parousia which had led them to give up their job. Paul had told them in his first letter to return to work, but evidently his directions had not been heeded.

What is striking now is not so much the instructions which Paul issues about them as the authority with which he does so. Nothing is more impressive in this chapter than the repetition of the verbs 'command' and 'obey'. 'There is a military ring' about these verses, Leon Morris writes.[26] For the words *parangellō* and *parangelia* were the usual terms for 'the commands given by the officer to his men'.[27] Five times Paul uses this language: 'We have confidence in the Lord that you are doing and will continue to do the things we *command*' (4). 'In the name of the Lord Jesus Christ, we *command* you, brothers ...' (6). 'For even when we were with you, we gave you this *command* ...' (10, RSV). 'Such people we *command* and urge in the Lord Jesus Christ ...' (12). 'If anyone does not *obey* our instruction in this letter, take special note of him' (14).

We have confidence in the Lord that you are doing and will continue to do the things we command. ⁵May the Lord direct your hearts into God's love and Christ's perseverance.

⁶In the name of the Lord Jesus Christ, we command you, brothers, to keep away from every brother who is idle and does not live according to the teaching you received from us. ⁷For you yourselves know how you ought to follow our example. We were not idle when we were with you, ⁸nor did we eat anyone's food without paying for it. On the contrary, we worked night and day, labouring and toiling so that we would not be a burden to any of you. ⁹We did this, not because we do not have the right to such help, but in order to make ourselves a model for you to follow. ¹⁰For even when we were with you, we gave you this rule: 'If a man will not work, he shall not eat.'

¹¹We hear that some among you are idle. They are not busy; they are busybodies. ¹²Such people we command and urge in the Lord Jesus Christ to settle down and earn the bread they eat. ¹³And as for you, brothers, never tire of doing what is right.

¹⁴If anyone does not obey our instruction in this letter, take

[26] Morris, TNTC, p. 143. [27] Morris, NICNT, pp. 120, 248.

special note of him. Do not associate with him, in order that he may feel ashamed. [15]*Yet do not regard him as an enemy, but warn him as a brother.*

It should be noted that there are five stages in Paul's handling of the problem posed by the *ataktoi*, and that in these he gradually narrows his focus from the church itself, through the loyal majority and the disloyal minority, to any individuals who (even after his admonition) may persist in their disobedience:

1. He expresses his confidence in the church as a whole (4–5).

2. He tells the faithful majority to keep aloof from the idlers (6–9).

3. He reminds them of the principle he had laid down during his visit (10).

4. He directly addresses the unfaithful minority, the idlers themselves (11–13).

5. He gives instructions about those individuals who may stubbornly reject his teaching (14–15).

At each stage, whoever is being addressed, he uses the same language of command and obedience.

First, Paul expresses his general *confidence in the Lord* about the Thessalonians, that they *are doing and will continue to do the things we command* (4). Even if Paul is tacitly associating Silas and Timothy with him, the 'we' is surely a plural of authority and indicates that the church lives under the teaching authority of the apostles. Paul's confidence in the Lord leads him to pray to the same Lord Jesus that he would *direct* their *hearts into God's love and Christ's perseverance* (5). It does not seem natural to interpret these two genitives as either objective (our love for God and 'patient waiting for Christ', AV)[28] or subjective (God's love for us and Christ's patience with us). This led Lightfoot to combine them. 'The apostles themselves', he wrote, 'availed themselves, either consciously or unconsciously, of the vagueness or rather comprehensiveness of language, to express a great

[28] *Cf.* 1 Thes. 1:3, 10.

190

spiritual truth',[29] namely that God's love for us arouses our love for him. Indeed, these two senses are so 'combined and interwoven' that it is seldom possible to separate them.[30] It is better still, it seems to me, to understand these genitives as qualitative. Then Paul's prayer is that the Lord will lead the Thessalonians into a love like God's love and a patience or constancy like Christ's. The context suggests that they will then express their love and patience in their obedience.

Secondly, Paul commands the loyal majority *In the name* (*i.e.* with the authority) *of the Lord Jesus Christ . . . to keep away* ('hold aloof', REB) *from every brother who is idle and does not live according to the teaching* (*paradosis*, 'tradition') *you received from us* (6). This apostolic teaching he had given them when he was with them, both by word of mouth and by his personal example. They should, therefore, obey his instruction and *follow* his *example* (7a). As for the model he gave them, he mentions two negatives. On the one hand, he and his fellow missionaries *were not idle* (7b), and on the other they did not *eat anyone's food without paying for it* (8a). They were evidently lodgers or paying guests in Jason's home.[31] And in order to be able to pay for their 'board and lodging' (NEB), *they worked night and day, labouring and toiling* (in Paul's case at his tent-making). The Greek assonance *kopos kai mochthos*, here and in 1 Thessalonians 2:9, has been rendered into English as 'toil and moil'[32] or 'slaving and straining' (JB).

Paul and his friends had two reasons for adding physical labour to their mission work. First, they did not want to *be a burden* on any of the Thessalonian Christians (8b), even though they knew they had *the right to such help* (9a). Paul gives no basis here for this right, although he had mentioned it in his first letter (1 Thes. 2:6b). It went back ultimately to the saying of Jesus that 'the worker is worth his keep',[33] and Paul was later to elaborate both his right and his renunciation of it.[34] The missionaries' second reason for earning their own living was in order to make themselves *a model* for the Thessalonians *to follow* (9b). In a word, their resolve was to be an example, not a burden.

Thirdly, Paul reminds them of the authoritative teaching

[29] Lightfoot, *Notes*, p. 127.   [30] *Ibid.*, p. 128.
[31] Acts 17:5–9.   [32] Lightfoot, *Notes*, p. 26.
[33] Mt. 10:10; *cf.* Lk. 10:7.   [34] 1 Cor. 9:3–14; *cf.* 1 Tim. 5:18.

which he had given them during his visit: *even when we were with you, we gave you this rule* (RSV, 'this command'; it is the verb *parangellō* again): *'If a man will not [i.e.* refuses to] *work, he shall not eat'* (10). There seems no need to speculate that this is an otherwise unknown epigram of Jesus, or to look for its antecedents in Jewish or Greek literature. For all cultures are likely to have a similar proverb. As Deissmann put it, 'St. Paul was probably borrowing a bit of good old workshop morality, a maxim applied no doubt hundreds of times by industrious workmen as they forbade a lazy apprentice to sit down to dinner.'[35] Whoever first uttered this sentiment, Paul adopted it and gave it his apostolic imprimatur. He apparently repeated it several times in Thessalonica (the imperfect tense of the verb 'we gave you this rule' suggests this), and now he reminds them of it again.

Fourthly, Paul directly addresses the disobedient minority, the idlers who (he had recently heard) were disregarding his teaching. *They are not busy,* he writes; *they are busybodies* (11). This pithy contrast neatly represents in English the play on words in the Greek sentence, not *ergazomenous* but *periergazomenous.* Having no work of their own to keep them occupied, they had become meddlesome in the affairs of others. In addressing them, Paul does not mince his words: *Such people we command and urge in the Lord Jesus Christ to settle down* (RSV 'to do their work in quietness', *cf.* 1 Thes. 4:11) and earn the bread they eat (12). He then addresses the rest of the *brothers*, who have not been infected with the virus of idleness, and exhorts them: *never tire of doing what is right* (13). Some have understood this as an appeal to them to be patient with the idlers. It seems more likely to be a plea that, in contrast to the idlers, they should persevere in doing good.[36]

Fifthly, Paul adds a further direction on how the church should treat those individuals who persist in disobedience: *If anyone does not* (RSV, 'refuses to') *obey our instruction in this letter, take special note of him* (14a). Perhaps the ringleader of the recalcitrant group is in mind. *Do not associate with him, in order that he may feel ashamed* (14b). At the same time, *do not regard him as an enemy, but warn him as a brother* (15), or 'admonish him as one of the family' (REB).

---

[35] Deissmann, p. 314.   [36] *Cf.* Gal. 6:9.

This verse contains some of the most important teaching in the New Testament on the subject of church discipline. How should the local Christian community handle a situation in which one or more of its members are guilty of serious misbehaviour? To be sure, many churches nowadays would do nothing. The administration of discipline has fallen into disuse, and the thought of reviving it is viewed with distaste. Our Lord and his apostles were of a different opinion, however, and 2 Thessalonians 3:14 lays down five practical guidelines on when, why and how discipline should be exercised.

1. The *need* for discipline does not arise from some trivial offence which can be dealt with discreetly in private, but from a public, deliberate and persistent disobedience to plain apostolic instruction. In the case of the *ataktoi* Paul had repeatedly communicated the apostles' teaching by word of mouth, personal example and letter. The Christian standard in this matter was not in doubt. But the culprits were showing a spirit of defiance. It was those who obstinately refused to obey (14) who, Paul said, must now be disciplined.

2. The *nature* of the discipline which Paul demanded was a measure of social ostracism. The idlers had already received a general admonition (1 Thes. 5:14). But now, because they had disregarded it, the loyal church members were to keep aloof from them (6). Then, if anyone continued in disobedience, they were to 'take special note of him', which implies 'some form of public censure',[37] and not to 'associate with him' (14). This verb is *synanameignymi*, to 'mingle or associate with' (BAGD). Paul will use it again later when telling the Corinthians not to have fellowship or even eat with Christian brothers who are openly guilty of such offences as immorality, dishonesty, idolatry and drunkenness.[38] But the verb may imply differing degrees of ostracism, ranging from the total separation involved in excommunication (as at Corinth) to the more moderate avoidance of free and familiar fellowship (as at Thessalonica). 'Let there be no intimate association with him'[39] is Paul's meaning here, rather than RSV's harsher expression 'have nothing to do with him'. For this injunction of the apostle's is qualified by the further one to continue regarding and treating him as a Christian brother (15).

---

[37] Bicknell, p. 94.   [38] 1 Cor. 5:9, 11.   [39] Frame, pp. 298, 308.

3. The *responsibility* for administering discipline to a persistent offender belongs to the congregation. Paul does not address his instructions to the elders of the Thessalonian church who are 'over' them 'in the Lord', even though they have a special responsibility of admonition (1 Thes. 5:12). Leaders may need to take the initiative, but then a corporate decision and corporate action should be taken by the whole church membership. Without this, rival factions are bound to develop.

4. The *spirit* in which discipline is to be administered must be friendly, not hostile. It is to be done 'gently'.[40] 'Do not regard him as an enemy' (15a), for that would be equivalent to treating him like 'a pagan or a tax collector',[41] that is, excommunicating him. Instead, 'warn him as a brother' (15b), continuing to give him fraternal admonition (the verb is *noutheteō*, as in 1 Thes. 5:12 and 14).

5. The *purpose* of this discipline is positive and constructive. It is not to humiliate delinquents, still less destroy them. It is rather to make them 'feel ashamed' (14b), that is, to shame them into repentance for the past and amendment of life in the future. Paul's intention is not that he be excluded from the community, but reinstated in it.[42] Jesus had made this plain by saying that if an offender listens to reproof, 'you have won your brother over'.[43]

4. Reflections on the authority of the apostles

Paul has clarified the three distinct media which he has used in instructing the Thessalonians. First, he had taught them the apostolic *tradition* (*paradosis*) verbally, and they had received it from him (6; *cf.* 10 and 2:15). Secondly, he had set them an *example*, which they were to imitate (7–9; *cf.* 1 Thes. 1:6).[44] Thirdly, he confirmed and elaborated his teaching by *letters* (14; *cf.* 1 Thes. 4:16), which he autographed personally (17) in order to distinguish them from forgeries (2:2). Thus it was by a combination of verbal teaching, visual example and written instruction that he directed the affairs of the Thessalonian church.

We have already noted that five times Paul resorts to the

[40] Gal. 6:1. [41] Mt. 18:17. [42] *Cf.* Gal. 6:1. [43] Mt. 18:15.
[44] *Cf.* also 1 Cor. 4:16; 11:1; Gal. 4:12; Phil. 3:17.

language of 'command' and 'obedience'. Moreover, these five verses may be divided into two categories according to whether he is addressing the obedient majority ('you') or the disobedient minority ('them'). He begins by saying in effect 'we command you and are confident of your obedience' (4, 6, 10), and then adds 'we also command them [*sc.* the idlers] and tell you what to do in case of their continued disobedience' (12, 14). Further, in issuing these instructions Paul dares to claim that his authority in teaching and commanding is the authority of the Lord Jesus himself. This is plain beyond question in what he writes to both the majority and the minority groups. To the former he says 'In the name of the Lord Jesus Christ we command you' (6) and to the latter 'Such people we command and urge in the Lord Jesus Christ' (12). It is also clear in his opening expression of confidence from its combination of noun and pronouns: '*We* have confidence in *the Lord* that *you* are doing and will continue to do the things *we* command' (4). It is truly astonishing that he says he is trusting the Lord Jesus to ensure that the Thessalonians will obey him. By these 'blunt commands . . . he appears to canonize his own doctrine and writings'.[45]

Now these are not the wild ravings of a demagogue. They are not the petulant reaction of a tinpot leader whose authority is being challenged and who over-compensates by reasserting it. Paul betrays no personal pique or anger, and no petty arrogance. On the contrary, he keeps his cool, continues to call them his 'brothers' (6, 13, *cf.* 15), and does not require of them an obedience which he is unwilling to give himself (6–10). Yet he makes the explicit claim that his commands are the Lord's commands, for he issues them 'in' and 'in the name of' the Lord Jesus Christ himself, that is, as his personal representative. It is another clear example of his self-conscious authority as an apostle of Christ. In an earlier letter he has commended the Galatians for welcoming him as if he 'were Christ Jesus himself',[46] and in a later letter he will refer to his insistence that Christ was 'speaking through' him.[47]

Nobody in the church today has this kind of authority or dares to use this kind of language. True, infallibility is still claimed by and for the Pope when he is speaking *ex cathedra*

[45] Markus Barth, *Ephesians 1 – 3* (Anchor Bible; Doubleday, 1974), p. 362.
[46] Gal. 4:14.   [47] 2 Cor. 13:3.

and (since Vatican II) in association with the college of Roman Catholic bishops. Yet, politely though firmly, we must reject this pretension. Indeed, even the Pope, although in his pronouncements he uses the plural apostolic 'we', never uses the vocabulary of commandment and obedience which Paul used. At the other end of the theological spectrum there are some very authoritarian leaders of the charismatic and house church movements, who claim to be 'apostles' and who, in the exercise of their so-called 'shepherding' ministry, lay down the law and require obedience. But we must emphatically reject their pretensions too. There is nobody in the church who has an authority which even remotely resembles that of the apostles of Christ; nor has there been since the last apostle died.

This fact was clearly recognized in the immediate post-apostolic church. The church leaders of those days knew that the apostles had no successors, and that they lacked their authority. Take Ignatius as an example. He was Bishop of Syrian Antioch at the beginning of the second century, and was condemned to die in Rome for his Christian faith. On his way there he wrote seven letters, in which his high view of the episcopate is evident. Yet in his letter to the Romans he wrote: 'I do not give you orders like Peter and Paul. They were apostles; I am a convict.'[48] He was a bishop. But he was not an apostle, and he lacked an apostle's authority to issue commands.

How then can we submit to apostolic authority today? Only by submitting to the New Testament. For the authority of the apostles (which is the authority of Christ) is undiminished. It is not, however, exercised through their supposed successors (whether Catholic bishops or charismatic leaders), since in their unique historical role as eye-witnesses of the risen Lord they have had no successors, but rather through the New Testament which preserves their teaching and through which they continue to instruct the church.

To be sure, there is an important work of interpretation and application to be done, in order that the apostles' teaching may be related to contemporary situations and cultures. Nevertheless, their essential teaching retains a permanent and universal validity. For if Christ spoke through them and they

[48] Ignatius, *To the Romans*, chapter 4, verse 3.

196

spoke in the name of Christ, to disagree with their teaching is to disagree with him.[49] The well-being of the church, in the twentieth century as in the first, depends on our listening to Jesus Christ and obeying him as his word comes to us through his apostles in the New Testament.

5. Conclusion: a threefold blessing (3:16–18)

Now may the Lord of peace himself give you peace at all times and in every way. The Lord be with all of you.

[17]I, Paul, write this greeting in my own hand, which is the distinguishing mark in all my letters. This is how I write.

[18]The grace of our Lord Jesus Christ be with you all.

The serious division between the workers and the loafers is threatening to split the Thessalonian church. There is a real possibility that disciplinary action may have to be taken. Paul has issued some clear instructions about this in case the disobedience of the minority persists. But he ardently hopes that the recalcitrant church members will repent without the need for discipline. So he pronounces a threefold blessing from Christ upon his church, which takes the form of being half prayer, half wish.

First, *may the Lord of peace himself give you peace at all times and in every way* (16a). In his first letter Paul wrote of 'the God of peace' (1 Thes. 5:23); here 'the Lord of peace' means Jesus Christ. For the Old Testament prophets depicted the Messiah as the 'Prince of Peace', who would inaugurate a kingdom of peace.[50] And so it proved to be. For 'he himself is our peace', who by his cross reconciled Jews and Gentiles to each other, and both to God, 'thus making peace'.[51] Because he is 'the Lord of peace', he is uniquely qualified to 'give peace', a pervasive peace 'at all times and in every way', or (reading *topos* instead of *tropos*, which Lightfoot favoured)[52] 'at all times, in all places'. Only his peace could bring an end to the Thessalonian conflict.

Secondly, *The Lord be with all of you* (16b). It is one thing to receive the peace of Christ as a gift; it is another to enjoy the presence of Christ himself in the midst of his people –

---

[49] *Cf.* Mt. 10:40; Lk. 10:16.   [50] Is. 9:6–7.
[51] Eph. 2:14–15; *cf.* Col. 1:20.   [52] Lightfoot, *Notes*, p. 135.

'all' of them, Paul stresses, 'the dissident brothers as well as the loyal and obedient'.[53]

Thirdly, *the grace of our Lord Jesus Christ be with you all* (18). The same wish concluded Paul's first letter (1 Thes. 5:28), except that here he adds the word 'all', as at the end of verse 16. Grace and peace are also united in the final greetings of the first letter (1 Thes. 5:23, 28), and at the beginning of both letters (1 Thes. 1:1 and 2 Thes. 1:2). They are pre-eminent gifts of Christ to his church, each involving the other, since there can be no peace without grace. And 'grace', the unmerited favour of God which secures and bestows salvation freely, epitomizes Paul's gospel. This must be why at this point, having thus far dictated his letter,[54] he takes the pen from his scribe and writes his final grace-wish with his own hand. It is *the distinguishing mark* in all his letters, he says. *This is how I write* (17). He is aware of the deceitful activity of forgers (2:2). So he adds his autograph as a 'mark of genuineness' (JB). 'This authenticates all my letters' (NEB). It became his regular practice.[55] In fact, he probably closed every letter in his own hand even 'without expressly saying so'.[56]

One cannot read the last three verses of this letter without earnestly desiring for contemporary churches what Paul desired for the Thessalonian church, namely the peace, the presence and the grace of the Lord. Is it possible? Only, I think, if these blessings are read in their context and if we share Paul's perspective on the primacy of the Word in the life of the church. Indeed, one of the perennial questions facing the church in every age and place concerns its relationship to the Bible. How do the people of God and the Word of God relate to one another? Did the Word create the church or the church the Word? Is the church over the Bible or under it? Roman Catholic, Orthodox and Protestant churches answer these questions differently, and our division at this point is arguably deeper and wider than at any other.

2 Thessalonians 3 throws a bright light on this controversy, since it gives pre-eminence to the Word. Its opening prayer that 'the word of the Lord may speed on and triumph' (RSV) puts all parochialism to shame and challenges us to develop

---

[53] Morris, TNTC, p. 151.   [54] *Cf.* Rom. 16:22.
[55] *Cf.* 1 Cor. 16:21; Gal. 6:11; Col. 4:18; Phm. 19.
[56] Deissmann, p. 172.

a global vision and a commitment to world evangelization. And Paul's repeated commands, with their expectation of obedience, also condemn those churches whose attitude to the Word of God appears to be subjective and selective. They wander at random through Scripture, choosing a verse here and discarding a verse there, like a gardener picking flowers in a herbaceous border. They have no concept of a thorough study of the Bible, or of a conscientious submission to its teaching. Let not such a church imagine that it will receive the blessing of the Lord! For to despise the Word of the Lord is to despise the Lord of the Word, to distrust his faithfulness and to disregard his authority.

To which kind of church do we belong? Is its vision global or merely parochial? Is its attitude to Scripture principled or unprincipled, obedient or disobedient? While history moves towards its denouement and we await the rebellion of Antichrist which will herald the revelation of Christ, can we say from the heart 'Let the Word of the Lord run and be honoured throughout the world' and 'Let the Word of the Lord be honoured and obeyed in the church'? For then, fully committed to the Lord and his Word, we can humbly expect to enjoy in our day his peace, his presence and his grace.

Study Guide
for groups or individuals

Introduction

It's all too easy just to skim through a book like this without letting its truth take root in our lives. The purpose of this study guide is to help you genuinely to grapple with the message of the letters to the Thessalonians and think about how their teaching is relevant to you today.

Although designed primarily for Bible study groups to use over an eight-week period, this series of studies is also suitable for private use. When used by a group with limited time, the leader should decide beforehand which questions to discuss during the meeting and which should be left for group members to work on by themselves during the following week.

To get the most out of the group meetings, each member of the group should read through the passage to be looked at in each study together with the relevant pages of this book. As you begin each session, pray that the Holy Spirit will bring these ancient letters to life and speak to you through them.

Part 1
The Message of 1 Thessalonians
The Gospel and the Church

STUDY 1
Christian Evangelism
1 Thessalonians 1:1-10 (pages 25-44)

Read 1 Thessalonians 1:1-4.
1. Paul addresses a church which is both in Thessalonica and 'in' God. 'Every church has two homes, two environments, two habitats' (p. 28). How does this fact both encourage and challenge your church?
2. John Calvin described 1:3 as 'a brief definition of true Christianity'. How would you explain this conclusion? (See pp. 29-30.)
3. God had 'chosen' the Thessalonians. Why? On what two grounds did Paul and his colleagues know this to be true (p. 31)?

Read 1 Thessalonians 1:5.
4. How had Paul and his fellow-workers presented the gospel in Thessalonica?
5. All too commonly churches and Christians emphasize one of these characteristics to the detriment of the others. How does this verse challenge you and your church in your practice of evangelism?

Read 1 Thessalonians 1:6-7.
6. How were the Thessalonians affected by their reception of the message?
7. How does your own experience echo that of the Thessalonians?

Read 1 Thessalonians 1:8-10.
8. John Stott emphasizes the importance of 'holy gossip' in

the spread of the gospel, even in an age of mass communications (pp. 36-38). What examples in your own experience would support this point?

9. Which comments in the section on pp. 36-38 are particularly relevant to your church as you seek to proclaim the good news?

10. John Stott picks out three steps in Christian conversion: 'you turned . . . to serve . . . and to wait . . .' (pp. 39-42). Trace this pattern in your own Christian experience.

11. How should this understanding of conversion shape our witness and evangelism? our nurture of new Christians?

12. In his conclusion (pp. 43-44), John Stott highlights two points arising from this chapter. In what ways do you and your church need to change in order more effectively to pass on the gospel and embody it?

STUDY 2

Christian Ministry
1 Thessalonians 2:1—3:13 (pages 45-74)

Read 1 Thessalonians 2:1-2.

1. As Paul begins his defence against those who were slandering him, to what two evidences of his sincerity does he appeal (pp. 47-48)?

2. In what ways are these points relevant to Christian leaders in our very different society today?

Read 1 Thessalonians 2:3-4.

3. Paul sees himself and his coworkers as stewards of the gospel whose hearts are continuously tested by God (pp. 49-51). How might an awareness of this stewardship, and of this continuous testing, guard today's Christian leaders against the unworthy motives disclaimed in 2:3?

Read 1 Thessalonians 2:5-8.

4. Into what temptations might Paul have fallen in his relationships with the Thessalonians?

5. How in fact did he relate to them (pp. 51-52)?

6. How does this speak to people engaged in pastoral ministry today?

Read 1 Thessalonians 2:9-12.
7. What motivated Paul as he supported himself, lived a holy life and ministered to the Thessalonians (pp. 52-54)?
8. How would you rank the importance of personal example (for good or ill) in the ministry of Christian leaders? Why?

Read 1 Thessalonians 2:13-14.
9. What can we deduce from these verses about the nature of Paul's apostolic authority (pp. 54-55)?
10. What are the implications for us today as we study his writings?

Read 1 Thessalonians 2:15-16.
11. How would you respond to someone who interpreted this passage as a violent anti-Jewish polemic? (See pp. 55-60.) a contradiction of what Paul wrote later in Romans 11?

Read 1 Thessalonians 2:17a.
12. What does this half-sentence tell us about the bond between Paul and the Thessalonians (pp. 61-62)?

Read 1 Thessalonians 2:17b-20.
13. What can you deduce about Paul's feelings on being prevented from returning to Thessalonica?
14. Elsewhere, he attributed similar blockages to God. How do you understand his attributing this one to Satan (p. 63)?

Read 1 Thessalonians 3:1-5.
15. What had it cost Paul to remain alone at Athens (p. 64)?
16. In sending Timothy to Thessalonica, what three objectives did Paul regard as of greater importance than his own need for fellowship (pp. 64-65)?

Read 1 Thessalonians 3:6-10.
17. What good news was Timothy able to report on his return?
Imagine the impact it must have made on Paul in his distress. What was his response, especially in his praying for the Thessalonians? (See pp. 65-66.)

Read 1 Thessalonians 3:11-13.
18. As Paul prays for the Thessalonians, what are his prior-

ities for them (p.67)?

19. How can these verses guide our prayers for the churches in which we minister or to which we belong?

20. 'The two chief characteristics of pastoral ministry are truth and love' (p. 70). How does John Stott arrive at this conclusion?

21. 'Yet this combination is rare in the contemporary church' (p. 70). Which aspect are you prone to emphasize at the expense of the other?

How can we develop a balance (pp. 70-71)?

STUDY 3

Christian Behaviour

1 Thessalonians 4:1-12 (pages 75-91)

---

1. How far would you agree (or disagree) with John Stott's remarks about contemporary evangelical Christianity on p. 76? Why?

2. On p. 77 he calls on Christians and pastors to give plain, practical, ethical teaching. Think of some ways in which your church and family could do more to meet this need.

Read 1 Thessalonians 4:1-2.

3. Most of us would probably react against anyone who told us how we should conduct our lives. Why should the Thessalonians - and why now should we - listen to Paul when he gives us instruction in Christian living?

4. What guiding principle does he set before us, and what are its implications? (See pp. 78-79.)

Read 1 Thessalonians 4:3-8.

5. Like the Thessalonians, we are surrounded by sexual laxity. How can Christians fulfill God's will in this area of life without being 'puritanical' and 'prudish' (pp. 81-82)?

6. How does the author reach the conclusion, from 4:4, that heterosexual and monogamous marriage is the only God-given context for sexual intercourse (pp. 82-85)?

7. In 4:4b-7, what standards does Paul set for sexual behaviour within marriage?

8. On what basis does he expect Christian couples to live according to these standards (pp. 85-86)?

Read 1 Thessalonians 4:9-12.
9. Whom did Paul have in mind when he penned 4:11?
10. In what sense was their conduct a breach of the brotherly love to which Paul urges his readers in 4:9-10?
11. What threefold instruction does he give them in 4:11-12, and what motives does he set before them? (See pp. 87-90.)
12. 'Paul the tentmaker reinforced the example of Jesus the carpenter and gave dignity to all honest human labour' (p. 90). What typical attitudes to work today are challenged by this statement?
13. In his conclusion, the author highlights two aspects of Paul's perspective on sex/marriage and work: unselfishness and growth (p. 91). Are there other aspects that struck you as you studied 4:1-12?

STUDY 4

Christian Hope
1 Thessalonians 4:13—5:11 (pages 92-116)

Read 1 Thessalonians 4:13.
1. Why does Paul turn his attention to the problem of bereavement (pp. 92-95)?
2. How do you understand his use of 'sleep' as a metaphor for death (pp. 95-96)?

Read 1 Thessalonians 4:14-15.
3. What do these verses tell us about the content of the Christian hope?
4. On what foundations is it based? (See pp. 97-98.)

Read 1 Thessalonians 4:16-17.
5. John Stott helpfully discusses these verses under the headings 'The Return', 'The Resurrection', 'The Rapture', and 'The Reunion'. How would Paul's description of these end-time events have allayed the Thessalonians' fears for those who had died (pp. 101-105)?
6. To which of the three temptations mentioned on p. 105 are you most prone?

Read 1 Thessalonians 5:1-3.
7. Paul uses two similes to teach about the timing of the Lord's return. Why do you think he uses similes rather than plain statements?
What does each one tell us (pp. 108-109)?

Read 1 Thessalonians 5:4-8.
8. How is it possible for some people to 'belong to the day' while others at the same time 'belong to the night' (pp. 110-112)?
9. How will your answers to questions 4 and 5 affect your own attitude as you wait for the Lord's coming?

Read 1 Thessalonians 5:9-10.
10. In what sense is salvation a 'helmet' (5:8) for those who belong to the day (pp. 113-114)?

Read 1 Thessalonians 5:11.
11. In what practical ways can your church fellowship do more to demonstrate mutual love and encouragement?
12. What is the basis on which all real Christian encouragement is offered (pp. 114-116)? (See also 4:18 and pp. 106-107.)

STUDY 5

Christian Community
1 Thessalonians 5:12-28 (pages 117-135)

Read 1 Thessalonians 5:12-13.
1. What is the meaning of Paul's threefold portrayal of responsible church leaders?
2. When tensions arise between pastors and people, how can Paul's words here guide them to 'live in peace with each other' (pp. 118-121)?

Read 1 Thessalonians 5:14-15.
3. Most of us find it all too easy to grow impatient with the church's 'problem children' (p. 122) and to hit back when someone hurts us. How do Paul's exhortations here challenge us? Where can we find the motivation to adopt a different attitude (pp. 122-123)?

Read 1 Thessalonians 5:16-22 and 27.

4. How does John Stott argue that these verses refer to public worship (pp. 123-124)?

5. Why does John Stott prefer the RSV rendering of 5:16 (pp. 124-125)?

Discuss ways in which this instruction is, or could be, put into practice in your church's worship.

6. John Stott writes of the 'prayerlessness of the people of God' (p. 125). How can your church begin to obey 5:17 more fully?

7. Reflecting on the variety of pleasant and unpleasant circumstances in which we might find ourselves, how can we give thanks in them all (see 5:18a and p. 126)?

8. Commenting on 5:20-22, John Stott writes, 'We are neither to reject [any utterance which claims to come from God] outright, nor to accept it outright' (p. 128).

9. On what grounds should we be ready to accept or reject such an utterance (pp. 126-129)?

10. By contrast, what conclusions do you draw from the authoritative note of 5:27 (pp. 129-130)?

11. Turning back to 5:19, how could your church increasingly develop forms of worship through which the Spirit can work and speak (p. 131)?

12. How do you think we can distinguish between worship that quenches the Spirit and worship that simply quenches our own preferences?

Read 1 Thessalonians 5:23-28.

13. What does Paul's concluding prayer teach us about God's purpose for his people?

Which main themes of the letter does it bring together?

Part 2

The Message of 2 Thessalonians
A Christian Perspective on History

STUDY 6

The Revelation of Christ
2 Thessalonians 1:1-12 (pages 142-155)

Read 2 Thessalonians 1:3-4.
1. What features of the Thessalonian Christians' life together made Paul so thankful?
2. What does this thanksgiving add to the parallel one in 1 Thessalonians 1:2-3 (pp. 143-145)?

Read 2 Thessalonians 1:5-10.
3. How did Paul discern God's justice in the injustice the Thessalonian Christians were suffering (pp. 145-147)?
4. How does this passage add to the knowledge about the Lord's return which we gained from 1 Thessalonians (pp. 147-150)?

Read 2 Thessalonians 1:11-12.
5. In what terms do you pray for the church of which you are a leader or member?
6. What can this prayer of Paul's teach you (pp. 150-151)?
7. In his conclusion, John Stott focuses on the glory of Christ as it relates to those who believe and those who do not (pp. 151-155). Trace this theme through 1:7-12.
8. What are the implications of this theme of the glory of Christ for our individual and collective witness and outreach

to unbelievers?
the motivation and quality of our Christian life together?
9. How seriously do we take these implications? Explain.

STUDY 7
The Rebellion of Antichrist
2 Thessalonians 2:1—17 (pages 156-180)

Read 2 Thessalonians 2:1-3a.
1. What false teaching had been perpetrated in Thessalonica?
How does Paul refute it?
2. How may we best avoid becoming 'unsettled', 'alarmed' or 'deceived' by erroneous teaching (pp. 156-159)?

Read 2 Thessalonians 2:3b-5.
3. What does Paul teach about the nature and purpose of Antichrist?
4. Why does John Stott caution humility in seeking to identify this figure? (See pp. 159-162.)
5. John Stott relates this difficult passage both to Daniel's prophecies about a figure who would set up 'the abomination that causes desolation' and to Jesus' Olivet discourse that takes up that theme (see pp. 162-165, and look up the references in footnotes 17-20, 22 and 25). Explain how the author reaches his conclusion that 'the biblical prediction of the Antichrist may during the course of church history have had (and still have) multiple fulfilments' (pp. 165-166) who may have been 'forerunners or anticipations of the final "man of lawlessness" ' (p. 167).

Read 2 Thessalonians 2:6-8.
6. What *facts* does this passage give us about the influence that is restraining the rebellion?
7. The author outlines three possible *interpretations*, and favours the third: Rome and the power of the state. Why does he argue for this view rather than the others?
What will happen when the restraining influence is removed? (See pp. 168-171.)

Read 2 Thessalonians 2:9-12.
8. How will the coming of Antichrist parody the return of Christ?
9. Trace the process by which those who are perishing become deceived. (See pp. 171-173.)

Read 2 Thessalonians 2:13-14.
10. 'Paul now gives a marvellously comprehensive statement of God's saving purpose' (p. 175). What does this passage tell us about the nature of God's purpose and the stages by which he accomplishes it in our lives (pp. 175-177)?

Read 2 Thessalonians 2:15.
11. If the sovereign God is working out his purpose for his people so certainly, why does Paul exhort them to stand firm?
What does this involve? (See pp. 177-179.)

Read 2 Thessalonians 2:16-17.
12. How does Paul's prayer for his readers relate to his exhortation in the preceding verse?
13. What does his prayer teach us about the nature and relationship of Christ and the Father? (See pp. 179-180.)

STUDY 8

The Responsibility of Christians
2 Thessalonians 3:1-18 (pages 181-199)

Read 2 Thessalonians 3:1-3.
1. Having prayed for his readers in the preceding two verses, Paul now solicits their prayers for him and his co-workers. What do the terms in which he makes his request teach us about his primary concerns and vision (pp. 184-187)?
2. What truths about the nature of Christian mission does John Stott draw out of this passage (pp. 187-188)?

Read 2 Thessalonians 3:4-15.
3. 'What is striking . . . is not so much the instructions which

Paul issues . . . as the authority with which he does so' (p. 189). Pick out the words that give this passage such an authoritative ring.

Why was it necessary for Paul to use such words?

4. John Stott notes that 'there are five stages in Paul's handling of the problem of the *ataktoi'* (the idle) (p. 190). Trace them through verses 4-5, 6-9, 10, 11-13 and 14-15 (pp. 190-192).

5. What guidance does 3:14-15 give us in the matter of church discipline (pp. 193-194)? In what ways does this challenge the practice of your own church?

6. How far would you agree with John Stott's 'reflections on the authority of the apostles' (pp. 194-197)?

7. In what sense should we submit to apostolic authority today?

Read 2 Thessalonians 3:16-18.

8. In what ways were Paul's concluding wishes particularly appropriate in the Thessalonian situation (pp. 197-199)?

9. John Stott concludes his exposition by inviting us to consider to what kind of church we belong. What steps could your own church take increasingly to conform to the vision of the local church presented in the Thessalonian letters?